The Essence of
Organizational Behaviour

The Essence of Management Series

The Essence of Organizational Behaviour

Shaun Tyson
and
Tony Jackson

Prentice Hall
New York London Toronto Sydney Tokyo Singapore

First published 1992 by
Prentice Hall International (UK) Ltd
66 Wood Lane End, Hemel Hempstead
Hertfordshire HP2 4RG
A division of
Simon & Schuster International Group

Typeset in 10/12 pt Palatino
by Photoprint, Torquay

Printed and bound in Great Britain by
BPCC Wheatons Ltd, Exeter

Library of Congress Cataloging-in-Publication Data

Tyson, S. (Shaun)
    The essence of organizational behaviour / Shaun Tyson and Tony
Jackson
       p.   cm. — (The Essence of management series)
    Includes index.
    ISBN 0–13–284837–6
    1. Organizational behavior. I. Jackson, Tony, 1944–
II. Title. III. Series.
HD58.7.T97 1992
302.3'5—dc20   91–25702
                                                         CIP

British Library Cataloguing in Publication Data

Tyson, Shaun
    The essence of organizational behaviour.
    – (The essence of management series)
    I. Title II. Jackson, Tony III. Series
    658.3

ISBN 0–13–284837–6

---

1 2 3 4 5   96 95 94 93 92

Contents

v

Contents

Contents

Acknowledgements

The authors and publishers wish to thank the following who have kindly given permission for the use of copyright materials. The President and Fellows of Harvard College for permission to use the diagram 'The five phases of growth' from L.E. Greiner's article which appeared in the *Harvard Business Review*, July/August 1972. Prentice Hall for permission to use the diagram by Henry Mintzberg from *Structure in Fives: Designing Effective Organisations*, 1973, p. 262 and the diagram from Hersey and Blanchard's book *Management of Organisation Behaviour, Utilising Human Resources*, 1977. Brooks-Cole for permission to use material from *Group Dynamics*, 2nd edition, 1990. Scientific Methods Inc. for permission to use 'The leadership grid' figure located on p. 29 in *Leadership Dilemmas – Grid Solutions*, 1985. McGraw-Hill Inc. for permission to use material from W. Reddin's *Managerial Effectiveness*, 1970. John Wiley for permission to use material from *Motivation to Work* by F. Herzberg, B. Mausner and B. Sniderman, published 1959. Cambridge University Press for permission to reproduce the diagram by S. Cytrynbaum and J. Crites on 'Adult life stages' and other extracts from *The Handbook of Careers Theory* by M. Arthur, D. Hall and B.S. Lawrence, 1989. Professor E. Schein and the *Journal of Applied Behavioural Science* for permission to publish an extract from *Career Dynamics* by E.H. Schein, 1978, and to Professor Andrew M. Pettigrew, Professor Andrew Kakabadse, Dr Kim James and Dr Simon Baddeley for permission to quote from their work.

Every effort has been made to trace all the copyright holders, but if any have been overlooked, the publishers will be pleased to make the necessary arrangement at the first opportunity.

The authors would also like to acknowledge the help received from Ann Davies, Jean Loughlan and Dorothy Rogers whose word processing and secretarial skills helped to create this book.

1

Introduction to the study of organizational behaviour

"What is the use of a book", thought Alice, "without pictures or conversations?"

Lewis Carol, *Alice's Adventures in Wonderland*.

This book is a comprehensive organizational behaviour text. However, Alice is right: life is too exciting, people are too colourful to be easily represented in a text. In this book we seek to describe the organizational terrain where people live out most of their active existence: the work organization is a source of identity, a forum for emotional expression, a place apparently rational, serving economic purposes, but which is a human construct. Offices, factories, hospitals, schools and shops are places of triumph and disaster, of alienation or fulfilment, where people often find their most vivid social experiences. Our book portrays the essential themes in organizational life, which are, like Alice's adventures, frequently paradoxical.

The study of organizational behaviour analyses and interprets behaviour in work organizations. This requires the application of sociology and psychology to the understanding of behaviour at work – the 'human side of enterprise' in McGregor's words. Sociology is the study of social action – that is, action which is directed towards others – whilst psychology is the study of personality and of individual and group behaviour.

There are, of course, common-sense theories which all people apply when interpreting their everyday existence. These theories require us to make assumptions about others and the situations in which we find ourselves. The study of organizational behaviour seeks to test these assumptions and common-sense theories in order to build up a store of knowledge about people at work. In this way, common-sense theorizing itself becomes the subject of research: the process by which we come to understand others as having 'typical' motives, the recipes for success we use in our everyday lives, in short, what is 'common' in our common-sense views therefore becomes the subject to be studied (Schutz 1970).

Organizational behaviour as a subject

Organizational behaviour is concerned to integrate the disciplines of psychology, social psychology, political science, sociology and anthropology in so far as they relate to people at work. What is sought is a shift from an intuitive approach towards a systematic approach to the study of behaviour which should enable managers to improve their capacities to explain and predict behaviour.

By and large, behaviour is not random; on the contrary, it is directed towards an end. Moreover, there are differences between people: in similar situations we do not necessarily act in similar ways. But there are fundamental consistencies which allow predictability, even across cultures, and by systematic study we can view relationships, in an attempt to attribute cause and effect, and draw conclusions based on evidence.

This is not to argue that intuition is outmoded. Rather, the argument is to base that intuition in a systematic procedure which allows for a greater awareness of where and to what extent chance may take over. There are not absolutes in organizational behaviour. People are complex, and some will act differently in different situations. Therefore, concepts must reflect situational conditions.

The study of organizational behaviour is based on the importance we all attach to understanding what happens to people in organizations, and to the causes of their behaviour. It is a scientific enquiry as much as a search for practical solutions to management problems in which knowledge has a value for its own sake. The behavioural sciences are still at the early stages of development, and do not yet offer 'universal laws' or golden rules; nor are research findings accepted at their face value. The science of organizational behaviour, as with many other sciences is founded on disagreement, controversy and alternative viewpoints: 'The key is to be able to decipher under what conditions each argument may be right or wrong' (Robbins 1989, p. 11).

One of our principal problems is that 'objectivity' in this science is impossible to achieve. We must consider research in relation to the values espoused by those engaged, because the standards of objectivity or independence between the scientist and the phenomenon under study do not exist in the same way in the study of organizational behaviour as in the natural sciences.

Indeed, even in the natural sciences, the processes of rationality although defensible in themselves are dependent on human observation and interpretation. Mathematics is a human invention in which all theories depend on 'givens' or theoretical assumptions. In the real world of human behaviour there is 'bounded rationality', that is, there are limitations on the person's world-view. There is always a reason for behaviour, but this reason is dependent upon the values, the experience and the intentions of the person. Emotional and intuitive reasoning is also an important causal agent, as when we marry, decide to have children, and perhaps even when we choose a career.

Simplistic models of decision-making which make assumptions about the motives of the actors in the organization, do not capture the complexity of the process. For example, this can be illustrated by subjective expected utility theory, in which it is assumed that the decision-maker has a well-defined utility function, that there is a well-defined set of alternatives from which to select, that a consistent probability distribution can be assigned to all future events and finally that the alternative chosen will maximize the expected value (Simon 1983). Each of these conditions would be difficult to meet in the everyday life of managers whose bounded rationality and personal situation condition the amount and the quality of information received and processed, even if we ignore other factors, such as the boss's opinion, the time frame in which the decision must be made, the pressure of other events and so on. This is one reason why economists such as Pareto and Simon found themselves drawn more into sociological and psychological explanations of behaviour.

The application of organizational behaviour

The questions we wish to explore in this book include the following:

- What are the significant differences between people at work?
- How does personality affect performance?

- How are employees motivated?
- How do we create effective work groups?
- What are the attributes of successful leaders?
- What are the effects of different organization structures?
- How can we manage change successfully?
- How can we design efficient and effective organizations?
- How does culture and international marketing influence organizations?

The benefit of our text for the reader will be dependent upon our facility in answering these questions. One can find many examples to show how the richness of organizational life can only be interpreted fully by an understanding of the major disciplines in the study of organizational behaviour. If anyone doubts, for example, the significance of personality and human emotions on behaviour at work the autobiography of Lee Iacocca is worth consulting. Iacocca started work for Ford in 1946. He was fired by Henry Ford, in 1978, after rising to become Company President. He recounts the interview in which his employment was terminated:

> 'What's this all about?' I asked.
> But Henry couldn't give me a reason. 'It's personal', he said, 'and I can't tell you any more. It's just one of those things.'

Iacocca goes on to explain to Henry Ford how much he has done for the company and to try to discover the reason.

> 'Your timing stinks', I said. 'We've just made a billion eight for the second year in a row. That's three and a half billion in the past two years. But mark my words, Henry. You may never see a billion eight again. And do you know why? Because you don't know how the . . . we made it in the first place.' (Iacocca and Novak 1986, p. 134)

Thus the conflict which emerges when two giant egos clash has a major impact on one of the world's largest businesses. At a more local level, we can see how language and conversation can be analysed to explain the deeper social structures and strategic interactions which are taking place.

In a major research study which examines interactions between doctors and child patients with Down's syndrome, and their parents,

Silverman analyses conversations and communications in order to reveal the social nature of medical discourse:

> After the normal exchange of greetings, this is how the consultant gets down to business:
>
> Doctor: 'Well, how is she? Dr X has written to me and has also sent the catheter films that were done in Othertown. Um, can I ask you a few questions? How is she in herself?'
>
> Mother: 'Well, I've been pleasantly surprised to be quite honest.' (She goes on to relate details of colds, chest infections and episodes of breathlessness.)
>
> Notice the format of the doctor's question: he does not ask 'Is she well?' but 'How is she in herself?' As a discourse of 'wellness' is avoided, so the ground is prepared for other, non-medical formulations of children. 'Parents of Down's syndrome children usually conspire with doctors to avoid reference to "wellness"'' (Silverman 1987, p. 143)

This is part of a strategically important set of conversations which serve to lower the parents' expectations for Down's syndrome children's life expectation, and to help the parents gradually to give up the idea of having a normal child. This is a 'demedicalization' process, this being the pressure in which decisions about possible operations take place. The purpose of such studies is not to argue for more medical treatment, but to examine and understand the situational contexts of social discourse.

Organizational occurrences are only explicable by reference to a mixture of psychological and sociological causes. For example, such complex events as strikes have multiple causes. The case of the strike at Pilkingtons which started on 3 April 1970 in the Flat Drawn department of the Glass Works, when a group of employees walked out over a wage miscalculation, illustrates this (Lane and Roberts 1971). The simple clerical error which occasioned the unofficial strike was put right immediately, but the strike lasted seven weeks and drew in the remainder of the plants. Within forty-eight hours, it had become a major dispute with strikers demanding a £10 increase on base pay.

The features of this strike were not unusual: there was an explosion of pent-up emotion behind the ostensible reason for the walk out at first, but morale in most of the plants was good, there were good employee relations, low labour turnover and there was no special increase in grievances. The only explanation seems to be that a combination of causes – the conditions in one department, opportunities to exploit the situation felt by the workers, a bureaucratic and non-responsive trade union which allowed unofficial action to gain momentum, the reliance by Pilkington on a paternalistic management style and the 'instrumental' attachment to work of the employees who felt underpaid and who wanted a better living standard – is the main reason.

Lane and Roberts go on to suggest that strikes are 'normal'. They are a natural expression by employees of their wishes, or desires, which may not be well articulated, a protest, a feeling against authority, and against control, rather than for anything in particular. There are many other aspects, of course, which contributed to the events – for example, the formation of an 'unofficial strike committee', the role of the media, the negotiating machinery and the organization's structure could all be included in the web of causes.

What matters here is that we go behind simplistic explanations which seek to 'blame' managers, trade unionists or militants, when there are clearly more social structural reasons. In order to determine causes, we may have to separate out issues for the purposes of analysis. In our book we divide the subject under particular headings. We do recognize, however, that causes interact and that problems present themselves to management without neat labels saying 'this is a motivation problem' or 'this is an organization design problem'.

As we move towards the end of the twentieth century, large organizations are considering what management structures, competencies, motivation, job design and organization structure they should adopt. They want to know how to become flexible and competitive. The move towards more flexible, *ad hoc* flatter structures, with devolved management systems and federal approaches to business organization is growing. Companies such as BP, Ericsson, SAS, IBM and British Airways have been going through these internal reviews, often in response to business needs, but especially in the spirit of long-term survival. What organizational theorists are now seeing as a connection with a post-modernist movement against rational explanations, is found in looser, network-based modular corporations.

The challenge for organizational development is to assist top teams to achieve these changes because leadership requirements for managers in the future seem likely to be even more challenging than in the past. Organizational behaviour studies are essential not just for those who aspire to the top, but they also offer insights for the increasing number of organizational roles where group working and influencing without direct authority are expected.

How to use this book

This book is intended for all students of organizations and is aimed at a postgraduate audience, with the MBA student particularly in mind. It is divided into seven main chapters covering individual differences and personality, motivation, group behaviour and leadership, careers, power and politics, organization theory and design and organization change and development. We have added a final chapter on the international dimensions to the study of organizational behaviour. As Figure 1.1 shows, we have followed a logical route through three levels of analysis.

Figure 1.1 Levels of analysis

We have set out the main theories and concepts with reference to the well-known authorities. Our intention is to satisfy the needs of prospective managers, although those who wish to follow up with further study in this field will find our guide comprehensive. In addition to placing the main theoretical precepts in context, we have also included new material drawn from our own research and MBA teaching.

At the end of some chapters, there are exercises or mini case studies which we suggest our readers undertake, to consolidate the learning and to provide a basis for discussion. Our book contains, we hope, a sufficiency of diagrams and conversations to meet the requirements implied by Alice. However, its usefulness will depend on how well we can engage the reader with an internal dialogue about the study of people at work.

References

Iacocca, L. and Novak, W. (1986), *An Autobiography* (London: Bantam Books).
Lane, T. and Roberts, K. (1971), *Strike at Pilkingtons* (London: Fontana).

Robbins, S.P. (1989), *Organisational Behaviour* (Englewood Cliffs: Prentice Hall, 4th edition).

Schutz, A. (1970), *On Phenomenology and Social Relations*, ed. H.R. Wagner (Chicago: University of Chicago Press).

Silverman, D. (1987), *Communication and Medical Practice* (London: Sage).

Simon, H. (1983), *Reason in Human Affairs* (Oxford: Basil Blackwell).

2

Individual differences and motivation

Definitions, both of personality and behaviour, are many and varied but in looking at individual differences we have to be concerned with such definitions. The problem, however, is that a particular personality psychologist will select or construct their definitions based upon their theoretical orientation. Thus those who are concerned with a deterministic or genetic orientation will choose a definition which emphasizes the operation of psychological processes. On the other hand, psychologists who view human beings as adaptive creatures whose behaviour is largely determined by experience will stress past learning and current situational factors. Mischel defines personality in terms of the distinctive patterns of behaviour (including thoughts and emotions) that characterize each individual's adaptation to the situations of his or her life. Other psychologists emphasize the measurement of personality in their theories. As a result they come up with definitions which stress the predictive utility of their measures. Raymond Cattell is such a psychologist, who defines personality as those aspects which permit a prediction of what a person will do in a given situation.

The issue then is one of the diversity of the definitions which are being used. We are left with the idea that to understand fully what a particular psychologist means by the term personality we have to examine that psychologist's theoretical approach.

Individual differences

In looking at individual differences we are concerned with the scientific study of human behaviour. In these terms behaviour is seen to be some kind of interaction between the organism and its environment which can be characterized in various ways. The most fundamental concept that we use to describe sets of behaviours is that of personality. At the simplest level we can say that personality is the characteristic way or ways in which the individual thinks and acts when he or she is adjusting to the environment. But personality is slightly more complex than this. It comprises many different behavioural characteristics which may be arranged in some form of hierarchy. In other words, we have characteristic ways of behaving but in part these are determined by the situation within which that behaviour is occurring. This idea will become clearer as we move through this particular part of the chapter. For the moment we can say that when dealing with personality, we should look at individual differences.

It would be easy to think of the study of personality as being a relatively new field, but the reverse is rather the case. We can certainly trace it back to the work of Aristotle and Plato, and perhaps even beyond. However, we do not need to go quite that far back in time to see some of the roots of early and mid-twentieth-century work. In essence we can determine at least three theories of personality, including static, dynamic and quantitative theories. It is probably easier to talk of these in concrete terms, but as an aside it is worth noting that although more comprehensive work can be found – some of which detail the work of some twenty major theories (Hall and Lindzey 1985) – our own review will be somewhat simpler.

Static theories

Static theories are almost inevitably based on observation. They tend to characterize types of people and the typologies are usually very broad and small in the number of elements. The earliest of these can be traced back to the first century AD, to Galen, whose theory was long lasting and talked about the humours. Four types were hypothesized. The Sanguine (based on blood) were the cheerful extrovert people, those of a highly outgoing and joyful nature who because they were doing much tended to be ruddy of face. The Phlegmatic type is based in Phlegm, or whiteness. Such people were perceived to be cold and aloof and more introverted: those who 'sat themselves in corners away from others'. Choleric (yellow bile) people were perceived to be much more impulsive in their behaviour, and being temperamental they were individuals who had sudden inspirations

ENDO . . .   MESO . . .   ECTO . . .

ENDOMORPHIC   ENDOMORPHIC   ECTOMORPHIC
MESOMORPH   MESOMORPH   MESOMORPH

4 – 6 – 1   5 – 2 – 1   2 – 5 – 6

Figure 2.1 Sheldon's morphological typology

to do things. It was difficult to judge precisely what they would do
next in these terms. The final type was Melancholic. Based in black
bile such people were seen to be depressives. With so many centuries
between it is difficult to know precisely what Galen meant by these
things but it does seem likely that he theorized that people's traits or
characteristics were derived from one or other of these humours.

This work was to see us through many centuries until the nineteenth
and twentieth centuries when it changed dramatically although it was
still of a static kind. Kretschmer in the early part of the twentieth
century created a static theory based on morphology (body shape),
specifically the limbs and trunk. He argued that morphology predis-
poses people towards specific personality structures and categorized
three major types. The first were Pyknic people (short limbed, thick
trunk, fat face), who were perceived to have wild mood fluctuations
and today would be thought of as manic depressives. The second

type was Asthenic. These were long limbed, narrow trunk people of thin face, who tended to be much more introverted and shy. Kretschmer also encapsulated them as schizophrenic in mind. The third type was Athletic, who were perceived to have balanced physiques and were likely to be energetic and quite aggressive in their behaviour. The problem with both this, and Galen's theory, was that these were perceived to be pure types and it is quite plain from a review of people around us that this is too simplistic a way of classifying people. That problem was perceived by Sheldon in the middle part of this century.

Sheldon described another type theory, again based in morphology and building on Kretschmer's work. As with Kretschmer, Sheldon argued that there were three basic types (Figure 2.1). In essence these were Endomorphs (soft and round, sociable), Mesomorphs (hard and square, extroverts) and Ectomorphs (tall and thin, passive). The difference with Sheldon's work is that these morphologies admitted that there could be mixes of each type. So that although we could take extremes as being of the 'true' type he did at least allow for different body types to imply different personality characteristics. However, as with many of these theories, there were some problems which remained unanswered. Sheldon, for example, failed to consider the age variable and indeed – possibly a most important thing at the time he did the research – environmental factors such as diet deficiencies and so on. Perhaps equally importantly there was a failure to consider the halo effect. In other words, there are perceptual and cultural expectations which are derived from stereotyping people in particular ways. One overall assumption found in all the static theories was that personality was a function of genetic make-up, that is, it was largely innate.

Dynamic theories

Whilst the notion of innateness has never been fully denied there was a movement away from that in the theories of Freud and the post-Freudians with their consideration of dynamic theories of personality. Freud's theory was essentially based on psychoanalysis. He had a driving need to conceptualize those areas of the mind which were not available to our conscious thinking. Indeed, in his early theory he simply named these as the unconscious (instinct, physiological needs and so on), conscious (logic, reasoning) and pre-conscious: the boundary between these two. In his later theory these were named the id, ego and super ego.

The id was a way of describing the instincts of the individual and was the location of the libido: the sex drive. These were the things that were not available at the conscious level of analysis. The ego, on the other hand, was that area of the mind which dealt with day-to-day events, or reality. The moral laws or conscience were provided by the super ego. This latter aspect of personality was determined by the socialization process, especially of the individual's early years. The energy to drive all these things was given by the libido.

Defence mechanisms
Almost any theory of personality can be criticized; Freud's ideas certainly no less than anyone else's. But one of the lasting creations which Freud brought to the world of psychology and individual differences was that of defence mechanisms, which would include such things as repression, projection, regression and rationalization. At the simplest level of analysis these have provided us with a very useful set of stereotypes of forms of behaviour which people show. Certainly, Freud's contribution was that he saw an interplay between innate and environmental factors. Moreover, while he recognized the importance of the maturation process itself in determining people's behaviour, on the other hand he attached very little importance to behavioural processes (which to Skinner were all important). In addition, his original sample was of middle-class Viennese at the turn of this century. These were people who had behavioural problems and therefore the generalizability of any theory which comes from his work has to be questioned in those terms. Perhaps most importantly, however, was the number of people who followed Freud's path, even if in the final analysis they were to divert from it; such people as Jung (1961) and Adler (1927) plainly fall into this category. It is, of course, Adler's work which in turn underpins that of Rogers (1947) and Maslow (1970) (see page 17).

Quantitative theories

Quantitative theories are based on some form of objective measurement of overt behaviour. In other words, the concern is with demographic data, questionnaire and interview data. The two major protagonists in this field are Eysenck and Cattell. Whilst there are some differences in their work, there are very broad similarities between them; for example, both the orthogonal characteristics of introversion and extroversion, stability and neuroticism are found in their respective theories. Of interest to us organizationally, is the point that these theories can be used, albeit in a simple way, to predict behaviour. Both admit that personality is a unique aspect of the individual and underpins much of that person's behaviour. If this phenomenon called 'personality' can be tapped then it allows us to talk about that individual's likely future behaviour. What is really interesting about these two theorists' views is the different bases from which they arrived at the broad similarities: Eysenck's original work was undertaken on normal and neurotic soldiers; on the other hand, Cattell used a working population. What has been derived from the work of these two psychologists is a degree of objectivity in the way that we actually measure individual behaviour patterns.

Dynamic versus static theories

Whereas Mischel was arguing for a very high position for situations as determinants of behaviour, other researchers were showing quite different results from research in personality and in the prediction of behaviour. Cattell has always argued that we may accept that personality, as he defines it, is relatively fixed; but *relatively* is the operative word. He argues that we are able to adapt and change as circumstances allow, but that such change will be by and large consistent with the individual's main personality attributes. In other words, if the person is already an outgoing individual then any change which may occur around him or her will be maintained within the notion of outgoing, although to a greater or lesser extent. On the other hand, Block (1973) argues from a quite different perspective. In a major longitudinal study the final emphasis of his research indicated that personality, as defined by a range of different instruments over an extended period of time, was relatively fixed. In other words the amount of change which may occur is relatively insignificant; we are what we are, we behave as we behave.

However, the indications really seem to be that personality as such simply lays down the guidelines within which behaviour is going to occur. It is the situation which determines the particular form of behaviour which each of us expresses. Taking this as the central theme, then, it indicates the importance of the situation within which we find ourselves and which may, by this analysis, either help or hinder our development over time. Indeed, it may well be that personality studies *per se* create better predictors of group behaviour than of individual behaviour. It is from this point that we are led to a consideration as to how, given some knowledge of people's behaviour, we can influence it in the most positive sense, for the good both of the individual and the organization. Such thinking plainly leads us into the area of motivation.

Today's debates

The concerns today in terms of individual differences are less with conscious versus unconscious issues but rather to what degree do unconscious factors determine behaviour and under what conditions? Almost all modern personality theorists accept the responsibility for dealing with acquisitions and the process of learning. On the other hand, some theorists such as Adler offer little specific treatment of learning. In general, what seems to happen is that people simply treat learning under the headings of maturation, individuation or self-actualization rather than provide a more detailed picture of that process.

Interestingly, the whole area of the genetic determination of individual differences is once more coming under scrutiny, this time from microbiology. Whereas at one stage Sheldon was one of the very few psychologists who was concerned with the centrality of genetic determinants of personality, a view that was not espoused by others, today the heredity versus environment issue is clamouring once more for attention. It might well be that we are the sum of our parentage and that sum may have an even greater claim than environmental factors in shaping our actual behaviours. In the same way, the arguments about whether early experiences are as important as, or more important than, current experiences are beginning to falter. Few, if any, would now argue that our early experiences in childhood, especially if quite traumatic, can quite dramatically emerge in later life as reasons for particular forms of behaviour.

There are also arguments about the holistic versus analytical way of dealing with individual differences. While some have argued that Cattell and Eysenck, among others, tend towards the analytical end of that spectrum, Cattell's arguments have always contained the idea that you cannot divorce the individual and his or her behaviour from the environment within which that behaviour takes place. In other words, the situation has to have some impact. That does not mean to say that behaviour cannot be analysed segmentally, rather the indications are that the whole must be put back together again.

This leads very neatly into what was a huge debate during the late 1960s–early 1970s of person versus situation. Mischel has, in part, been much maligned on this issue. Today, the position is very much one of interaction, in which an individual's disposition or traits will help to determine their situations as well as the stimuli in the environment to which they attend. In these terms both traits and situational variables will play a role in determining the behaviour.

In much the same way, another argument has been about purposive behaviour versus mechanistic. The problem here is whether the individual is seen as a thing which reacts to particular stimuli or whether he or she has some kind of purpose and goal. Few would argue with the latter idea. Indeed the debate goes further than that, for there are implications for the motives which people bring to particular situations. Again there are arguments between the ideas of having either a few or very many motives. Communicators such as Adler and Maslow (at least in their earlier works) would argue for unitary motives. On the other hand, there are those such as Murray, McClelland and Cattell who would call upon a large number of motivation variables to explain behaviour.

In many ways one of the most contentious of the dimensions under which personality and individual differences are looked at is that of normality versus abnormality. In part, the difficulty lies in determining where each begins and finishes. For example, it would be simple to put Freud and Adler on the abnormal end of the spectrum, given that they were writing strongly and theorizing about those who were psychologically distressed. Maslow and Cattell, on the other hand, are concerned primarily with normality. Yet even this distinction is not so clear-cut. Thus, for example, Maslow was also concerned with the rehabilitation into society of those people who were, in some way, mentally ill. But the roots of this contention go deeper. For it is easy, in distinguishing between people's behaviour, to ascribe normality or abnormality labels to them. The issue, then, is, what is abnormality? What we note over time is that our definitions of these terms change, almost markedly; what was abnormal behaviour yesterday, is no longer the case today.

The knowledge base which we have about the manner in which biological factors influence and are influenced in their turn by behaviour is increasing dramatically. Biology is plainly going to have a major impact on individual differences: already we are looking at evolutionary theory and the way it applies to complex behaviour such as aggression, competition, cooperation and so on. In the past, these have been seen as being very much behaviour shaped by the environment within which people are socialized. It now appears that this view may be far too narrow. It is worth noting that more and more research is being done on people in late adulthood, and we are getting better ideas about the development cycle both of behaviour and personality through the life cycles.

Motivation

Needs

Needs theories, so far as motivation is concerned, can be simply traced back to Maslow's original work, which was undertaken with the rehabilitation of all people in mind. Today, it is often quoted for use in management and worker motivation. One thing which ought to be remembered beyond this is that the original hierarchy did not have five, but six, elements in it. The five which are most often quoted are those of 'physiological', 'safety', 'belonging', 'esteem' and 'self-actualization'. What are ignored are what Maslow called Meta needs, comprising a range of different needs such as 'cognitive' and 'aesthetic' which exist between esteem and self-actualization. What the original theory did recognize, however, was that people's needs varied at different times, and in different circumstances one or other of these might come to the front. But what was also needed was for these concepts to be translated into the world of work.

Maslow's 'Hierarchy of needs' is so called because it works on a very simple basis: a satisfied need is no longer a motivator. Moreover, his original argument was that the two basic needs had to be achieved before the individual could move on to higher order needs: that is, we need to look after our physiological and safety needs before entering into those of social or self-fulfilment, and so on. However, a far better way of seeing these needs is to deal with them in terms of the organization and its environment. The list below shows what is meant by this. For the sake of simplicity, the five major characteristics which Maslow's hierarchy contains are as follows:

- **Self-fulfilment** – personal or professional growth, autonomy, worthwhile job.

- **Self-esteem** – being consulted, rank, success, achievement, encouragement, recognition, perquisites.

- **Social** – joint tasks, appreciation, sharing offices, recognition, team membership.

- **Stability and security** – job descriptions, regularity, role clarity, structure, communication, safety report meetings, agreements, contracts.

- **Physical** – decoration, vibration, temperature, space, noise, gas, canteen facilities.

If such things as decoration, vibration and temperature are not kept within reasonable bounds, then they can have an important and deleterious effect on performance. Although that does not mean to say that getting these things right will necessarily ensure a good performance, at least they provide the environment in which a good performance may occur. Moreover, if we go into the world of ergonomics, we know that excessive noise does not just affect behaviour generally but actually creates the potential for mental breakdown. It was no accident that one of the areas in the United Kingdom where the incident of nervous and mental breakdowns was found to be highest was around Heathrow Airport.

It is even possible to look at Maslow's 'Hierarchy of needs' over the lifetime of individuals. In the early years, that is in our late teens, the two main elements are those of relations and basic needs. It is a time of change, during which new patterns of relationships are being laid down. At the same time, the individuals are leaving, or taking a new place in, the family home. For the first time, they have a degree of independence which is marked by their capacity, or otherwise, to earn money. This changes as they progress in their career, so that by the early–mid twenties the concern is much more with autonomy and their own self-esteem. As a result, these two aspects, so far as motivation is concerned, come to the fore. With the advent of family, there is a regression to the original starting-point, in which basic needs and relationships emerge, once more as being fundamentally important to the individual.

Thus different cycles can be acknowledged over the working life of individuals within the organization. Even the so-called mid-life crisis can be seen in motivational terms, for it is at this time that relationships, and basic needs, suddenly re-emerge as crucial aspects of the individual's motivation pattern. In part, this stage is reinforced by a need to come to terms with things which are happening in their career as well. Since the individual is now likely to be seeing people coming through from beneath him or her, who have, in the past, been juniors.

Maslow's work was simplified by Aldefer whose ERG theory gained some credibility, if for no better reason, than for its simplicity. ERG was simply the way of reducing the words: 'existence', 'relatedness' and 'growth' into a single unitary concept. 'Existence', in Aldefer's terms, accounted for the physiological and safety aspects under Maslow's work. 'Relatedness', on the other hand, was a direct cross to Maslow's 'belonging'. Maslow's 'self-actualization' related to Aldefer's 'growth', which included both 'self-esteem' and 'self-actualization'. In a sense, Aldefer's work suffered from similar problems to that of Maslow; it was difficult to relate it to the world of work. Moreover, both its predictive capacity and its ability at least to give clues as to how people should be motivated were severely limited.

The work of Murray, which was taken up by McClelland, derived a quite different form of needs. Their arguments were very simple and straightforward. As individuals, we each have multiple needs; they are not so simple as those identified by Maslow and Aldefer but take many different forms. The best known of these are the needs for achievement, power, autonomy and affiliation. The argument they put forward is that if you could in some way codify the individual's needs, then you could begin to predict the likely way in which that individual would work. For example, someone with a high need for achievement is likely to be self-motivated, whereas a person with a low need for achievement requires much closer supervision by his or her boss. But even this does not quite go far enough. Belbin and Hartston (1976) used a particular form of personality inventory which actually tapped need for achievement. This they broke down into four elements: competitiveness, attainment, determination and consistency. Their argument in defence of this breakdown was that whilst it was quite possible to set one's own goals and targets (need for attainment) without the necessary determination to see them through, they were unlikely to give rise to effective results. In just the same way, some people's need for achievement can be broken down quite simply into need for competitiveness. The implication of this is that they have a high need to do better than other people. Now, the only way to determine whether this can be effective or not, is to look at the direction in which the competitiveness is aimed. If it is within the individual's own group, then, plainly, this is much more likely to be a dysfunctional aspect of behaviour. In other words, even the simple concept of need for achievement can be broken down into many constituent parts which, in turn, will determine whether these particular forms of behaviour will be effective.

Money and social comparison theory

There is a vociferous group of psychologists who have argued that money is not a motivator, but their arguments often fall on stony ground and deaf ears! It would be foolish to deny the power of money in terms of motivation. However, the actual time-frame and direction in which money works need to be carefully looked at. When this is done, then we see that money is not a continuing motivator, not, that is, in the same way that other aspects of motivation work. Perhaps one of the best examples of this lies in the work of John Stacey Adams. His equity theory looked particularly at the ratio of input, that is, effort in relation to outcomes (such as pay). His argument was that people actually look at these and compare them with similar ratios of a relevant other person. In the case of an organization employing many people, then the relevant other person may well be an individual within the comparer's own organization. Where the position is unique, at least to the host organization, then the comparator group is drawn from outside. Adam's argument is that people make the comparison and, if they are worse paid than the comparator group or individual, then this has a demotivating effect. Strangely, an additional argument is put forward that if people are better paid than their comparator groups, this will also be demotivating; it is almost as if individuals begin to relax their effort. The time when equilibrium is created is where the two are roughly in comparison one with another.

Social comparison theory takes a similar view, except that here the orientation is very much towards the group and the way the group influences our perceptions of others and the rewards which they gain. But the theory of group comparisons breaks down in that it ignores one facet of human behaviour: pay is rapidly internalized. In other words, individuals quickly shift their mode of living in order to take account of their new standard of income.

What may happen is that money may act as a pull or push incentive to leaving a particular job for another. The effect of using money as a motivator is very short term. There is other evidence which indicates that this might be the case as in Figure 2.2a which shows the effects on performance of putting in some kind of performance-related element of pay at a fixed point in time. What seems to happen, is that people have a level of performance which they act

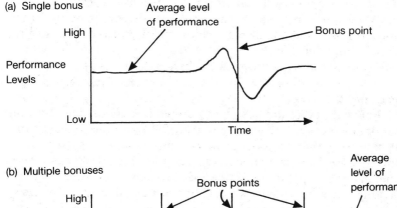

Figure 2.2 Bonus payments and performance levels

towards. Any surge in performance is paid for by a decrement in that performance at a subsequent time, and the overall effect is of an individual level of performance within the job which takes account of the level of competency (a point to which we shall return later). Having noted the phenomenon, some organizations determine that they will put in a series of bonus points in the calendar. Figure 2.2b shows the resulting performance levels of individuals.

What we do know about money, and its immediate effects on people, is that, whether we are talking about salary or bonus, the more individually oriented is the system, the greater will be its effectiveness. Bonuses have been found to have the best effect but, unfortunately, also the most side-effects. Generally, the side-effects are caused either through the setting of low norms, or the perceived subjectivity of the measures being used. What is known is that a relationship of trust is vital, so far as the payment of bonuses is concerned. What needs to be seen by the members of the organization, is that the bonus and salary system is as objective as it can be. Within some organizations, payment of a bonus acts as a useful stem to the tide of turnover within the organization. This is especially the case where the bonus is reasonably substantial and is paid at a certain date in the calendar. There are organizations whose turnover falls to nil within a couple of months of this bonus becoming due, but whose turnover rises rapidly as soon as the bonus itself has been paid.

Expectancy theory
Undoubtedly, one of the best of the dynamic theories of motivation is Vroom's expectancy theory (see Figure 2.3). It is a cognitive theory which is very process-oriented. It is based on people having (a) motivation, (b) some ability and (c) a clear role within the organization, such that a prescription can be derived as to how best to deal with the individual. The argument put forward is that motivation is based heavily on people's expectations, i.e. that individuals will associate an outcome with some action and will assign some probability value to this expectation. The profile then runs that people will put some effort into their performance, and that effort or performance will lead to a specific outcome.

The relationships between those things are multiplicative. Probably the most important aspect of all this is the concept of valence, which is the value which the individual attributes to the particular outcome. It is in the combination of the elements that the richness of the theory emerges. Plainly, if I place a high value on something, then it would lead to greater efforts and potentially lead to those outcomes which are actually desired. However, there is a set of assumptions which underpins the theory, some of which may not be apposite for everybody within the organization. In essence, the assumptions boil down to autonomy, conscious choice and rationality. Whilst all of us

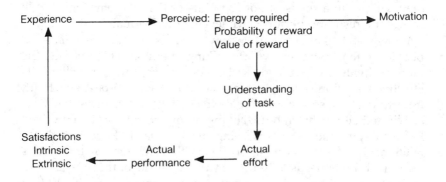

Figure 2.3 Diagram of expectancy theory

have a higher degree of autonomy than we might believe within an organization, few of us take advantage of it. Similarly, both rationality and conscious choice may not always be at work in the individual. Whilst this does not deny that there are some rational people within organizations, there are equally some who make their decisions based on emotion and subjectivity.

Reinforcement

A psychologist whose research is little known but who made a massive contribution to the area of psychology generally, and motivation specifically, was G.B. Watson. Watson was strictly a behavioural psychologist. His concern was to see what the reactions of the individual were to particular stimuli. Unfortunately, some of his original research apparently went beyond the bounds of sexual propriety at that particular time (the late 1920s), as a result of which his career was capsized. Watson's work was taken up by the late B.F. Skinner, whose initial work took him into the area of rats and pigeons and their particular behaviours.

The behavioural theory of motivation is concerned, quite specifically, with observable behaviours. The mind, it was argued, simply does not exist. What these theorists worked on was a black box theory of how humans work. The nature of the theory, therefore, takes specific types of behaviour which may, or may not, currently exist in the repertoire of the individual and, through a series of rewards, predicts that the likelihood of a particular behaviour occurring is increased. In essence, a relationship is created between the behaviour which is required and its outcome. In most cases, this relationship is bonded by the use of a reward system, though not necessarily a reward in the monetary sense.

Clearly, in this theory, the manager's behaviour is crucial. It is assumed that the environment itself is being controlled by the manager, and that the reward system is within his or her gift. The implication is that the manager must recognize and reward good behaviour. Reward in most cases, when looked at in behavioural terms, is concerned with the giving of praise and, in these terms, is seen as positive feedback. Behaviourist theories do admit to the use of punishment as a way of negatively rewarding a particular outcome, but Skinner's major argument is that, if we reward the positive behaviours that we wish to see, then the chances of other outcomes arising are substantially reduced. There is an acknowledgement in these theories that the reward schedules themselves may be varied; typically, they include: fixed interval, variable interval, fixed ratio and variable ratio. Examples under each of these headings might be as follows:

- **Fixed interval** – weekly wage

- **Variable interval** – praise, visits or walkabout

- **Fixed ratio** – piece work

- **Variable ratio** – this is the most interesting and involves the reward being given around some known ratio, e.g. 5:1, but where the reward occurs sometimes on the third occasion, sometimes the seventh, and so on, the average ratio is the fifth.

Variable ratio is perhaps the most powerful reinforcement schedule that exists. In essence, the reward is gained but precisely when it will occur is not known. It is the reward schedule which underpins gambling and, in part explains why gambling is so difficult a habit to break. The roulette wheel works on a variable ratio reinforcement schedule so you may well win, but what you do not know is precisely when that win will occur.

Job satisfaction

The relationship between job satisfaction and work performance is one which has puzzled people for many years. The real question that we have to start with, however, is whether it matters that jobs are unsatisfying. There are two distinct ways of looking at this question. First, a moral view, in which the answer to the question is plainly in the affirmative, that is, yes it does matter. Secondly, the view is an economic, or perhaps pragmatic position, in which the benefit to the firm is looked at, as well as the benefit to the individual through job satisfaction itself. In this latter context, if it were seen that job satisfaction was able to reduce labour turnover or improve productivity, then, plainly, it would be important for the organization.

Job satisfaction is related to behaviour at work in the following ways: quality and quantity of output, as well as cooperation, are related quite directly to effort and purpose. These latter two aspects could be defined under the general heading of motivation. Job satisfaction, on the other hand, can equally be related to the liking, or otherwise, for the job, signs of which might be accidents, cheerfulness, lateness, absenteeism, labour turnover, etc.

We may actually look at the reverse of job satisfaction at work, i.e. frustration. Frustration can take one of the following four major forms:

- Fixation.
- Regression.
- Withdrawal.
- Aggression.

Fixation is to be seen where people continually repeat arguments in meetings, or continue to attempt to solve problems, using solutions which have already been shown to be inadequate. Regression, on the other hand, is to be seen in behaviour such as sulking, tantrums or immature behaviour generally. Occasionally, of course, it may come out as crying and depression. Withdrawal, on the other hand, is concerned with attempts by the individual to actually remove his or her behaviour from the workplace and would include absenteeism, turnover and even such things as extended lunch hours and tea breaks. Finally, aggression can take the ultimate form: that of sabotage or damaging equipment; alternatively, it may take a slightly less visible, yet no less deadly, form of malicious gossip or simply of voicing superficial grievances. It may also be seen in excessive criticism of 'them'; the problem then becomes how to turn this into something which has a more positive aspect for use within the organization.

No chapter on motivation can be written without at least visiting Herzberg's work. His original work was published in 1959 and involved him in examining sources of job satisfaction and job dissatisfaction. His original research was undertaken using ninety engineers and accountants in the United States. They were all men. The particular methodology he used was interviewing respondents who were asked to think of incidents in the job that made them feel good or feel low. The analysis was undertaken on a content analysis basis, in which the incidents themselves were classified by their content. In other words, the concern was whether the incidents were related to praise, working conditions, success, and so on. The findings are well known and are reproduced in Figure 2.4.

In essence, what the figure attempts to show is that there are certain aspects of work which, if insufficient attention is paid to them,

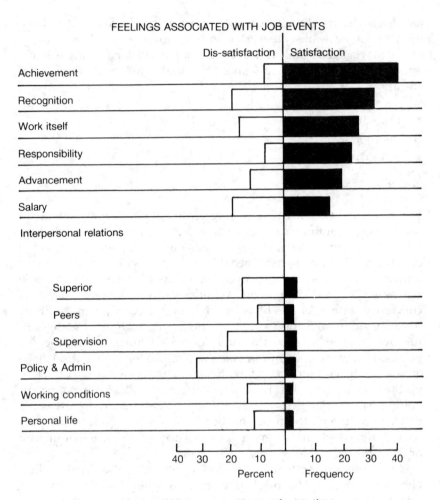

Figure 2.4 Herzberg *et al.*'s two-factor theory

act as demotivators or sources of job dissatisfaction. If they are well dealt with in the organization, they have little, if any, motivational effects. These are known as the 'hygiene factors'. Other aspects, if badly dealt with, have some demotivational effect but, if they are done well, have enormous motivational impact so far as people within the organization are concerned. Subsequent attempts to replicate Herzberg's work have met with mixed success. In part, this might be simply because of the different time frames within which the work was actually done. The 1950s and 1960s, both in Europe and in the United States, were times of relatively low unemployment. Moreover, inflation was also relatively low. In fact, these two decades were quite unusual in Western history, certainly over the last three or four hundred years. As subsequent replications were attempted, these factors changed quite markedly, and it may be that as a result of this we find things like job security, for example, becoming far more important when the unemployment rate climbs rapidly. Nevertheless, the research does allow us to see that there are factors which impinge upon performance, other than those which are carried inside our own heads.

Job design

Eric Trist's work brought a new flavour to motivation theories. The concept which was captured by this work is probably caught today in the notion of human resources management. In essence, Trist, through his research, said that people prefer reasonably demanding work with some variety.

We explain the organizational consequence of what came to be known as socio-technical systems theory in Chapter 6. Here, we should say that many would see work as giving them the opportunity to learn, as well as giving them the opportunity to make decisions. What is also required and what is reflected in other theories of motivation, is the need for social support and recognition. Moreover, people do not purely have a present orientation but, rather, the significance and meaning that they would like to see within the context of their work, should also lead to some desirable future; that is, people actually have a future orientation.

This led Trist to the whole idea of job design, which required looking at the work that was involved for the individual and seeing what the contribution to the product was going to be. Both quantity and quality of results were important as was, possibly more important than everything else, feedback. It was also felt that people would work better if they had a meaningful 'whole' task. This does not necessarily mean that they should undertake the whole of the construction of the product but that they should understand where their particular part fitted with all other elements, although there was an inherent belief that it was better if this part was a 'whole' part. Such work was seen to include, not just the actual manufacture but also the planning and evaluation stages of the work itself. It was found that this variety led to much more satisfying work by those who were involved.

Trist's work led to a range of different methodologies to try and improve morale, job satisfaction and motivation. All have been tried with more or less success. They include such things as the following:

- Job rotation.
- Job enlargement.
- Job enrichment.
- Job redesign.

Job rotation

Job rotation was one of the earliest attempts to do something about the monotony engendered in many jobs. Essentially, the aim of job rotation was to conquer monotony by providing people with a variety of work. It cannot be denied that many of the jobs which have to be done are intrinsically boring, but it was simply felt that, by giving variety, boredom would be reduced to the minimum. The operator would, therefore, move from one (dull) job to another. It was felt at the outset, and subsequent research seemed to indicate this, that improved performance could occur with rotation. There were, however, drawbacks. It was often forgotten, in undertaking a job rotation scheme, that those people who are intimately involved at that level in the organization do actually perceive a series of status steps, even within jobs which are declared to be equivalents. A problem then occurs when a switch has to be made from a perceived high status task into one which is of lesser status. This is especially the case when people progress in time through the status oriented pieces of work. Under such circumstances, job rotation fails.

Job enlargement

Job enlargement is the opposite of fragmentation and involves the operator taking on more of the actual assembly task. In essence, no more authority or responsibility is given; rather, the number of short-term tasks which have to be undertaken by a single individual is increased. The theory was that, with the increasing number of different tasks, albeit monotonous ones, the variety would actually provide some kind of stimulus for the operator. There is some evidence that there has been success here. However, social disruption can often be quite enormous and work methods upset, with subsequent implications for overall productivity. Perhaps, and perhaps most strangely, this method prevents daydreaming. Broadbent's work at Cowley at Oxford showed the particular benefit of daydreaming. When this was, in fact, taken away from people, by virtue of their doing a variety of simple repetitive tasks but for which they had to think, the organization found that there was an increased proclivity towards mental breakdown. Daydreaming, in effect, is a non-disruptive release from the monotony and boredom of the work which we have to undertake.

Job enrichment

Job enrichment, on the other hand, is not job enlargement, although it embodies some aspects of the latter. The individual is given more to do, but this time in a vertical rather than a horizontal direction. In essence, controls are removed from the individual, who is given increased accountability and authority to undertake the work which is being done. He or she becomes actively involved in the planning and evaluation of that work. Moreover, quite often, new and more difficult tasks are involved which give the individual an opportunity to become an expert in that particular job, or part of the job. This has all the hallmarks of a good delegation system. What has been found, where this has been enacted, is a reduction of boredom and a quite marked increase both in motivation and productivity. In addition, where absenteeism was a problem, this was also reduced substantially.

Job redesign

Job redesign became the *cri de cœur* during the late 1960s and 1970s. The work itself is rooted in ergonomics and in social theories of motivation at work. The essence of job redesign is to design jobs that use the individual's abilities in terms of judgement and decision-making. Mechanical, routine, repetitive operations are allocated, so far as is possible, to machines. The job itself is meaningful in exactly the same way as it is under a job enrichment scheme. The idea is that, as the job grows, and the worker learns, then he or she gains recognition and support. In this way, the social context of the job is

29

enhanced. Moreover, the redesign has direct implications for the career prospects of the individual.

Job redesign has been brought in by organizations for one of two major reasons, either operational or personnel. Operationally, the organization may have been concerned to reduce such things as costs, down-time, bottlenecks, and so on. As people took more control for their work within the organization, it was held that such things as these and delivery times and reject rates would be reduced substantially. In this way, it was felt that improvements could be made to such things as customer service and cost control. Moreover, productivity and quality could both be increased quite dramatically. In the longer term, it was felt that what was also being generated was a more adaptable form of staff. In these terms, people became much more of a resource to the organization itself.

On the personnel side, it was hoped that job design would reduce such problems as turnover and absenteeism. In the short term, there may well have been an increment in training costs but, in the longer term, these would reduce. Demarcation problems and overtime could also be curtailed, as could complaints and grievances. Improvements, so far as the personnel side of things was concerned, would be in an area such as recruitment and timekeeping. Both industrial relations and skills development could also be improved quite dramatically. Job redesign also had implications both for management development practices and, therefore, training in the longer term as well as flexibility of behaviour within the organization. But these were not the only reasons why job redesign was brought in. Occasionally, it was introduced purely on an experimental basis or in association with a development of industrial democracy and the growth of participation. Sometimes, it was brought in alongside, or even as a result of, job evaluation or work study. At other times, it was brought in as a potential solution to difficulties over pay or with changes in the size of the work force itself.

Stress

We cannot look at motivation without also considering the stress symptoms which appear in behaviour from time to time. Typically, you can divide signs of stress into two major categories: physical and mental. Under physical, you would look under such things as insomnia, gastric disturbances, heart disease, migraines, excessive smoking or drinking and lethargy. Even some forms of phobia may be reactions to stress. Thus, in the City of London, one particular person's reaction to the stress which 'big bang' brought to that area in 1986/7, was the onset of claustrophobia. Given that the individual's journey necessitated travelling on the London Underground at rush hour periods, it was not to be wondered that there was a marked, and very noticeable, downturn in performance. This complaint, whilst having its physical side, was, in fact, better encapsulated under the generic heading of mental problems. Typically, stress comes out in mental fashion through anxiety, tension or mental illness at the extreme. Boredom and worry about the future, equally, may be seen in this particular light, as may that most debilitating of mental problems, depression. It is because of all this that we cannot simply look at motivation as having positive implications. We must also look at the downside risk inherent in people's behaviour at work, if we are properly to consider the whole arena of motivation.

Traditional view

Up until the late 1920s or early 1930s there was a traditional view of the people at work encapsulated in Taylorism. Taylor based his theories of people at work on a series of assumptions. These, in turn, led to a series of policies and a set of expectations. The essence of these is contained in Figure 2.5, and we look at the organizational implications of Taylor's ideas in Chapter 6.

Assumptions

People:
1. Dislike work
2. Work only for money
3. Are incapable of self-control or self-direction.

Policies
1. Simple repetitive tasks.
2. Close supervision tight control.
3. Extra effort will lead to greater reward.

Expectations
1. If closely controlled people will meet the standards.
2. Firm, but fair, supervision will be respected.

Figure 2.5 Traditional view of motivation

The impact of Taylor's original conceptualization should not be underestimated. It underpins many working practices today. The whole idea of differentiation and integration within an organization could be laid quite firmly at Taylor's feet. Indeed, had he not been so politically naïve when he came across the unions at the Watertown Arsenal in the 1920s, his impact might even have been greater. In the relative chaos of his era, he brought alternative ways of dealing within organizations to ensure high productivity. Moreover, despite the fact that we might argue that he was taking advantage of people's inability to bargain for themselves, none the less people were substantially better off under his particular method of working. This was especially the case where piece-work systems were introduced, for it enabled people to increase their productivity substantially and, thereby, their take-home pay. The cynics among us might well argue, however, that the amount of productivity increase was not exactly matched by the amount of wage increase.

Human relations

The roots of the human relations school of thinking can be quite plainly seen in the work of Mayo and his colleagues; however, it took another eighteen years for its impact to begin to be felt within organizations (see Chapter 7). Figure 2.6 captures the essence of the human relations school.

Assumptions
The people want:
1. To feel important.
2. Recognition.
3. To be controlled.

Policies
Managers should:
1. Discuss the plans which have been made.
2. Be prepared to listen to any objections put forward by the staff.
3. Allow self-control on routine tasks.

Expectations
1. Participation increases satisfaction and morale.
2. Subordinates would willingly cooperate.

Figure 2.6 Human relations view of motivation

This school of thinking grew out of the experimentation undertaken by Mayo and his colleagues at Western Electric in Chicago, whose work involved them in intimate contact with a range of different people within that organization. Their published findings had major implications for a range of quite different organizations in the Western world and led to a whole new way of thinking about people at work. What has to be placed in context is, however, the fact that during the time in question people working within the organization did so under the most pitiful conditions. In essence, they worked in sweatshops where hours were long and conditions were not good.

It is today somewhat difficult to conceive of this situation yet it could be encapsulated in the remark during the Second World War between two flight sergeants in the RAF. One of them turned to the other and asked how he had been able to shave a tapering octagonal piece of metal to fit precisely over the spar of a wing. The answer which he received says it all: 'Where I worked before the war, if you spoilt a piece of metal you got the sack. As a result you did things both quickly and accurately.'

For the people working in Western Electric to have these white-collared academic researchers being attentive and giving them feedback on their performance was a major change. In practical terms it led to improved performances – performance improvements which were deemed to have been created by means other than straightforward knowledge of results (feedback). One underestimated result of the original research is quite interesting, for the organization actually brought into existence the role of counsellor. This was somebody to whom any member of staff could turn at any time in order to discuss problems from whatever source in total confidence that the inform-ation would be treated as sacrosanct. It was a role which was maintained until the early 1950s and it is re-emerging in today's organizations (for a fuller description of the Hawthorne studies, see Chapter 6, below).

The best of the results of this school of thinking emerged as quite different ways of treating people within the work situation. This plainly had very positive benefits both to the organization and to its members, especially in motivational terms. There was, of course, a downside to this. As the idea caught on that people might want some involvement in the decision-making process, managers became more manipulative in the way they discussed their own plans and listened to suggestions and objections from members of their staff. In turn, this at least in part led to a diminution of the effect which this theory might otherwise have had in the longer term.

Assumptions: People
  1. Want to contribute.
  2. Can exercise broad self-direction and self-control.
  3. Represent an untapped resource.

Policies
  1. Create a climate in which everybody could contribute.
  2. Develop full participation on important problems.
  3. Continually broaden the area of self-direction and self-control.

Expectations
  1. Direct improvement in decision-making and control.
  2. Increase in job satisfaction as a by-product of what is occurring.

Figure 2.7 Human resources view of motivation

The shift from human relations to human resources occurred during the period of the 1950s to the late 1960s. The roots of it can be seen in the work of Trist and Bamforth. The idea that people from the lowest organization level to the highest had something to contribute beyond actually doing their job has had some interesting implications for many organizations during the last two decades (see Figure 2.7).

Whilst advocates for this view can often be found at the most senior levels of an organization, and at the most junior, the major difficulty is convincing those people in the middle of the organization. This gross and occasionally unjust generalization about middle management and their unwillingness to access junior levels for suggestions and alterations to the methodology of working is actually quite a well-known phenomenon within organizations. Having said that, if we actually expect middle management to change their behaviour then we must change the situation within which they work in order that new behaviour can be reinforced.

When it comes to dealing at the individual level, so far as motivation is concerned, both theory and practice go back, not just decades, but centuries. Robert Owen's work in Lanarkshire at the turn of the nineteenth century used very simple behaviour reinforcement in the shape of coloured counters. These were used to provide feedback on performance for the individuals undertaking the work. Different colours represented different standards of performance and were plainly visible, both to the job incumbent, as well as to other people on the shop floor. As an aside, Owen actually did a great deal more for his workers and was, to put it mildly, an extremely enlightened employer. Moreover, he was sufficiently successful to draw attention to his work from the Yorkshire and Lancashire areas of the country. In the final analysis, it was the other mill owners who finally put paid to his experimental work.

Part of the managers' responsibility within the organization is to look after its resources, one of the most expensive of which is, of course, people. A major part, therefore, of the managers' work is to ensure that those people for whom they are responsible are performing at appropriate levels and it could well be argued that they need to keep in fairly close contact with them in order to do this. There must be a two-way flow of information in which managers should listen to the staff and at the same time keep them informed of intentions, at least so far as they are able. This does not always imply that the manager has to give all available information to the subordinate. Plainly there will be things which, by their very nature, have to be withheld, but the better people are able to contextualize their actions the greater the likelihood that they can behave appropriately. Moreover, if that leads to greater performance then the evidence from a great deal of research comes into its own. Quite specifically, the research indicates that high performance leads to job satisfaction. The reverse, whilst sometimes being true, does not necessarily follow: that is, feeling satisfied does not necessarily lead to high performance.

One of the major motivation issues is how to determine the frequency with which the manager should be concerned with this so far as the staff are concerned. What we should never lose sight of is the fact that motivation is almost inevitably levelled at individuals, since while there are things that you can do at the group level of analysis, by and large we are dealing with individuals. The complexities in dealing with individuals are many and varied. Both our priorities and our aspirations change; the changes in these will depend upon our age, the job level and other social factors even outside the organization itself. Indeed, more and more in today's world managers must face the fact that there will be times when they should be prepared to question people about issues which are beyond the work place and are in the social environment of that individual. From a simple review of the literature we can see the variation in motivating factors, including the following (but there are many more):

Motivators
- Challenge.
- Intellectual content.

- Social satisfaction.
- Security.
- Creativity.
- Responsibility.
- Money.
- Status.
- Autonomy.
- Promotion.
- Benefits.
- Aims.
- Recognition.
- Variety.
- Pride.
- Achievements.

The factors are varied and we shift between them depending on what is going on around us and depending at what stage in our lives we are. In other words, what motivates an individual at a particular point in time may, or may not, be the same motivator at some subsequent moment.

Demotivators

Nor should we simply consider looking at those things which act as motivators to performance. There are things within the organization which lead to decrement in performance: the demotivator factors. Again, as the theories show, these factors can be broken down under a series of broad headings. The first of these might be aspects to do with the environment or within which the work is taking place and would therefore include such things as poor working conditions. Others would have to do with the people side of the business and would therefore include such things as poor training, interpersonal clashes, poor leadership, inadequate staffing levels, and so on.

Inadequate staffing levels is an interesting case in point. Where this exists in the organization it is quite possible to compensate through the use of overtime. However, whilst people can maintain fairly high levels of overtime in the short term it is not a tactic to be utilized for continuing staff shortages. Evidence from research strongly indicates that performance under excessive overtime practices will fall quite markedly. Finally, the other broad category lies within the individual. Here we would include such problems as sickness, insecurity and personal problems. The effect of any of these should not be underestimated.

Stereotyping

At the individual level of analysis there is little doubt that stereotyping and labelling people can have direct effects on their overall performance. These effects can be in either direction, that is, leading to poorer or better performances. It has been known for a long time that by rewarding those things which we do properly we increase the chances that they will occur in future. This was the sort of thinking which underpinned much of Skinner's work. Blanchard and Johnson's *The One Minute Manager* (1982) includes the phrase 'help people reach their full potential, catch them doing something right'. It has been well known for centuries; it has been written about in detail for the last fifty years. Yet still the lesson needs to be taken up by people in the work place.

Labelling is another unfortunate habit much akin to stereotyping. Whilst it can have quite positive effects, e.g. if the person is labelled as a high performer, it can also have quite negative effects. The question is: Why do these effects occur? The answer is simple and straightforward. If we label somebody as good, what we then do is look for those behaviours in the individual which say that that person is a good performer. These behaviours are rewarded. The behaviour continues, the person performs well and the label has become a self-fulfilling prophecy. The reverse is equally the case. When someone has been defined as a poor performer what tends to happen is that those aspects of his or her behaviour which indicate poor performance are the only aspects which are monitored. The self-fulfilling prophecy works equally well in this direction. The history of research in this area is again strong and follows the same line as expectancy theory. It shows the impact of expectations on performance. Blanchard encapsulates this as: 'Everyone is a potential winner, some are disguised as losers, don't let appearances fool you.' Those people who have been intimately involved in selection work will know this phenomenon particularly well.

Perhaps the classic piece of work undertaken in the area of motivation was to do with appraisal and was carried out by Meyer *et al.* (1965). Their research was purely concerned with looking at the effects on individuals of various management practices and their ultimate findings are as valid today as they were then. In summary, what they found was that systems in which more than two elements of criticism were given were actually perceived by the recipients as a reprimand. Even if the criticisms took the form of a critique and were accurate in their representation, the end result was not in the direction which the manager had hoped for. Praise, too, was found to be desperately underutilized. Indeed, where it did occur, it was of such a general nature that there was virtually no effect.

What the researchers were advocating from their work was something which, today, we take for granted – in research terms at least, i.e. that any criticism or praise should be undertaken keeping the four Ps well in mind. The four Ps are as follows:

- Personal.
- Proximate.
- Precise.
- Private.

What is meant by these is that any praise or criticism should relate to the individual rather than necessarily the group or wider set of people (personal); it should also follow as closely as possible the event to which it refers (proximate). Taking this into the world of appraisals, for example, there should be no surprises at the annual review of performance. The feedback should delineate exactly what has been done well or done badly (precise); in the initial stages, additionally, it should also be done with the individual him- or herself (private). This goes as much for praise as for criticism. There may be occasions when the praise itself is then made known to the wider group, but in the initial stages it should be given specifically to the individual.

Meyer and his colleagues went on to define other aspects so far as motivating people was concerned. They argued that any goals that were going to be set for the individual, and his or her performance, should both be mutually agreed and be as specific as possible. They also went on to argue that the manager's job involved them in managing the total resources of the organization. The implications of this were that the manager should be a human resource manager which would involve the manager in coaching those under his or her control. Meyer *et al.* were also categorically determined that any appraisal system should separate out the performance side of things from other elements. Certainly, if the attempt is being made to motivate people to increase performance levels, there should be no confusion between the coaching side of things which looks at the subordinate's day-to-day performance and the review of the degree to which they met the objectives set, which in turn determines the level of reward which is gained (see Jackson 1985).

Randell's model

Randell's equilibrium, or steady state theory attempts to pull together many of the different strands of motivation theory into a single model. The model is reproduced in Figure 2.8 and begins with the

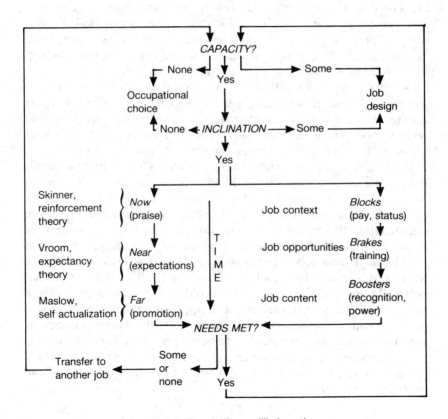

Figure 2.8 Randell's equilibrium theory

first question: Does the individual have the capacity to undertake the work or not? If the answer is 'no', and there is little chance of him or her creating the capacity, then the question has to be asked whether they have made the right occupational choice. If the answer is 'some', then there may be things that can be done in terms of job design. If the answer is 'yes', the second question then needs to be asked is: Do they have the inclination to actually undertake the work? If the answer here is 'no', then the implication is either, go for occupational choice or perhaps for job design. On the other hand, if the inclination exists, then we have to look at other aspects to see whether that inclination can be put to effect.

Down one side of the model are work technique aspects which can hold back or enhance performance. These would include such things as the job context and opportunities, as well as the content of the work itself. Down the other side of the equation are person-centred aspects of motivation on a time dimension. Some things we need to do immediately, for example, praise and criticism would fall into this category and the work of people such as Skinner would be pertinent. On the other hand, people will often do things for rewards which exist in the near future as opposed to the immediate present. In this area we are concerned with people's expectations and Vroom's work plainly fits. Some people have much longer term goals in mind and are concerned with individual growth and, in Maslow's terms, self-actualization. The way we would deal with the individual, therefore, under each of these time dimensions, might be quite different.

The model then goes on to ask the question as to whether the needs both of the organization and of the individual are met. If the answer here is 'no', then it may have implications again for a job design or even, at the opposite extreme of this, the restructuring of the organization. If some of these needs are met, and there is no chance of any increment in this, then there may be implications for the individual in that job – perhaps involving transfer to some other work. If the answer is actually 'yes', then we still do not stop at that point. Because of the dynamism, both of the individual and the situation within which they are working, the whole thing needs to be continually gone through. In other words, the model is a loop in which the actors are continually changing and, therefore, the needs, inclinations and capacities are also changing. It is the manager's task to make sense of these for the benefit both of the players and the organization at large.

References

Adams, J.S. (1965), 'Inequity in social exchange', in L. Berkowitz (ed.), *Advances in Experimental Social Psychology*, vol. 2 (New York: Academic Press).

Adler, A. (1927), *The Practice and Theory of Individual Psychology* (New York: Harcourt Brace and World).

Aldefer, C.P. (1972), *Existence, Relatedness and Growth* (New York: Free Press). Press).

Belbin, R.M. and Hartston, W. (1976), *Personal Preference Questionnaire Manual* (Cambridge: Industrial Training and Research Unit).

Blanchard, K. and Johnson, S. (1982), *The One Minute Manager* (London: Willow).

Block, J. (1973), 'Lives through time', *Contemporary Psychology*, vol. 18, No. 12, pp. 600–1.

Broadbent, D.E. (1961), *Behaviour* (London: Eyre and Spottiswoode).

Cattell, R.B. (1966), *The Scientific Analysis of Personality* (Chicago: Holme).

Hall, C.S. and Lindzey, G. (1985), *Theories of Personality* (New York: Wiley,

Herzberg, F. Mausner, B. and Snyderman, B. (1959), *The Motivation to Work* (New York: Wiley).

Jackson, A.P. (1985), 'Performance appraisal, counselling and management by objectives', in B. Livy (ed.), *Management and People in Banking* (London: Institute of Bankers, 2nd edition).

Jung, C.G. (1961), 'The theory of psychoanalysis', in *Collected Works*, vol. 4, (Princeton: Princeton University Press).

Kretschmer, E. (1925), *Physique and Character* (New York: Harcourt Brace Jovanovich, 2nd edition).

Maslow, A.H. (1970), *Motivation and Personality* (New York: Harper and Row, 2nd edition).

Mayo, E. (1933), *The Human Problems of an Industrial Civilisation* (New York: MacMillan).

Meyer, H.H., Kay, E. and French, J.R.P. Jnr (1965), 'Split roles in performance appraisal', *Harvard Business Review*, vol. 43, pp. 123–9.

Rogers, C.R. (1947), 'Some observations on the organisation of personality', *American Psychologist*, vol. 2, pp. 358–68.

Sheldon, W.H. (1942), *The Varieties of Temperament* (New York: Harper & Row).

Steers, R.M. and Porter, L.W. (1979), *Motivation and Work Behaviour* (London: McGraw Hill, 2nd edition).

Trist, E.L., Higein, G.W., Murray, H. and Pollock, A.B. (1963), *Organisational Choice* (London: Tavistock).

Vroom, V.H. (1964), *Work and Motivation* (New York: Wiley).

3

Group behaviour and leadership

Interactions between people in groups are fundamental within the world of work, where we are concerned with looking at the ways in which people influence one another's behaviour. These interactions might be by talk, by occasional smiles or other non-verbal behaviour. The conclusion from all the literature is that the behaviour of every group member potentially affects all the other members of that group. The interaction may be discontinuous or short-lived but whatever interaction does occur (physical, verbal, non-verbal, emotional, etc.), is a key feature of group life.

Definitions

In trying to define what we mean by a group, we naturally understand that if three people are seated in separate rooms with no means of communication, they can hardly be considered a social group, for their isolation prevents any form of interaction. The moment we allow for some interaction, by letting at least one person influence, and be influenced by, the others, then we may well consider these three people to be a rudimentary group. In these terms, therefore, we can follow Forsyth (1983) in defining a group as two or more individuals who influence one another through social interaction.

A group is a collection of individuals who have relations to one another that make them interdependent to some significant degree (Cartwright and Zander 1968). By a group, we mean a number of persons who communicate with one another, often over a span of time, and who are few enough so that each person is able to communicate with all the others, not at second-hand through other people, but face to face (Homans 1950). There will be two or more persons who are interacting with one another in such a manner that each person influences, and is influenced by, each other person (Shaw 1981). A group is a social unit which consists of a number of individuals, who stand in (more or less) definite status and role relationships to one another, and which possesses a set of values or norms of its own, regulating the behaviour of individual members, at least in matters of consequence to the group (Sherif and Sherif 1956). A group is a number of people in interaction with one another, and it is this interaction process that distinguishes the group from an aggregate (Bonner 1959). For a collection of individuals to be considered a group, there must be some interaction (Hare 1976).

Structure

Almost all groups develop a structure of some kind. What is meant by structure is a stable pattern of relationships among the members of the group. The three major terms which are used to describe such structures are roles, norms and inter-member relations. Roles are the behaviours expected of people who occupy different positions in the group. Norms are the rules which identify and describe appropriate behaviours (see below). Inter-member relations may be based on many factors such as authority, attraction and communication. They will be looked at in more detail as we progress through this chapter, starting with norms.

Norms

Rules are established within groups and concern how individuals are expected to behave. These rules are called norms, and serve as standards by which people will regulate their own behaviours and, through this means, improve their coordination. Typically, norms fall into one of two quite distinct patterns: prescriptive (those behaviours which should be performed) and proscriptive (those which are to be avoided). There is an element of evaluation contained in norms. It is, by this means, that people who transgress are considered to have behaved badly and leave themselves open to sanction by other group members. Such norms are often adopted implicitly rather than made explicit within the group. Norms appear rapidly, even where the group begins with little, or no, consensus and perhaps with great variability in behaviour. What happens is that members structure their experiences until they conform to some standard developed within the group. Sherif's work on the autokinetic effect is an example of what happens as a result of group pressures. In the experiments, subjects looked at a stationary light source in a darkened room; they reported a pendulum type movement of this light – even though the light did not move. What he found was that, although there may initially be a wide dispersion of judgement, after three or four sessions and where people interact with each other, there was an almost unbreakable pattern of consensus among the subjects of the experiment, that the light source had moved. This leads us directly to a concern with the system of communication within the group.

Studying norms experimentally
Experimentation in group work finally took off during the mid-1930s with Sherif's work on social norms. His experimentation, in which social norms in a group setting were both created and manipulated, was a major breakthrough for social psychology and established experimentation as a suitable method for group dynamics research. What Sherif was able to show in his work of 1936, is that group concepts, such as norms, could be experimentally manipulated. Moreover, he was able to show that meaningful research could be conducted in a laboratory setting. Perhaps most importantly, two other factors emerged. First, it was not always necessary to look at naturally occurring groups – the groups could be *ad hoc* assemblies of people. Secondly, providing that the setting itself was carefully controlled, the impact of the so-called 'Hawthorne' effect could be minimized. The Hawthorne effect occurs when the subjects under study change their behaviour because they are being studied (see Chapter 6 below).

Communication networks

Plainly, the format of communication within a group directly affects its effectiveness and efficiency. Communication has direct implications for problem solving, leadership and member satisfaction. It does appear that network efficiency, in terms of the different forms of communication, is related to information saturation. The more complex the issues involved, then, as the work progresses there is an increase in the number of communications routed through the central member. The result is a saturation in which the individual can no longer efficiently monitor, collate or route incoming and outgoing messages. Saturation may, of course, occur in decentralized networks but it is much more likely to occur in centralized ones. In this latter situation, the hub receives, and gives out, a huge range of communications on many different channels. Typically, in real-life situations, central position occupants report they are satisfied with the group's structure; more peripheral members emphasize their dissatisfaction. For the majority of people, it appears that a decentralized network is preferable, as this would encourage independence of action, autonomy and self-direction.

Interpersonal exchange

Within the notion of interpersonal exchange, the major theory is that of social exchange. It is an interesting idea, for it assumes that, as individuals, we actually balance the costs against the rewards of membership of certain groups. There is certainly strong evidence that the value of rewards decreases with the number of times that the reward is actually given. Generally, we can say people will gain more from coming into groups less frequently and for shorter periods of time. Moreover, this points to the fact that people can be a source of comfort, encouragement, approval and support. There are two other aspects. The first is the notion contained under the heading 'social approval', which is a positive means of providing social support for others by showing them that you approve of them as people. Also involved in this is the notion of reciprocity, that is, 'I like people who like me, and I dislike those who do not.' Secondly, there is a notion of belief confirmation. This is concerned with the similarity in terms of values, beliefs and interests in people who come together in groups. It is this agreement which assures group members that their beliefs are acceptable and accurate and in many ways, it paves the way for conflict-free and rewarding future interactions. Group members tend to give back very positive self-evaluations. Moreover, as Festinger's cognitive dissonance theory would have us believe, disliking people who share our beliefs would lead to a cognitive imbalance. Because such imbalances are uncomfortable we work to avoid them, and therefore reconcile our views by creating reasons for liking such people.

Perceiving groups

In order for us to believe that a group is actually a group, we require certain cues to be available to us. The three basic principles of organization of our perceptions of groups are as follows:

- Common fate.
- Similarity.
- Proximity.

By common fate, what is meant is the extent to which individuals in the group seem to experience the same, or interrelated outcomes. Similarity is concerned with the extent to which the individuals display the same behaviour or resemble one another in some way. Finally, proximity is concerned with the spatial distance among individuals in that group. It is by using these cues that we determine whether a group exists, or whether it is simply a collection of independent individuals.

Forming a group

When people encounter ambiguous situations, then the overall finding is that they will join with others as a means to a better understanding of the reality of the situation in which they find themselves. This is a force which enables people to join and work together, and as such, it might be considered to have motivational value. In which case, we would turn to Maslow's original hierarchy of needs to discover that it is the need for information (a cognitive need) which is a major driving force for people when working together.

Two other factors are involved in people coming together in groups. The first of these factors is the competence of individuals, and the second is physical attractiveness. In the case of the former, competent, intelligent and perhaps task efficient people are viewed as more desirable group members than those who are incompetent. Strangely, with this particular aspect of people's behaviour, extremely competent people may well feel rejected simply because of their infallibility. There is some evidence to suggest that highly competent people who reveal their fallibility through some minor errors, are often better liked than unerring group members. Physical attractiveness, especially in informal groups, seems to rate as a major asset and is a commodity which can be traded during social interaction. However, the evidence here is less concrete than that for other aspects of group interaction.

Groups exist for a reason. People join groups in order to achieve goals that they might be unable to achieve on an individual basis. This sharing of common goals is one of the major unifying factors within groups and shared goals motivate individual group members to behave in ways which can result in the successful completion of the group's goals. Group formation also is made more easy when group membership is able to facilitate the attainment of desired goals. To be quite specific about this, the use of the word 'goals' refers, in the main, to goals which can be achieved only through group membership. Under these circumstances, groups can form and become highly

Table 3.1 The relevance of the study of group dynamics for academic disciplines and for organizations

Discipline	Some relevant topics
Psychology	Social facilitation, problem-solving, attitude change, perception of others, social comparison
Sociology	Coalition formation, influence of norms on behaviour, role relations, deviance
Anthropology	Groups in cross-cultural contexts, societal change, groups based on sex/age/race
Political science	Leadership, inter-group relations, political influence, power
Speech and communication	Information transmission in groups, problems in communication, communication networks
Business and industry	Motivation, productivity, improving organizational effectiveness, structuring goals
Social work	Improving adjustment through group participation, family counselling
Education	Classroom groups, team teaching, class composition and educational outcomes
Clinical counselling psychology	Therapeutic change through group counsellings, sensitivity training, encounter groups
Criminal justice	Organization of law enforcement agencies, gangs, jury deliberations, patrol team effectiveness
Sports and recreation	Team performance, effects of victory and failure, cohesion and performance

cohesive. Indeed, groups can often put away frictional aspects of their behaviour in order to deal well with the goals which actually are faced by the group.

Groups are relevant to many applied areas. We have certainly been occupied with research on groups in the work setting since the late 1920s to the early 1930s. Plainly the classic research from that time was that of Mayo and his cohorts at the Western Electric Company in Chicago. Forsyth (1983, p. 14) has compiled a table in which topics in group dynamics are laid out (see Table 3.1). The listing shows quite strongly that groups, and the study of them, is not limited to a single field.

Primary groups

Perhaps the father of group work and research is Emile Durkheim, who attempted to show that society is based on fundamental solidarity among people. He suggested that solidarity is derived from interpersonal relations among members of primary groups. For him, the primary group was defined as a small group of people who are characterized by face-to-face interactions, interdependency and strong group identification. Plainly, such groups would include families, peer groups, groups of business colleagues, etc.

Dynamics
It is worth noting that group dynamicists recognize that groups do change all the time. Conclusions based on observations earlier on may not be valid for the same group at a later stage. Two explanations are usually quoted to account for this change. The first of these is a recurring phase theory, which is concerned with the suggestion that certain issues tend to dominate group interactions during the phases of group development, and that these issues can recur later in the life of that group. Thus, if the group was concerned to balance task-oriented and emotionally expressive behaviours, then it may oscillate between these two concerns, first achieving high solidarity, then shifting towards a more work-centred focus.

The second explanation is that of sequential stage theory. This is the work of Tuckman (1965), who developed the concepts of 'forming', 'storming', 'norming' and 'performing'. In fact, he added a further one to these in his later work (with Jensen) in 1977, that of 'adjourning'. These frameworks provide perspectives from which we can understand group development. The actual differences between the two approaches are minor, but both agree that, because the issues inherent in group behaviour are never completely resolved, the stages can recur.

Industrial research
The Hawthorne studies, during the late 1920s and early 1930s, were the first attempt to look at group interactions within an industrial setting (see Chapter 6). As a result of their initial work, the focus of research shifted to the social organization of the group, group norms and the attitudes and motives of workers. Despite some concerns over the years as to the validity of the Hawthorne studies' findings, what cannot be denied is the impact which those studies have had on research into human behaviour within the work situation. What also was demonstrated was that group members act differently when they believe they are being observed by others who are interested in their behaviour. This change in behaviour, via observations, is now known as the Hawthorne effect. It may well limit the generalizability of research findings, based on field and laboratory situations, in which people know they are being studied.

Group think

The notion that groups can be so powerful that they influence the thinking process of group members was explored by Janis. The unfortunate thing about group think is that as a concept it is used to describe two almost opposing hypotheses. The original work of Janis (1972) was concerned with, in his words, 'a deterioration of mental efficiency, reality testing and moral judgement that results from in-group pressures'. Unfortunately, as with many concepts, other researchers have used the same word to describe a more positive aspect of group behaviour. Underpinning their ideas is the belief that synergy is a positive force, which improves group decision-making. In this case, the exact reverse of that described by Janis occurs and the group emerges in its decision-making at a much higher level than the people comprising that group could do in their own right (Belbin 1981).

Source of conflict

For some considerable time, the evidence concerning the characteristics of people within groups, and how these influence conflict in a group, was perceived to be too complex. For this reason, general conclusions have been, to date, difficult to formulate. However, armed with the research which was undertaken by Belbin *et al.* (1976) we can now begin to move to some predictions about where potential conflict can arise within groups. These are detailed below. As a result of the work of Belbin *et al.*, we can add a predictive quality to Blake and Mouton's (1964, 1978) basic assumptions that conflict was a function of the importance of the production of results and the importance of the feelings of people in disagreement. And, indeed, one of the major aspects of conflict within a group is the amount of anxiety which is to be perceived within the group itself.

Misunderstandings and misperceptions: attribution theory

Before we examine Belbin's findings, we should first consider the problems we encounter when trying to interpret behaviour. In order that people can begin to make inferences about the causes of behaviour, what they tend to do is to formulate causal hypotheses which are based on intuition. These are then used to understand, and predict, transpiring events within the group. Naturally, these causal beliefs more often determine group members' perceptions of other people's motives and intentions. What attribution theory tells us is that if group members attribute disagreement merely to the group's attempts to make the right decisions then such disagreement does not turn into conflict. On the other hand, conflict escalation occurs when the attribution for the disagreement is based on incompetence or argumentativeness. Moreover, there are some errors which tend to occur when we attribute causal relationships between things. In essence, the attributor will overestimate the causal importance of personality, beliefs, attitudes and values, whilst, at the same time, underestimating the importance of situational pressures. The overall perception, so far as attributions are concerned, is that these are more often than not biased in a negative direction; people tend to assume the worst about other group members. In fact, we can differentiate competitive people from cooperative people. The latter tend to be more accurate in their attribution, whereas competitors tend to assume that others are also competitive.

Conflict and values

Nor should we assume that conflict is necessarily a bad thing. There is some evidence which suggests, quite strongly, that a degree of tension and, therefore, conflict is necessary for a group to perform at an adequate level. In part, of course, what we are looking for are frequent episodes of conflict which have positive consequences, e.g. the clarification of goals, increased understanding of differences, etc. What may well have happened, under such circumstances, is that the group may have developed norms and techniques which limit escalation of the conflict. By controlling the magnitude and extent of conflict, group interaction is maintained at a lively level.

Intra-group conflict exists whenever the actions or beliefs within the group are incompatible, or are resisted by others within the group. We can identify the following five stages in this process:

- Disagreement.
- Confrontation.
- Escalation.
- De-escalation.
- Resolution.

Upon examining the nature of the disagreement, and the creation of the belief that the issue is important enough to require resolution, then group members will tend to confront the problem through active discussion. During this confrontation, people become more intensely committed to their respective viewpoints and this may, in turn, lead to coalitions being formed within the group. The third stage, i.e. escalation, then occurs and this is typified by an upward conflict spiral often fed by misunderstandings, distrust, frustration, hostility, and so on. In time, hopefully, de-escalation of the conflict begins as the group attempts to reach agreement on the issues. Negotiation is plainly important here, as is the development of trust. If the groups cannot solve the problems internally, then third party intervention may be necessary. If this is at all successful then the group should reach conflict resolution. As a result, and throughout the sequence, a host of factors may be working to increase conflict among members and these will include such things as interdependence, personal characteristics, the influence strategies adopted, the magnitude of misunderstandings and misperceptions, etc. Finally, research indicates that conflict is both natural and necessary and an essential part of group dynamics. Confronting conflict may well create very strong feelings of group unity. It can also serve as an avenue, or release valve, for interpersonal hostility.

The evidence suggests that this course of conflict is spiral in nature, that is, having satisfactorily dealt with conflict at one level it will re-emerge, in a different form, and at a different level, at a later stage. In a sense, the resolution part of the conflict cycle is a crucial aspect, for it may equally be looked at in terms of learning ability so far as the group as a totality is concerned. Unless the group has the capacity to actually learn and work through the conflict, then schisms will occur within that group which, in the end, will lead to its destruction. The question, therefore, is: How can conflict be allowed to emerge in a non-destructive way? To answer this we need to look at how conflict emerges.

Once a group has begun to settle to the work which has to be done, and has agreed a series of norms, albeit covertly, it frequently emerges that disagreement exists between two or more members. At this stage, the rate of interaction slows and the attention of the group tends to focus on the source of conflict. The end result of this is extensive discussion as clarification of the problem is attempted. It is at this stage that other, previously unnoticed, issues of disagreement may also begin to arise. The discussion of disagreement and conflict within a group becomes quite fundamental to its ultimate health, for it may lead to other, more basic, points of contention which, if dealt with adequately, can begin to ensure that people are actually pulling in the same direction.

Confrontation conflict
The escalation of disagreement will show real differences existing between two or more people. It is, at this stage, that we shift from disagreement to confrontation. At this point, true conflict is said to exist within the group. As Forsyth (1983) points out, 'the actions and/ or beliefs of one or more members of the group are incompatible with – and hence are resisted by – one or more of the other group members.' As a result of this, discussion focuses more and more on substantive issues.

In the early stages of confrontation, what tends to happen is that there is an intensification of commitment by each of the parties to their own view. In part, this is based on a logical process of committing the strengths of each person's position to a verbal display. Having spoken the words, people simply become more committed to them. Such commitment is based in rationality. How-ever, the commitment itself is enhanced because, as a generality, individuals begin to doubt the veracity of information which conflicts with their stance and, as a result, increase their dedication to their original position. The greater the degree of escalation which occurs, the greater the degree of tension. As a result, emotions run much higher and this, in turn, may lead to the formation of a coalition within the group.

Escalation

It is at this point that a mini spiral may well occur within the group, i.e. conflict leads to more conflict which creates even more conflict. Group unity is shattered at this stage, as exchanges become increasingly hostile and emotional. Coercion, rather than persuasion, becomes the order of the day and promises are often replaced by threats. The conflict itself is often fed by distrust and frustration on the part of the members. In part, this escalation is due to the so-called norm of reciprocity. The implication of this is quite simple for what tends to happen between people is that any aggression shown by one person to another is likely to be reciprocated. This might well be deemed to be one of the norms of behaviour. To make this slightly clearer, if the norm within the group is one of competitiveness, then that becomes the way that any new member will behave. If, on the other hand, the norm is one of cooperativeness, then that norm will predominate over all others.

De-escalation

De-escalation tends to occur when people recognize that time and energy are wasted by the continuing debate. In any case, from psychological theory, we know that high levels of tension and emotional frustration cannot be maintained indefinitely. At that point, people once more become rational and understanding in the way that they deal with the particular conflict. What also may help is the fear of undermining the foundations of the group itself. De-escalation will then involve the participants in a negotiation which, in turn, can lead to the building of trust within the group. Whilst the initial conflict may not involve the disruption of trust, if trust has been built within the group, it can be destroyed only once. The rebuilding of it a second time is a near impossible task.

Resolution

Conflict can be resolved in a number of ways. First of all, it might be for the sake of group unity, or in the interest of saving time, that one of the participants withdraws from the conflict arena. Secondly, it may be that the group leader or some other authority figure may be persuaded to take one side in the issue and then mandate a decision.

An alternative method, under this same heading, is to simply vote on the issue and go with the deciding vote. The group may also work towards some kind of arbitrary decision made by flipping a coin or whatever. Agreement can be achieved through compromise.

Consensus decision-making

In this case, compromise is reached by both sides conceding points which they find more favourable, until, finally, agreement is reached. In a sense, this stage involves often quite deep bargaining and negotiation by the parties themselves. The group's dilemma could be solved by the conversion of one side to the point of view expressed by the other. This might be simply through the power of logic, persuasion or even, perhaps, promises. Finally, conflicts may be resolved through the dissolution of the group itself; that is, under the extreme pressure of apparently insoluble conflict the group itself will splinter into sub-groups. It is something which can sometimes be seen in very senior board level groups within organizations.

Roles

Any group has, of course, some form of structure. The uniformity of behaviour, regulatory standards, authority relations, attraction relations and communications all comprise, in their totality, the structure. Of these, two are key: those of role and norms. The latter has been dealt with above. By and large, we understand the word 'role' to denote those behaviours which people perform as group members. However, it could well be argued that this definition is somewhat narrow. Biddle (1979, p. 68) defines roles as 'behaviours that are characteristic of persons in a context'.

As the group begins to form, so roles also form within it. This is a process called role differentiation. Whilst, in part, role differentiation is based on the task and processes which the group will undertake, there are some roles which are common to all groups. The leadership role is an obvious one, yet even this may be discriminated into two quite different aspects: task and process. It may well be that, in some groups, both of these tasks are undertaken by a single person; in others, two or even more people will perform these functions.

One of the major actors in defining roles is Bales. Based on his original work with groups, he concluded that three dimensions would be needed to describe fully the structure of roles in groups (Bales 1980). Using these three dimensions, he has created a new measure of group interaction which goes far beyond the original Bales

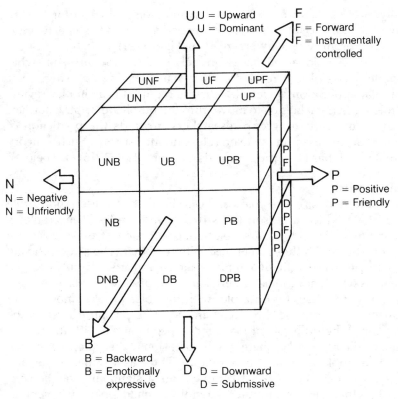

Figure 3.1 The SYMLOG model of group roles (Source: Bales 1980)

U	Active, dominant, talks a lot		N	Unfriendly, negativistic
UP	Extroverted, outgoing, positive		NB	Irritable, cynical, won't cooperate
UPF	A purposeful democratic task leader		B	Shows feelings and emotions
UF	An assertive business-like leader		PB	Affectionate, likable, fun to be with
UNF	Authoritarian, controlling, disapproving		DP	Looks up to others appreciative, trustful
UN	Domineering, tough-minded, powerful		DPF	Gentle, willing to accept responsibility
UNB	Provocative, egocentric, shows off		DF	Obedient, works submissively
UB	Jokes around, expressive, dramatic		DNF	Self-punishing, works too hard
UPB	Entertaining, sociable, smiling, warm		DN	Depressed, sad, resentful, rejecting
P	Friendly, equalitarian		DNB	Alienated, quits, withdraws
PF	Works cooperatively with others		DB	Afraid to try, doubts own ability
F	Analytical, task-oriented, problem solving		DPB	Quietly happy just to be with others
NF	Legalistic, has to be right		D	Passive, introverted, says little

analysis of groups from which he created some nineteen or twenty different roles. Using the three-dimensional model, some twenty-seven different roles may emerge (see Figure 3.1).

For organizational purposes, models such as this are somewhat complex. Useful for research, they have less value when their practical application is viewed. What is required is a simpler review of roles which enables us to move from the purely descriptive format, used by most of the group researchers, towards the prediction of group output based on the team roles and interactions. Such a theory is that which has been propounded by Belbin *et al.* (1976) (see below).

Role conflict

There are two forms of role conflict. The first of these is inter-role conflict, in which a person plays two or more roles. The problems occur when the behaviours associated with one of these roles are incompatible with those associated with the other. The incompatibility here is within the individual him- or herself and arises simply because the roles which have to be undertaken are mutually exclusive in some way, as is the case, for example, with the roles of wife, mother and manager. Given these three roles in the same person, there will be occasions when the role of manager is incompatible with the role of wife; in the same way, there will be occasions when the role of wife is incompatible with the role of mother. Thus, as a manager she may have to remain at work to complete an assignment, yet be torn between that and, as a mother, attending a child's parents' evening.

Examples

A second form of conflict is that of intra-role conflict which this results from contradictory demands within a single role. In this case, the demands are those placed first by the individual who is undertaking the role and/or by the other members of his or her group. Roethlisberger's work on 'Foreman: master and victim of double talk' (1947), expresses this idea quite succinctly: within the single role of foreman, he is both perceived as a worker by management, and as a manager, by the work force. This raises tensions and conflicts within that individual trying to undertake this somewhat paradoxical role within the organization.

Performing

Critics of groups are sometimes right. There are times when people work very ineffectively as members of groups. Yet the antithesis of this is also true; groups can work effectively. Arguing that groups are always bad makes little sense: claiming that they always work well is equally nonsensical. The key question, therefore, is not whether groups are effective but rather when, or under what circumstances, are groups effective? One of the crucial concepts here is that of coaction.

Coaction occurs whenever we are performing a task whilst others around us are doing a similar thing. In the early days, it was believed that coaction actually facilitated better performances. However, subsequent work has, as with many aspects in social theory areas, shown there to be differing results under differing conditions. In some instances, coaction actually leads to performance decrements. What seems to be the case is that the presence of other people creates a sense of increased drive in the individual concerned in the task. This state of arousal increases the chances that dominant, as opposed to non-dominant, responses will occur. What is meant by dominant here is those behaviours which are uppermost in the individual's total repertoire of responses. If those dominant responses are then deemed to be appropriate, then the presence of any kind of audience will increase the likelihood of correct responses occurring. On the other hand, if these so-called dominant responses are inappropriate in the particular situation, then the presence of an audience will increase the likelihood that incorrect responses will occur.

In many ways, the notion of dominance can be replaced by the idea of familiarity of task. The more familiar the thing that has to be done, then the better it will be done in front of an audience. The less familiar, the more mistakes are likely to occur: i.e. mistakes beyond the number that might occur anyway in undertaking that particular task alone. It does appear that the presence of others facilitates well-learned responses and inhibits unfamiliar ones. The three factors which appear to be involved in this are as follows:

1. Arousal (that is, the mere presence of other people has arousing effects on the actor).

2. Concern about evaluation (a concern which is linked to the experience which all of us have had, that when we are watched by other people we are inevitably evaluated in our performance, either positively or negatively, by them).

3. Distraction.

On more complex tasks, the increase in drive is insufficient to offset the effects of distraction and, in turn, performance may be impaired. A key response to the question of the circumstances in which groups are effective, is Steiner's typology of tasks. He began with the notion contained in the following three questions:

1. Can the task be broken down into sub components?

2. Is quantity or quality of performance more important?

3. How are individual inputs related to the group's product?

In answering the first question, the two answers available are 'divisibility' and 'unity'. In terms of the second question, the two responses are concerned with maximizing (quantity) or optimizing (quality). In the third instance, we may relate individual inputs as being either additive, that is, adding even more to what is already occurring within a group, or as requiring the summing together of individual group members' inputs to maximize the group product.

Compensatory tasks are those which require the averaging together of individual judgements to yield the group's product. Disjunctive tasks, on the other hand, require an either/or answer. In disjunctive tasks, groups outperform individuals, although time costs are much greater within group settings. Conjunctive tasks, on the other hand, are tasks in which all people have to complete or at least contribute something to the total task. Under such circumstances, the group inevitably performs at the speed of the slowest member. Only if such tasks are divisible can the speed of completion, or whatever criteria is being used, be increased. Discretionary tasks are those which members can perform using their own preferred combination of procedures.

With Steiner's work, task classification is important. Different types of task require different sorts of resources (skills, abilities, tools, materials, equipment, time, etc.). If these resources are available, then the group may be successful, if not, then failure is likely. Steiner's work allows us to begin to predict whether a group will be successful at the task in hand. However, even more information is actually required if this is to make sound final sense. The other element which we need to know is whether decisions should be delegated. What is certain is that a group-centred approach to decision-making is a better strategy when issues are complicated, especially where members have a stake in the outcomes. However, delegation, although it takes away some of the decision-making power from members, actually saves a great deal of time and this may well justify the delegation. This is particularly the case when tasks are routine or extremely technical or, indeed, where group commitment to the decision is of little importance.

In a similar vein, averaging is an alternative way of dealing with decision-making within the group. Faced with a series of projects, by working out a ranking for those projects from each person, an overall ranking for the projects can be obtained. This is undertaken without discussion and there is, therefore, a danger that people may end up feeling little responsibility for implementation. An alternative to this is that of balloting, which is not dissimilar in terms of its effects within a group. People may feel alienated by such systems.

Consensus is the final notion. The unanimous agreement of all group members appears to be an ideal procedure. In the main, it is the in-depth discussion which binds members to the group and to the decision itself, which is so helpful. However, reality sometimes works against such a stratagem. It is in these instances that we find pressures to conform or to manipulate other people coming to the fore and this may result in decisions becoming railroaded through the group.

The communication process

It has often been held that having good communication within a group will make for a more effective group. Whilst this may be so, there will be occasions when having good communication may actually hold up the effectiveness of the group. The problem is in the definition of the word 'communication'. It covers a great deal. It includes, not only the actual words used, but, also, tone of voice, pitch, situation in which it takes place, and so on. It is precisely because of the interpretative quality of communication that we do not know whether it works for group betterment or to the detriment of the group.

Thus, we may communicate efficiently, but what we may communicate are things which work to the detriment of the task which actually faces the group. In a sense, communication is like conflict. It is a two-edged weapon. It has both negative and positive aspects to it. Thus, although we may reduce conflict by communicating, we may also increase the level of dispute within the group by outlining feelings of hatred, annoyance, etc. As a result, we can discriminate two quite different aspects of communication, first its content and secondly, how it is received by others. Of these, it is probable that how the message is received is the more important.

Process-planning

Groups rarely show much interest in process-planning. The reality, for most groups when they get together, is that they work almost immediately on the task in hand, rather than consider process-related issues. People believe that planning activities, except those which relate quite dramatically to the task itself, have a low priority, even when cautioned that advanced planning is critical. Where some procedure or other has already been devised, then this is leant on as a crutch without further amendment.

In a sense, the concept of process can be strictly allied with strategic planning. There is a great deal of evidence from the literature to suggest that the use of process-planning within groups makes them much more productive, especially when they are encouraged to discuss their performance strategies before working on the tasks which require coordination and cooperation within the group (Hackman, Brousseau and Weiss 1976). The further suggestion is that groups can enhance their effectiveness quite markedly by simply planning their performance strategies, rather than by simply letting the process unfold.

Systematic working procedures

When confronted with a task, groups need to go through the following steps:

- **Study and clarification**: the group needs to determine where the ambiguities in what they have to do may be. They must also look at what needs to be sorted out before they can move further. What is required is to achieve sufficient clarity and agreement within the group so as to be able to tackle the next step.

- **Setting objectives and criteria**: the group here is concerned with precisely what they are trying to achieve. At this stage, they are determining what the output or outcome of their work will be and in this way they will be able to ascertain, not only what success is, but how they can judge it at the end of that task.

- **Collecting information**: here the concern is rather with what is available within the group, or what is available to the group through its external contacts. What they may be concerned with are things like the facts, ideas and opinions contained within the group, relevant to the objectives which they have now set.

- **Deciding what has to be done**: in the light of the information that they have now gathered together, the group here is concerned with determining the actions and activities which are relevant to the achievement of the objectives. During this stage, what they have not got to lose sight of is the criteria which they would also have established.

- **Planning**: the concern here changes in emphasis. Questions now involve 'who' rather than 'what'. Planning embraces more than people, for there are also time and place dimensions to it. Who has to do?, What do they have to do?, When should it be done? and Where?, are really the crucial questions which face the group.

- **Action**: this speaks for itself and involves simply the carrying out, but, most importantly, the monitoring, of the plan.

Performance improvement planning: the group process
What objectives and plans for improvement can be carried forward by the group? is the final question. It is one which is often missed out. Yet reality, and research, tell us that this is possibly the most important aspect of any group work. It leads into a discussion of the very next aspect of the group performance which is concerned utterly with process. We may well have a systematic approach as the one outlined above, but it is quite another thing to make it work. Working systematically is what the group does; process tells us how it goes about doing this. As with systematic working, so with process there are things to which the group will need to agree to in advance.

- **Systematic working procedure**: this is concerned, as we have already outlined, with ensuring that groups stick to a commonly agreed approach to the task in hand.

- **Time**: probably the most underestimated of all the resources available to the group – this needs to be looked at most carefully. The group requires to forecast, divide up, plan and monitor its use of time. With some exceptions, it should be noted that of all the resources, this is the one which despite the number of reminders given to the group will be the least heeded and worst utilized.

- **Leadership**: the determination of leadership is crucial. A longer section on this area is included below. However, within the group situation, it is necessary to think of the type of leadership which is required and precisely what is expected of that leader. The assumption here is that leadership will emerge from within the group. Quite often this is not the case, for groups working within organizations have a leader imposed upon them. However, there may well be times when that leader delegates some of the leadership aspects to one, or more, members of the group, in order to ensure that the task is done in as effective a way as possible.

- **Decision-making**: plainly, the decision-making process is crucial in a group. How should they decide things: by vote or by consensus, or should they rely simply on the leadership making the final decision? Whichever way they decide, it will have direct implications for the way the group performs. It should be said that, in part, it will be determined by the kind of task which actually faces the group.

- **Delegation**: concern here is with the way in which jobs will be allocated to the people concerned. There will be a marked difference within the group as to whether it uses a volunteer base for the best use of skills, or by direction from the group leader him or herself; whichever it is going to be, some agreement has to be reached at the earliest stage of the group's formation.

- **Scribe**: within many groups, the idea of a scribe, or writer, for the group is one which arises only when the need actually to interface becomes paramount. However, the implications of the task should not be underestimated. And, indeed, if presentation is required from the group at some stage, the scribe might well be the best person to undertake that work. Again, following Belbin *et al.* (1976) we can begin to discriminate, through personality characteristics, the sort of person who would best make a scribe. In these terms, what is required is someone who has the capacity to listen to things said, to watch what is being done, and to reflect these back accurately.

We may well think of other matters which the group needs to consider. However, if it is to be successful in carrying out tasks, it will certainly need to invest effort in getting its process, i.e. the ways and means through which it works, right.

Performance improvement

This is a simple, but important, concept. It is based on the idea that a team improves, both rapidly and substantially, by reviewing its successes and failures, and setting new objectives to build on the successes and remedy its failures. After each task completion, it should review its performance and, over a series of reviews, it will then be able to build up a robust set of rules for higher performance. It is, in many ways, a continuous stage or part of any management work. And, in the manager/subordinate relationship, has implications which are often encapsulated in the word 'coaching'. We can see four main stages in any performance improvement planning work as follows:

Stage 1: reviewing the tasks which the group has worked upon and allowing the team to identify significant factors which have contributed to the success of, and those which have impeded, the task.

Stage 2: from the successes and failure factors, select those which are practical and remove those which have been found to be of no value.

Stage 3: the group then has to agree as to how precisely it will build on these factors and dispense with the others.

Stage 4: not only has this got to be done at a group level of analysis, but also at the individual level. Agreement needs to be determined as to how each individual will act or work differently to achieve any objectives which may now be set for the group. By and large, performance improvement sessions are concerned with performance and time management. They are important for establishing codes of practice for exactly how the group wants to manage itself effectively.

Brainstorming

One of the best known ways of attempting to increase the productivity of a group is to enter into a procedure which we today know well,

63

that of brainstorming. It was Osborn (1957) who set a series of rules together in an attempt to stimulate divergent thinking. His systematic procedure involved the following four rules:

1. **Expressiveness**: any idea which comes to mind can be expressed no matter how strange, wild or fanciful. Freewheeling is to be encouraged and constraint has to be avoided.

2. **Non evaluative**: ideas should not be evaluated in any way during the generation phase. All ideas are treated as having value. Criticizing anyone else's viewpoint is not allowed.

3. **Quantity**: the more ideas the better. Quantity is desired. It increases the possibility of generating better solutions.

4. **Building**: it is recommended that other people's ideas are both modified and extended. Brainstorming is conducted in group situations precisely so that participants can draw from one another.

There are further recommendations which have been made in terms of brainstorming. These include such things as asking questions, recording all people's ideas in full view of everybody and even, on some occasions, utilizing a turn-taking procedure. This latter course of action is particularly useful if interactions are becoming too unequal. A similar notion was utilized by Gordon (1961) who, together with other people, derived a procedure which they called Synectics to describe a not dissimilar approach to brainstorming. The only difference or, at least, the major difference, between it and brainstorming, as such, is that they attempt to stimulate divergent thinking by adding certain creative features to the actual process itself. These may, for example, take the form of expression of feelings as well as going on so-called excursions. The latter is an attempt deliberately to distract the group from the issues and problems which it currently faces. In this way, it can often provide an opportunity for creative thought, which often involves metaphor, analogy and even fantasy. However, it is well known that there are two features which are quite important for successful using of Synectics. In the first place, a fairly open cooperative group membership is a useful starting base. Perhaps more importantly, a skilled group leader or facilitator is also needed. Group members must be willing to follow the often unusual suggestions of the leader. Any refusal will disable the creative process.

Originator compatibility

From Schutz's (1958) work, the notion of compatibility between the members of a group of people who intend to work together is derived. It is in this notion of compatibility that some of the roots of Belbin's later theories can be seen. What Schutz argued was that it is possible to predict how well a group will come together by looking at the compatibility of the group members. Thus, in his terms, originator compatibility occurs when people who are prepared to initiate things work with those who wish to be included in such activities (inclusion). In addition, two other aspects are required to be present. The first of these is when you have those who wish to dominate and control the activities of others, working with those who wish to be controlled (control); secondly, when those who wish to give affection work with those who wish to receive it (affection).

However, Schutz does not stop there but moves on to talk about interchange compatibility. In a sense, the concern here is with the degree of compatibility which occurs. In simple terms, if you have two people coming together, one of whom believes that a great deal of affection should be exchanged, and the other who believes that only a small amount, if any, should be exchanged, then these two individuals' needs would be incompatible. Were this to be an existing framework, the chances of the group actually coming together are reduced. Moreover, Schutz's theory allows us to make predictions. It also allows us to describe what we should do within the structure of the group in order to enable it to perform reasonably well. People would have to agree on the amount of involvement that they have with others. They have to agree about the degree and formation of control, that is, how authoritarian or *laissez-faire* the control structure of the group is going to be. Furthermore, there has got to be at least an implicit agreement on the degree of closeness in terms of the personal feelings of the members of the group.

Predicting their performance

Until the mid-1970s, the work which had been carried out with groups allowed us to describe individual and group behaviour. From that, the change agent, consultant, observer, or even participant, was able to intercede in order to look at the effects of current behaviour in the group so far as its overall performance was concerned. The idea of such an intercession was to ensure that the group moved to a higher level of performance. However, from an organization's viewpoint, whilst the development of a team *in situ* is something which is plainly to be applauded, it would be far more helpful if a collection of individuals could be put together to form a group task force and for the organization to be able to know in advance the way such a group would perform. This notion of predicting the likely outcomes from a group was a problem which had beset social psychology for some decades. The work of Belbin (1981) and Belbin *et al.* (1976) finally gave practitioners the opportunity of putting teams together to ensure success. Based on a longitudinal study of senior-level managers from many different disciplines and many cultures, the predictive validity of the theory is high. Moreover, the theory does not move a great distance from the earlier theories of roles and the classifications of behaviours.

The original work delineated eight different team roles, and to these has now been added a further three. Nor are the roles themselves mutually exclusive: people may have a number of roles available to them. The clarifying concept is perhaps role dominance. In other words, each of us has a hierarchy of behaviours available to us and dominant behaviours are those which we utilize most quickly in most situations. For those who do have a repertoire of roles, this does not deny that they can dip into the other team roles when the occasion demands. Team roles themselves are described in the list below.

Over time, additional complexities have been added to the theory. Whilst the original work argued for an overall balance in the team, subsequent work showed how with known imbalances corrective action could be taken, for example in training terms, to ensure the success of the group. It was also found that different tasks may well require a different make-up of the team roles themselves. In other words, as with much human behaviour in the work situation, there is a situational, as well as individual, set of factors which must be accounted for in attempting any predictive work.

In many ways, it is the simplicity of the theory which lends it power. The team roles themselves can be classified under three major headings. The headings are no different, at least in two cases, from those which were derived from the Ohio Studies in 1940s. As ever, task orientation and people orientation emerge as fundamental aspects of people's behaviour. What Belbin adds to that classification is the notion that some people are ideas-oriented. In terms of these three headings (task, people and ideas), only three roles fit absolutely into one of those three categories. All other roles are, so to speak, tainted by more than one aspect. Taking each of the three overall headings in turn, the following picture emerges:

- **People-oriented roles**

  Team worker
  Company worker
  Chairman
  Resource investigator

- **Task-dominated team roles**

  Completer finisher
  Company worker
  Chairman
  Shaper
  Monitor evaluator

- **Ideas-oriented team roles**

  Plant
  Monitor evaluator
  Resource investigator

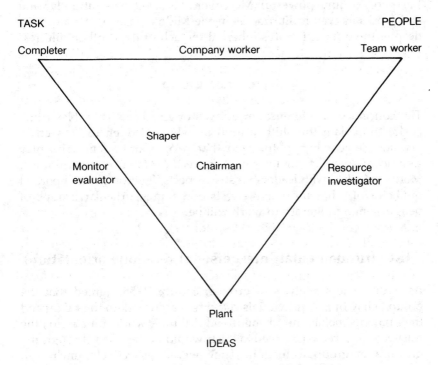

Figure 3.2 Team roles

The Essence of Organizational Behaviour

In each case, the first name 'team role' is the one which is, so to speak, pure. The other are mixes of the three orientations. Rather than show these linearly, we could, with better effect, show them as points on a triangle (see Figure 3.2).

By plotting the team roles of a particular group membership into this triangle, we can begin to make predictions as to the possible strengths and weaknesses of the group as a working entity. A proliferation of Plants would indicate many ideas, very little listening and the possibility that, without a Monitor Evaluator, they would quite suddenly run with one idea without any firm indication of how they came to choose it. Lack of a team role, for example, a Completer, would indicate that the group itself might have some trouble ensuring that the final details had been fully dealt with. In other words having monitored the make-up of the group in team-role terms, all that would then need to be done would be to work out, given the behaviours inherent in each of the team roles, the likely effects of having too much, or not any, of particular styles of behaviour. Work undertaken in a large range of organizations seems to indicate that the theory is quite powerful. Moreover, it is also cross-culturally valid and works as well in Europe as in the Middle East, or the Far East, despite the different mores inherent in each of these other cultures.

Reference group

The concept of a reference group was originally used by Newcomb (1943) to explain the shift in attitude which is often to be seen in people. Newcomb hypothesized that people around us who play significant roles in our lives can indirectly influence our attitudes. Moreover, allied with leadership style aspects, it becomes an important predictor of what the likely effects of having particular groups of people coming together to work will be.

FIRO (fundamental interpersonal relations orientation)

As with Freud's analysis of groups, Schutz (1958) agreed that the group behaviour of individuals could be traced back to their own and their parents' behaviour in childhood. Schutz's work emphasized the existence of three basic needs which would be satisfied through the medium of group formation. They were, respectively, inclusion, control and affection. The first of these, the need for inclusion, is concerned with the finding of a sense of belonging. The relationships which are involved in this need for inclusion are reciprocal, i.e. 'Not only do I need to feel accepted by others but I need also to accept them.' The second aspect, the need for control, is concerned with leadership in the group. Leadership, in these terms, is concerned with the group's process. Again, the concept, as a concept, can be split into two quite different aspects, submissiveness and leadership, i.e. the need to be controlled and the need to control. Finally, Schutz described the need for affection as the final element in this triumvirate. As with the other factors, there is a duality in its definition for it involves a desire to like others as well as a desire to be liked by them.

Leadership

There are many misconceptions about leadership. It might be helpful to get some of these out of the way at an early stage. What we certainly do know is that the very nature of leadership is imperfectly understood. Most common-sense conclusions about leadership appear to be based more on myth than on reality. For example, the notion that leadership is power over others can, at one level, be seen to have some relevance. However, its relevance occurs where the power base is with the people rather than over them.

The notion of leadership involves some kind of reciprocal relationship between those who lead and those who are led. In similar vein, the idea that some people are simply born leaders does not help to explain the fact that, in the majority of cases, the ability to lead can be seen to be acquired through practice. The search for personality variables to predict effective leadership has, in the main, proved fruitless (Stogdill 1974), but the search continues. The more accurate view seems to be that leadership is rather an achievement than a happy accident or a birthright. Nor can we assume that someone who is a good leader in one situation will necessarily prove to be a good leader in another. Such an idea undervalues the power of environmental circumstances in determining leader effectiveness.

Getting to a working definition of leadership is not so simple. There are almost as many definitions as there are theoreticians in the field. Certainly, one common aspect on which authorities will agree, is that leadership is some form of process of legitimate influence. Many would also agree that there is some notion to do with reciprocity contained in the definition. This reciprocity involves the leader (the director), where the leader acts as guide and facilitator for the group's behaviour.

These two notions of leadership (influence and reciprocity) are taken from Grimes (1978) and Hollander (1978) respectively. But there are two other aspects which are important in leadership. The first is that the right to lead is often voluntarily conferred upon the leader by some, or all, members of the group. Secondly, leadership involves the motivation of group members to expend some energy in attaining the goals of the group.

Whilst we can define leadership as a process of influence involving ongoing transactions between leaders and followers, others have argued that three minimal conditions need to be satisfied if leadership is to be confirmed as having taken place. These conditions are:

● The leader must be shown to have caused something to happen.

● The relationship between the leader's behaviour and its effects must be observable.

● There must be substantive changes in the behaviour of organization members and in the ensuing outcomes, as a consequence of actions by the leader.

Leadership traits

Whilst the common notion is that Stogdill's work disclaimed any relationship between traits and leadership, that is not actually the result of his work. In reality, his work indicates that several personality factors are certainly stronger in leaders than in followers, and this is also corroborated by the work of both Cattell and Belbin (1981). Unfortunately, because the work is correlational, we cannot indicate more than a relationship between variables, a relationship which may, or may not, be causal. However, we do know that the need for achievement, adaptability, alertness, energy, responsibility, self-confidence and sociability are all positively correlated with leadership. Dominance (i.e. bossiness) is negatively correlated with leadership. Interestingly, the relationship between emotional balance and leadership and between extroversion and leadership is unclear. The reason why personality data *per se* may show inconsistently across studies is that there is a situational aspect to leadership which is not always apparent in personality studies.

Gary Yukl (1989) argues that there are six main elements which interact with one another and which impinge upon the effectiveness of a leader, as follows.

● **The leader's traits and abilities**: which would include such things as his or her physical attributes, drive, personality, knowledge and technical skills.

● **The leader's power**: which can be analysed under such forms as position power, reward power, cohesive power, expert power, personal power, etc. (see Chapter 4).

● **The leader's actual behaviour**: the concept concerned here is whether that behaviour is oriented towards the task to be performed, towards people, towards political activation, or towards the culture of the enterprise itself.

● **The intervening variables**: such as the nature of the organization, the skills and efforts of subordinates and the relationship between the leader and subordinates. This would also include the nature of support services and other resources available to the leader.

● **The situational variables**: where concern is both with external and internal variables such as economic, political and social forces, as well as technology and the needs, values and personalities of subordinates.

● **The organizational culture**: which should not be missed and finally, yet no less importantly, the *short- and long-term end results*.

Leadership dimensions

The classic study which attempted to define the major aspects concerned in leadership was that carried out by the Ohio State University in their leadership studies which were reported in 1950. Descriptive phrases, used to distinguish leadership behaviours, grew so long that the researcher got concerned to reduce the various types of actions down to the key dimensions of leader behaviour. Today, such work would be undertaken using the competencies approach. However, the questionnaire approach was adopted by the Ohio State University, in which they developed a list of nine key types of behaviour that appeared to characterize military and organization leaders.

Using factor analysis, the original nine elements were narrowed down to four factors or dimensions (consideration, initiating structure, production emphasis and sensitivity). The first two of these accounted for more than 80 per cent of the variation in follower's evaluations of their leaders:

Consideration: (alternatively called relationship orientation, supportive, employee-centred, relation-skilled or group maintenance-oriented) the meaning given to this was the degree to which the leader responds to group members in a warm and friendly fashion; the degree to which he or she involves people in mutual trust, openness and a willingness to explain decisions.

Initiating structure: (alternative labels for this are task-oriented, goal-oriented, work-oriented, production-centred, administratively skilled or goal achiever) conceptually, this means the extent to which the leader organizes, directs and defines the group's structure and goals; the extent also to which he regulates group behaviour, monitors communication and reduces goal ambiguity.

The two dimensions then alternately became called relationship orientation (consideration) and task orientation (initiating structure). These two basic concepts underpinned almost all the leadership study work which continued through the 1950s and 1960s.

Problems occur when we attempt to check, via observation, whether reality agrees with this theory. Reality does not necessarily correlate closely with the theoretical perspective. The major differences found between leaders and followers was that leaders tend to give more direction and interpretation to the problem than subordinates. In a sense, therefore, leaders not only facilitate goal completion and maintain relationships, but also appear to act in ways which make them stand out in a group. It may even be, as Forsyth (1983, p. 209) states, 'the two dimensional theory of leadership behaviour may actually be a theory of followers' perceptions of their leaders'.

Leadership models

The Ohio State studies led to a great deal of further work on leadership. Throughout the 1960s there was an emergence of a series of theories, each of which built on the preceding one. Blake and

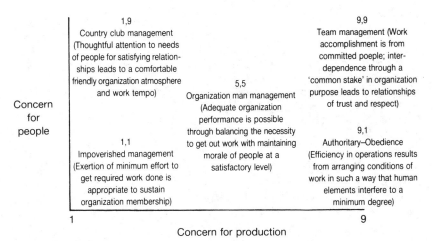

Figure 3.3 Blake and Mouton's managerial grid (Source: Blake and Mouton 1964)

Mouton's (1964) managerial grid can be seen as the start of these (see Figure 3.3).

The two axes of the diagram are comprised of 9-point scales which are attitudinal and which reflect degree of concern for task and degree of concern for people (relationships). They held there would be different leadership styles and that these could be conceptualized into five or more different aspects on the Grid. Blake and Mouton's theories held that the most effective style was the 9,9 style which represents attitudes or assumptions that lead to an integration of high concern for task (production) and high concern for relationships (people). Theirs is not a situational or contingency theory. They held that the 9,9 style is the most effective regardless of situation although the tactics of implementing it (as opposed to its underlying principles) may vary depending upon factors such as maturity level of subordinate time, and others. Work which they undertook was built on by Reddin (1970). His three-dimensional grid (see Figure 3.4) added an effectiveness dimension to Blake and Mouton's work. The hypothesis now was that, for each of the four major styles of leadership behaviour, there would be more or less effective styles contained within each of the four.

The encapsulation of a situational factor was left to Fiedler (1971) and his contingency model. We shall look at this in some detail.

Fiedler's contingency model

Fiedler's concern was to differentiate the motivational style of the

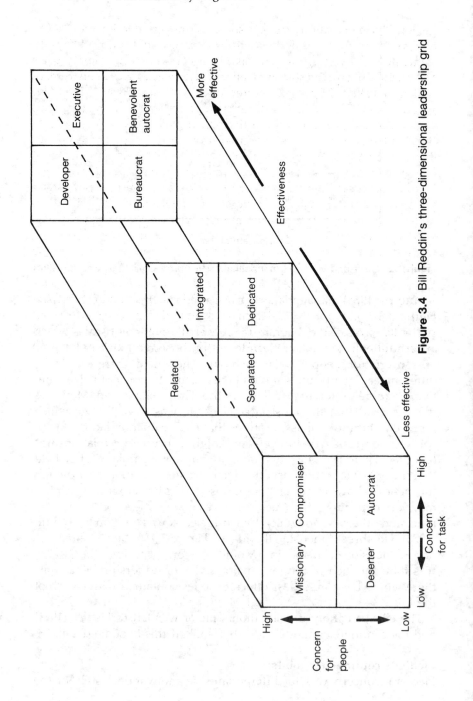

Figure 3.4 Bill Reddin's three-dimensional leadership grid

leader. His explanation was that some leaders are relationship motivated (wish to find acceptance within their groups), others are task-motivated and concentrate on task completion as the primary goal. His method of tapping this motivational style was to use an instrument which he called the least preferred co-worker scale (LPC). Literally, respondents were asked to rate the person with whom they had worked in the past and whom they liked least well, or with whom they had experienced most difficulty in working to get the job done. The rating scales were of such items as: pleasant to unpleasant, tense to relaxed, supportive to hostile, trustworthy to untrustworthy, etc.

It has been held by many other researchers that the instrument, as such, was a better measure of personality than it was of leadership style. Leaving that aside for one moment, Fiedler then argued that it was necessary to know more about the situation within which the leadership was to occur, in order to begin to make predictions of how well the leadership style would accord and gain results. He felt that three aspects were crucial (see Figure 3.5). The first of these was leader–member relationships, the second, task structure and the third, position power. Leader–member relations were good or bad dependent upon the degree of cohesion, degree of conflict and cooperation. Task structure, on the other hand, was concerned with

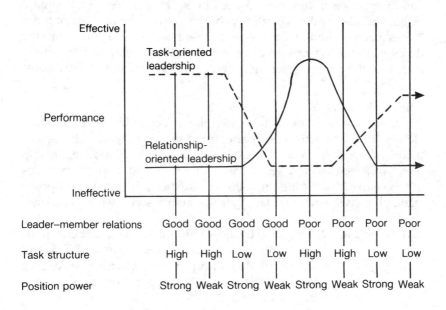

Figure 3.5 Fiedler's model of leadership

how easily the solutions to problems were checked and the degree of ambiguity which was contained in the particular situation. The final element, position power, refers specifically to the leader's power over the other group members. This was perceived to be either strong or weak, and was determined by the amount of control which the leader had over rewards, punishments, salaries, hiring, etc.

Overall, the model predicts that the low LPC leader (task-motivated) will be most effective in situations that are highly favourable or unfavourable. On the other hand, the high LPC leader (relationship-motivated) will be most effective in the mid-range situations. Forsyth (1983) indicates, from his review of research, that the model is reasonably predictive.

There are, however, some criticisms. One of the major criticisms is the simplest of all: because the early research relies heavily on correlation findings, cause and effect conclusions may be inappropriate. Indeed, as we have mentioned earlier, it may well be that the LPC scale is a better measure of the personality of the individual than it is a description of leadership behaviour through motivation. There is another aspect to the correlations themselves. There are some people who would utterly reject them on the basis that they do not always reach conventional levels of statistical significance. Perhaps the most damning criticism, however, is the LPC scale itself. Any scale should be both reliable and have validity, but in view of the number of times it has been modified in research, there are suggestions that the different versions themselves are incompatible. It may well be, therefore, that they are measuring different things in different situations.

Situational leadership
An attempt was made to take a totally eclectic view of leadership. Hersey and Blanchard (1977) attempted to band together the major theorists' work into a behaviourally based situational leadership theory. To four basic styles of leadership they added four typologies of followers. By defining the follower situation, the most appropriate leadership style emerges. The four leadership styles were as follows:

(S1) **Directing**: high directive/low supportive leader behaviour. The leader tells the follower what, how, when, and where to do various tasks. Decision-making is initiated solely by the manager. Communication is largely one-way.

(S2) **Coaching**: high directive/high supportive behaviour. The leader

still provides a great deal of direction but also attempts to hear the followers' feelings about decisions
as well as their ideas and suggestions. Control over
decision-making remains with the leader.

(S3) **Supporting**: high supportive/low directive leader behaviour.
Control for day-to-day decision-making and problem-solving shifts from leader to follower. Leaders
provide recognition and actively listen and facilitate
problem-solving.

(S4) **Delegating**: low supportive/low directive leader behaviour.
Leader discusses the problems with subordinate(s)
until joint agreement is achieved. The decision-
making process is delegated totally to the follower.

Hersey and Blanchard found the greatest impact on choice of
leadership style to be the follower(s). The amount of direction or
support that a leader should provide depends on the development
level that the follower(s) exhibits on a specific task.

Development level
Development level is defined as the competence and commitment to
perform a particular task without supervision. Competence is a
function of knowledge or skills which can be gained from education,
training and/or experience.

Commitment is a combination of confidence and motivation; a
measure of a person's feeling of being able to do a task well without
much supervision and their interest and enthusiasm in doing that
task.

Situational leadership identifies four development levels: low (D1),
low to moderate (D2), moderate to high (D3), high (D4). Each of these
development levels represents a different combination of competence
and commitment. The total picture, of leadership style and development level, is illustrated in Figure 3.6.

By learning to enact the various leadership styles, and by learning
to define the follower situation, appropriate leadership behaviour can
be shown. The implication of Hersey and Blanchard's work is not
only that these behaviours can be acquired, but, also, that effective
leaders are those having the greatest range of style flexibility.

The leader's behaviour can be analysed in further detail in terms
of its orientation. It is easy to think of the usual two aspects of
behaviour: that is, task-oriented, which would include such things as

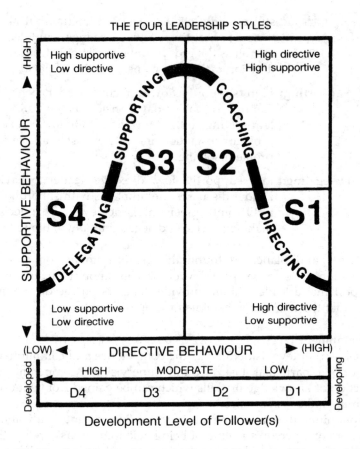

Figure 3.6 Situational leadership model (Source: Hersey and Blanchard 1982)

setting goals, planning, clarifying roles, coordinating, problem-solving, etc., and person-oriented behaviour which would include such things as delegation, training and coaching, praising, constructively criticizing, giving information, etc.

However, there are two other aspects of leader behaviour which also are important. The first of these is politically oriented behaviour. This represents the individual's capacity to promote the unit within which he or she works and to represent it within the organization. It also implies, quite rightly, forming networks and alliances, managing conflict and initiating change. The second aspect, which again can often be underestimated and indeed missed from leadership theories, is that of culturally oriented behaviour. This is where the leader affirms corporate values and will often perform and function as a figurehead. Such individuals are capable of inspiring others with a vision of the future.

The model indicates that the ability of the leader to influence the intervening variables may be assisted by personal skills and either helped or hindered by situation variables. While leadership is concerned with strategic issues, it is more and more common for leaders to influence those who exercise political constraints or who control the allocation of valuable resources within the organization and externally from it.

Nor can the importance of the leader's own behaviour be underestimated in setting an example in establishing and maintaining high standards of performance. It is plainly important that the leader obtains material and human resources which will enable other people, in subordinate roles, to perform to those standards. Where the external world becomes harder and economic reality impinges upon organizational life, then the leader may have to maintain morale and still maintain at the same time high standards of performance.

Bennis and Nanus (1985), in their study of ninety business leaders, identified the following five key leadership skills; the skills are quite different from those which we normally associate with leadership behaviour:

- The ability to accept people as they are.

- The capacity to approach relationships and problems in terms of the present rather than the past.

- In many ways quite at odds with the way people often behave, is the ability to treat those close to the managers with the same courteous attention that they extend to strangers and casual acquaintances.

- The ability to trust others.

- The ability to do without constant approval and recognition from others.

In a sense, the important thing is not really whether leaders are liked but rather the quality of the work which results from collaborating with them. As with many writers in this area, Bennis and Nanus conclude, quite rightly, that each of us has leadership potential, and the capacities and competencies of leadership can be learnt. In a sense leadership is 'full of trial and error, victories and defeats . . . there is no simple formula, no rigorous science, no cook book that leads inexorably to successful leadership' (p. 48). What they conclude is that learning simply takes place during the experience itself.

Belbin team roles as they affect a senior management production team

A divisional director, Stewart, and the six people who reported directly to him were reviewed on the Belbin team roles. What emerged from the analysis was the matrix shown in Table 3.2.

The question was, given their undoubted technical competence, how might they behave as a team? Using their dominant team roles, and plotting these into the role triangle, we obtain Figure 3.7. If all their roles are plotted, including those which they would have to work hard to undertake, Figure 3.8 is obtained.

The picture emerging from the dominant roles figure in terms of potential weaknesses is of a group which is unlikely to follow through or to attend too well to detail. Most importantly, there will be no evaluation of the alternatives which face the group from time to time. The picture changes little in the all team roles figure, though some potential to attend to detail is visible.

The wider picture portrays a group which, in undertaking a task or project, move too rapidly towards action without giving due consideration to the different aspects of that task. Once an idea is taken on there will be no attempt to determine whether it is appropriate as circumstances change. Moreover, the attention to detailed elements of the task will be left to others in the group – the problem being that everyone will take that approach. It is actually a listening group, but not until some of the initial excitement that they will feel with a new task has died down.

If we were to advise them how to improve, two aspects are important. First, they must appreciate the powers which the leader, Stewart, brings to bear by virtue of his position (and expertise) and learn to deal with this in an appropriate way. If not, they may well follow his enthusiastic starts without question; and his enthusiasm (and rapidly waning interest) need to be dealt with. Secondly, Ruth, whose team roles include chair, company worker, completer and plant, would be the most easily trained to perform the role of monitor evaluator. Failing her, Paul, as shaper, chairman, company worker and plant might also be able to cope with a monitor evaluator set of behaviours, a behaviour set which is necessary to the group's organizational well-being.

Table 3.2 Analysis of team roles

	Shaper	Chairman	Resource investigator	Team worker	Company worker	Completer finisher	Monitor evaluator	Plant innovator
Stewart			Dominant					Plant
Gary		Chairman	Dominant		Company worker			Plant
Ruth		Dominant			Company worker	Completer finisher		Plant
Paul	Dominant	Chairman			Company worker			Plant
Alex		Chairman	Resource investigator		Dominant			
Kate		Dominant	Resource investigator		Company worker			
Ed		Chairman	Resource investigator	Dominant	Company worker			Plant

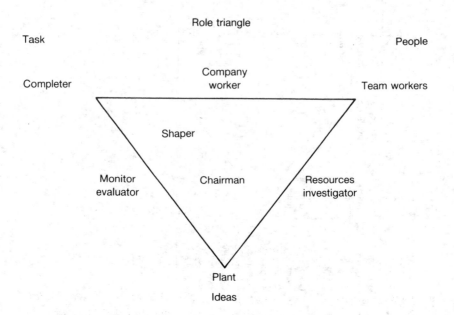

Role triangle

Task

People

Completer

Company
worker

Team workers

Shaper

Monitor
evaluator

Chairman

Resources
investigator

Plant
Ideas

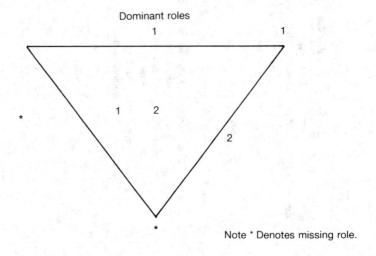

Dominant roles

Note * Denotes missing role.

Figure 3.7 Dominant team roles

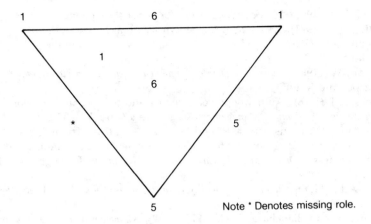

Note * Denotes missing role.

Figure 3.8 All team roles

Failing this, they may have to force themselves to develop some form of systematic way of working to compensate for their team role lack. In a similar way, they might be advised to allow Ruth or Kate to chair their actual team meetings in order to make more effective use of their personal team skills.

References

Bales, R.F. (1980), *Symlog Case Study Kit* (New York: Free Press).

Belbin, R.M. (1981), *Management Teams: Why they succeed or fail*, (London: Heinemann).

Belbin, R.M., Aston, R.B. and Mortram, D. (1976), 'Building effective management teams', *Journal of General Management*, vol. 3, no. 3, pp. 23–9.

Bennis, W.G. and Nanus, B. (1985), *Leaders: The strategy for taking charge* (New York: Harper and Row).

Biddle, B.J. (1979), *Role Theory: Expectations identities and behaviour* (London: Academic Press).

Blake, R.R. and Mouton, J.S. (1978), *The New Managerial Grid* (Houston: Gulf).

Bonner, H. (1959), *Group Dynamics: Principles and applications* (New York: Ronald).

Cartwright, D. and Zander, A. (eds) (1968), *Group Dynamics: Research and Theory* (New York: Harper and Row, 3rd edition).

Cattell, R.B. (1965), *The Scientific Analysis of Personality* (Penguin).

Fiedler, F.E. (1971), *Leadership* (Morristown: General Learning Press).

Forsyth, D.R. (1983), *An Introduction to Group Dynamics* (Monterey: Brooks-Cole).

Gordon, W. (1961), *Synectics: The development of creative capacity* (New York: Harper and Row).

Grimes, A.J. (1978), 'Authority power influence and social control: a theoretical synthesis', *Academy of Management Review*, vol. 3, pp. 724–37.

Hackman, J.R., Brousseau, K.R. and Weiss, J.A. (1976), 'The interaction of task design and group performance strategies in determining group effectiveness', *Organizational Behaviour and Human Performance*, vol. 16, pp. 350–65.

Hare, A.P. (1976), *Handbook of Small Group Research* (New York: Free Press, 2nd edition).

Hersey, P. and Blanchard, K.H. (1977, 1982), *Management of Organisational Behaviour: Utilising human resources* (Englewood Cliffs: Prentice Hall, 3rd edition).

Hollander, E.P. (1978), *Leadership Dynamics: A practical guide to effective relationships* (New York: Free Press).

Homans, G.C. (1950), *The Human Group* (New York: Harcourt Brace and World).

Janis, I.L. (1972), *Victims of Groupthink* (Boston: Houghton-Mifflin).

Newcomb, T.M. (1943), *Personality and Social Change* (New York: Dryden).

Osborn, A.F. (1957), *Applied Imagination* (New York: Scribner).

Reddin, W.J. (1970), *Managerial Effectiveness* (New York: McGraw Hill).

Roethlisberger, F.J. (1947), 'Foreman: master and victim of double talk' in G.F.F. Lombard (ed.), *The Elusive Phenomena* (Boston: Harvard Business School, 1977).

Schutz, W. (1958), *FIRO: A three dimensional theory of interpersonal behaviour* (New York: Rinehard & Co.).

Shaw, M.E. (1981), *Group Dynamics: The psychology of small group behaviour* (New York: McGraw Hill, 3rd edition).

Sherif, M. and Sherif, C.W. (1956), *An Outline of Social Psychology* (New York: Harper and Row, revd. edition).

Steiner, I.D. (1972), *Group Process and Productivity* (New York: Academic Press).

Stogdill, R.M. (1974), *Handbook of Leadership* (New York: Free Press).

Tuckman, B.W. (1965), 'Developmental sequences in small groups', *Psychology Bulletin*, vol. 63, pp. 384–99.

Tuckman, B.W. and Jensen, M.A.C. (1977), 'Stages of small group development revisited', *Group and Organizational Studies*, vol. 2, pp. 419–27.

Yukl, G.A. (1989), *Leadership in Organizations* (Englewood Cliffs: Prentice Hall, 2nd edition).

4

Power and politics

Everyone knows how praiseworthy it is for a ruler to keep his word, and to live with integrity, and not by cunning: nevertheless experience shows that in our own times, princes who have cared little about good faith, and have used cunning to confuse the minds of men, have achieved great things: so that in the end they have outstripped those who founded themselves on honesty.

(Machiavelli 1981, p. 104)

A prince therefore need not have all the good qualities we mention above, but he must seem to have them. I will even venture to say that if he has them and always practises them they will harm him, whereas if he merely seems to have them he will do well out of them.

(Machiavelli 1981, p. 105)

All the other theories put forward in our long conversation have been refuted, and this conclusion stands firm, that one should avoid doing wrong with more care than being wronged, and that the supreme object of a man's efforts in public and in private life must be the reality rather than the appearance of goodness.

(Plato 1971, p. 148)

We all have a sneaking feeling that success in business is not about 'playing by the rules', but that it has more to do with changing the rules to suit oneself. Entrepreneurial ability seems to derive more from a desire to exercise power over one's life, and over the working environment than from any moral principle. The self-interest may be enlightened, but it is firmly rooted in survival at all costs. The provision of work for others, and the output of goods and services are worthy, that is, socially acceptable objectives. However our

suspicion that they are a by-product, almost an unintended consequence, of the desire for money, power and status underlies much
of the debate about power and politics in organizations. The quotations
from two famous sources at the start of this chapter take us to the heart
of the debate. The early Quaker employers, Rowntree and Cadbury,
for example, were conscious that potentially there was a conflict
between the search for profit with the consequent exploitation of
people to make money for their employers, and the great Christian
teachings on which their own religious faith was founded. They
resolved this conflict in their minds by stressing the benefits employees
enjoyed, such as an improved standard of living and welfare services,
and pointed to the benefits for the community and society at large
which came from capitalism.

People who exercise power over others require some socially
acceptable justification if that power is to be regarded as legitimate.
In Machiavelli's experience, the means used by rulers justified the
end if the consequences were beneficial to the rulers. But, in order to
convince the populace, a prince must take on the appearance of
goodness. This could be seen as the essential political act – the effort
expended 'to sell' ideas, to convince others, to seem to act in good
faith. Because of the duplicity of others, it is argued, the ruler who
always strives to act in good faith is soon trapped, and loses his power.
This hypocrisy was anathema to Socrates, who believed that an
attempt to persuade an audience through oratory to agree to something which the orator knew to be untrue, was an act of dishonesty;
that bad faith was always not acceptable.

It is difficult in the technically sophisticated world we now live in
to see the simple truths of our ancestors. The moral order in our post-
industrial society has yet to emerge. The nearest we can observe to a
principle which can be used to guide conduct is the notion of
agreement or consensus, a form of democracy which managers must
exercise if they are to gain the support of their staff. Therefore,
persuasion is necessary, and the debate in the *Gorgias* is still significant
today. A number of important questions remain: What are the political
processes which are justified? In what ethical context should managers
take decisions? What personality, team and situation variables need
to be taken into account when analysing power in organizations?

Definitions of power

The concept of 'power' is central to understanding organizational life, because people devote much of their energies at work to trying to accomplish tasks either for themselves or on behalf of other people. Intended behaviour or 'social acts' can only be interpreted as meaningful if the power or capacity of the individual or group can be understood. The problem with attempting to define 'power' is that it is both a word used to describe the physical, mental and collaborative resources available or attributable to the person, and it is itself desired by people who wish to possess more of these resources and is therefore the object of intended behaviour. Power is often described as the capacity to impose one's will upon others. Another formulation would be to see 'power' as an origin of energy both outside and within the self. Power must thus be both a physical property and also a function of influence over events and behaviour whose source may be rational or non-rational.

'Power' is a multifaceted concept, which has been analysed from a number of perspectives: as a characteristic of the individual, as an interpersonal influence process, as a commodity to be traded, as a type of causation and as an issue in the study of values and ethics (Cavanaugh 1984). All of these views of power are correct. Personality does affect the possession of power (as we explained in Chapter 2), it is a process, in that it can only be seen in use, it is sought after and is therefore the subject of economic exchange. The exercise of power does explain why events occur, and the way power is used inevitably raises ethical and value questions. In order to use the idea of 'power' we need to develop a framework which will explain the relationships between these different aspects of power.

In attempting to create this framework we have made a number of assumptions. First, we only conceive of 'power' in relation to humans, and it is to the power exercised by people in organization settings that we have addressed ourselves. Secondly, we believe power can only be defined in use. At other times, power remains an abstract quality which, if discussed at all, is discussed in relation to its use as an enabling capacity. It must, of course, derive from particular sources. French and Raven (1959) and Raven (1965) put forward the following six bases for power:

1. **Rewards**: this power source derives from the person's control over resources, for example to control manpower, to give pay increases and to effect control over promotion and status.

2. **Coercive**: the power to punish or reward, the power to threaten and to use one's position to force others to take action is this source of power.

3. **Legitimate**: the power which is exercised in accordance with organizational rules. This is power which is exercised with the authority of the organization.

4. **Referent**: this depends on the charisma or personal attraction of the individual. Interpersonal skill and emotional support from others are the source of power for this person.

5. **Expert**: power which derives from knowledge. Sometimes called sapiential authority, this is power based on an acknowledgement of another's expertise.

6. **Information**: information set in context, about people, events or other facts assists prediction about future behaviour or events.

It is clear from these sources as we have defined them, that power only exists within the interaction between those exercising and those responding to power. Power is the capacity to mobilize these sources for effective use. This capacity is also a function of personality and of the perceived effectiveness of the source in the view of those subject to the power act. The perceived effectiveness depends upon:

● The asymmetry of power relations between the two 'actors' – which results in control (March 1955).

● The acceptance of the legitimacy of the source mobilized.

● The desirability of the outcome – that is the mutuality of interests between the parties.

'Power' is a multiplier process, which is the capacity to mobilize these sources for effective use. The mobilizing capacity depends on the situational context, and the personality of the persons involved. We can express this relationship between sources and effectiveness of power as in Figure 4.1.

Power capacity is conditioned by the situational context which provides opportunities or restrictions on the use of power sources, and on the personality of those wishing to exercise power. The effectiveness of the attempt to exercise power is a function of the perceived differences between the power of the different parties to the relationship. As simple examples: overwhelming numbers of people in one group will give that group perceived power effectiveness over a smaller group and those who are perceived to have influential friends may be seen to be more powerful than simpler folk. Physical or psychological advantages over individuals are likely to

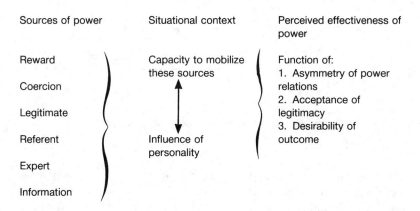

Sources of power	Situational context	Perceived effectiveness of power
Reward	Capacity to mobilize these sources	Function of: 1. Asymmetry of power relations
Coercion		2. Acceptance of legitimacy
Legitimate		3. Desirability of outcome
Referent	Influence of personality	
Expert		
Information		

Figure 4.1 Sources and effectiveness of power

result in the acceptance and reinforcement of the power sources. For example, sportsmen or women often are accorded charisma because their expert skills give them a physical advantage – and this in turn reinforces the differences between the champion and the challenger: the Wimbledon tennis champion who steps on to the court carries an aura which gives an initial psychological advantage and acknowledgement of this aura by the challenger makes the champion different, better.

The acceptance that the power is being exercised legitimately is a strong indicator of its likely effectiveness. The power of military and political leaders often relies initially upon this notion of legitimacy. If legitimacy is challenged, those granting it argue, the whole system will be reduced to chaos; only those with stronger physical power would succeed: might would overcome right. The belief in what is ordered can result in a simple acceptance of authority:

'If I were fierce and bald and short of breath
I'd live with Scarlet Majors at the Base
And send glum heroes up the line to death'
Siegfried Sassoon, 'Base Details'.

For power to be exercised effectively in a democratic society, there needs to be some mutuality of interest between the parties. Those seeking to exercise power effectively need to convince the people they seek to influence that the power is utilized for their benefit. Trade union leaders are only able to be effective in their leadershp role if the members believe it is in their interest to follow. Therefore,

		Technical System	
		work individually	*work together*
Skill level	Unskilled	Apathetic	Erratic
	Skilled	Conservative	Strategic

Figure 4.2 Sayles' strategic workgroups

trade union power is a variable, according to the issue in dispute. Whilst it may be possible to motivate members to take strike action over pay and benefits, the same members may not support the same leader over an issue of principle, such as the dismissal of a fellow worker.

It is a necessary, but not a sufficient condition for power to be used effectively, that there are one or more sources of influence, the sufficient condition will be dependent on the perceptions held by those over whom power is to be exercised. The mobilization of the capacity for power, whether or not it is effectively used – that is whether or not it leads to a change in the desired direction – is dependent on the situational context.

These situational contexts have been described as 'strategies' or 'tactical' opportunities for power to be used. In the instance of work groups, Sayles (1958) described the technological settings and skill levels of work groups as key contextual factors which influence the capacity to use power. Figure 4.2 illustrates his four types of work groups.

Workers with lower group solidarity (as in those who work individually) do not have the same opportunities to use their power as do groups of workers who are required to interact continuously through the technical system, and who have high skill levels. Strategic groups are calculating and exploitative in their use of power. 'Conservative' workers, possessing power through high skill levels, maintain solidarity because of an identity of interest with other skilled workers, and tend not to use power except to maintain traditional wage differentials. Erratic groups develop solidarity over particular issues, but do not use their power strategically.

Although Sayles' analysis only uses two situational variables, skill level and degree of interaction required by the work system, it does demonstrate how contextual variables influence the capacity to use power. Other contextual variables include geographical location (for example, remoteness from a head office) and the traditions and history of a company (for example, the management philosophy and organizational culture in companies such as the John Lewis Partnership, IBM, Shell, etc.). The degree of change in technology and in product or service is also important (for example, legitimate power sources may not be so significant as expert power sources in a computer software company).

Personality and power

In the model we have developed, the two main intervening variables which condition how power sources are used, we suggest, are the situational context and the personality of the person using the power. These variables interact, but for the purposes of analysis, we should first consider personality factors separately from the situations where they are expressed.

We all attribute special qualities to people in power. Prime Ministers, Presidents, military and business leaders seem to grow in stature after they have been appointed. But are these personality characteristics which single out these powerful people: do they possess special qualities? The 'great' man or woman theory of leadership has already been dealt with in our chapter on leadership. Here, we will look at what Adler described as the goal of superiority: 'Every neurosis can be understood as an attempt to free oneself from a feeling of inferiority in order to gain a feeling of superiority' (Adler 1929, p. 23).

Whilst Adler saw the pathological states which arose from inferiority complexes developing during childhood, we must turn to the broader questions of whether the desire for power is a normal state for most people, and if so why do some people seem to be more successful at achieving power than others? Control over one's own destiny is an end which most people seek. The problems we all face are how to achieve control, and how to cope with setbacks which are part of the human condition.

In Chapter 2 we described how David McClelland sees power motivation, and the need to achieve as strong motivations for most people. However, he differentiates between power which is desired for its own sake, power which is used to have an impact on others and the integration of power with higher goals such as a sense of duty. Maturity and effectiveness therefore is determined by selecting appropriate forms of power use. Managers are said to be high on power motivation, but low on affiliation motivation (i.e. they have less need to be liked, and a stronger desire to exercise power) (McClelland and Burnham 1976).

Overweening ambition is present in some people – what Mulder has described as an addiction to power, where the striving for success becomes a dominant passion (Mulder 1977). Ambition is normal; the problems arise when power over others is an end in itself, rather than a means to an end. For top entrepreneurs such as Robert Maxwell, Rupert Murdoch, or Tiny Rowlands, there seems likely to be a mixture of motives, which include altruistic desires to improve living standards, to protect their shareholders, and work force, as well as pleasure at beating rivals and outmanoeuvring the competition.

Although evidence of personality attributes in the study of success is clouded, there is more evidence to show how personality relates to leadership failures and managerial weakness. The study of military incompetence by Norman Dixon explains how the very features of the military culture such as orderliness, a love of hierarchy and controls and an over-obedience to orders, attracts individuals with particular personality characteristics, acquired during childhood. Unfortunately, these same characteristics are partly responsible for terrible blunders in wartime, when senior officers have to tolerate uncertainty, need spontaneity of thought and action and an open mind ready to receive novel and threatening information (Dixon 1976).

A study of redundancies among managers and senior executives examined the question of whether the selection for redundancy was random, or whether a choice was made according to the characteristics of the people concerned (Tyson, Barclay and Handyside 1986). This survey showed redundant managers were more socially bold, uninhibited, more imaginative and unconventional, but were less shrewd, more forthright and less self-aware than executives who had not been made redundant. The overall findings support the view that it is those executives who lack 'political' skills, that is executives who do not fit the 'organization man' image who are most prone to be selected for redundancy. A similar study by Hartley (1980) revealed that the least conventional, most assertive, imaginative and independent were most vulnerable to redundancy.

From these findings we may conclude that there are personality traits which contribute to managerial success, but leadership effectiveness is dependent on the mix of intrinsic abilities and situational determinants.

Situational determinants of power – the political dimension

Politics is about access to power. How organization structures and the opportunities available diminish or enhance access to power is therefore of considerable importance. For example, experts are often not called in to the decision-making bodies, the dominant coalitions, and feel excluded and powerless. Their power source, expert power, cannot find an expression in these circumstances. An opposite case, the Civil Service, sees advice-giving raised almost to an art form. Ministers may have to rely heavily on civil servants for advice, and civil servants can use their gatekeeper roles to keep out other potential advisers, and by making information secret are able to prevent others from competing for power.

People in professional occupations such as the law and medicine have long followed this strategy to the point where professions have been described as conspiracies against the laity. A secretary also has a gatekeeper role, admitting or denying access to the boss, and any person who has discretion in his or her role has choices which can be used tactically to their own advantage.

The positional sources of power are clearly dependent on the rules and demands of the job, but these are not fixed and can be manipulated.

Contextual determinants of relationships between departments within an organization centre around the degree of interdependence between departments. This is an area where power relationships are frequently expressed. Such relationships can be collaborative or conflictful depending upon a number of variables (Walton and Dutton 1969). Chief among the variables is mutual task dependence. This is an 'incentive for collaboration, but also an occasion for conflict and the means of bargaining over interdepartmental issues' (p. 73). Where there is asymmetrical interdependency, such as where departments have different responsibilities for solving common problems, there will be conflict. For example, production departments prefer long economical production runs, whilst sales departments want flexibility and a quick response to customer demands. Increased differentiation to meet customer requirements results in more internal differentiation between departments, through adapting to customers and to uncertainty. Dependence on common resources also gives rise to interdepartmental conflict when resources are scarce.

Role problems cause interdepartmental frictions. Blocked promotion, ambiguity about one's role and about the criteria to be used to evaluate performance leads to scapegoating. Walton and Dutton accept, however, that interpersonal skills are also important, and that a lack of shared experience is a typical source of communication problems: people who only have a narrow range of behavioural skills are not likely to adapt or to be flexible when dealing with other departments.

Hickson *et al.* (1971) followed up this work and suggested that the control of the contingencies described above is the crucial issue. 'Sub-units control contingencies for one another's activities and draw power from the dependencies thereby created' (p. 222). A sub-unit's power, they argue, is related to its coping with uncertainty (which includes preventing uncertainty), to substitutability (whether there are alternative means of performing the operation) and to centrality (the degree to which a sub-unit is linked into the organization's systems, for example through workflow). This is perhaps a more formal statement of Crozier's conclusions, whose study of a clerical agency and a tobacco factory showed how groups of people who have different interests try to preserve and expand their discretion, and thereby to limit their dependence upon others (Crozier 1964).

Organizational politics

When examining how power is used in organizations we inevitably enter the debate about organizational 'politics', or what could be seen as the strategies individuals and groups adopt in order to maintain their power, to prevent others from taking their power, or to enlarge their power. What we are describing is an influence process, through which power is exercised.

Politics can be defined in terms of our model as a particular form of the influence process itself. Whilst like other influence processes, it is exercised according to the power source, and the perceived effectiveness of power, political action seeks to gain an increase in power and utilizes one or more ploys to do so.

A range of strategies is available. These operate at two levels: first, at the strategic level, the long-term manipulation of relationships in order to improve one's position, or the position of one's own group we have already encountered in our description of Sayles' classification of work groups. There is also the behavioural level, where short-term tactical advantages may be gained by trying particular ploys as in Stephen Potter's 'one-upmanship' approach.

Power and politics

Table 4.1 Strategies used by executives

Strategic rejection	If executive is self-assured and powerful, rejects the report
'Bottom drawer it'	Executive sends a memo praising the specialist's technicality, and then puts it away and forgets it
Mobilizing political support	Executive 'calls in the credits' from colleagues
Nitty-gritty tactic	Minor details are questioned, and mistakes in details are raised to try to discredit the whole report
Emotional tactic	Relies on appeals to emotional states – such as personal consequences of action
But in the future . . .	Argument that data may be historically accurate but does not consider future changes
Invisible man	Avoidance, often with the support of a secretary, so no discussion can take place
Further investigation required	Specialist is sent away to collect more information, either because terms of references are changed, or to follow up the more interesting issues raised in the report
Scapegoat	A suitable scapegoat, who is raised as a threat to any change proposed
Deflection	Discussion is deflected away from the main areas by concentrating the attention on less crucial matters

Source: Pettigrew 1974, pp. 24–30.

A catalogue of ploys was set out by Pettigrew (1974) in his examination of the influence process between specialists and executives. He describes the way specialists' credibility is undermined by the tactics deployed by executives who can block changes, by preventing the written reports sent by specialists from having any effect (see Table 4.1).

At the micro level of behaviour analysis, we can therefore distinguish 'political' from 'non-political' behaviour. This still leaves us with the questions about whether such behaviour is ethical, and if there is a relationship between personality and 'political' behaviour at work. After all, if political behaviour is a necessary outcome from our model, we should presumably be teaching it at business schools to those people for whom it does not come naturally.

On the ethics of political behaviour it is worth considering the notion that politics is about overcoming the problems inevitably found in organizations because people belong to different interest groups. 'Politics' is seen as a way to manage situations where the various organization members bring different values to their work

95

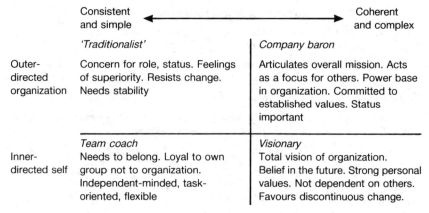

	Consistent and simple ← → Coherent and complex	
	'Traditionalist'	Company baron
Outer-directed organization	Concern for role, status. Feelings of superiority. Resists change. Needs stability	Articulates overall mission. Acts as a focus for others. Power base in organization. Committed to established values. Status important
Inner-directed self	Team coach Needs to belong. Loyal to own group not to organization. Independent-minded, task-oriented, flexible	Visionary Total vision of organization. Belief in the future. Strong personal values. Not dependent on others. Favours discontinuous change.

Figure 4.3 Action strategies (Source: Kakabadse 1983, pp. 19 *et seq.*)

and consequently do not share meanings with each other (Kakabadse 1983). This is a pluralist as opposed to a unitarist view. It implies that 'organizational politics' should not be interpreted as a pejorative phrase.

In an attempt to bring together the personalities' influence, and the situational determinants of political action, Kakabadse sees dominant values leading to particular attitudes and styles which are put into practice as opportunities arise. In this way, personality as expressed on the axis outer- (or organization-) directed and inner- (or self-) directed, is contrasted with action strategies which can be simple or complex, giving a mix of four personality/action strategy types (see Figure 4.3). Although this framework uses simplifying assumptions about personality and power, it is valuable as the first real attempt to indicate how particular personalities will seek out and use opportunities for action strategically.

Whilst accepting that 'political' behaviour is inevitable, it can be argued that there are some forms of political behaviour which are unethical, and other forms which are acceptable. Baddeley and James (1990) seek to distinguish between 'politicking' and 'manoeuvring'. The former they regard as acting in a self-oriented way, where people seek to defend their own ego, which requires 'game playing'. The latter approach is distinguished by the sense of personal integrity, where conscious choices are made on the ethics of the situations faced. The other main dimension is the extent to which a person is able to interpret or understand an organization's influence and decision processes: how good they are at 'reading' a political situation (see Figure 4.4).

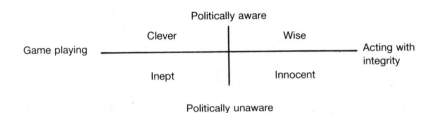

Figure 4.4 Reading political situations (Source: Baddeley and James 1990, p. 45)

Each of the four boxes in Figure 4.4 presents behaviours – clever, inept, wise or innocent, depending upon the person's capacity to read situations, and their propensity to play games or to act with integrity. Teaching people appropriate behaviours in business schools thus centres on helping them to understand and to interpret organizational life and so to become politically aware. If students can also be encouraged to act with integrity, they have at least the possibility of behaving wisely.

The idea behind the plea by Socrates, to avoid doing wrong with more care than being wronged, which suggests it is in one's own self-interest to avoid wrong doing, is consistent with the wisdom of acting with integrity. Although Machiavelli's Prince may have been clever, one wonders how he was able to survive in an environment where he was not trusted. How could one trust a person who 'cared little about good faith'? Without trust, how will it be possible to receive accurate information, and without accurate information, how will it be possible to make good decisions? Ultimately, ethical issues are settled by making personal decisions which can be scrutinized by other people, and in which the needs and rights of others are fully recognized (Cadbury 1987).

In business life, confidence is all, and to shatter that confidence, to break one's word, is to risk being left out of the game altogether. To exercise power, a person must have access to the decision-making caucus, and the amount of influence will depend on the opportunity to give advice, and the degree of joint decision-making which occurs (Heller *et al.* 1988).

Conclusion

This chapter has set out a model to show how sources of power and the perceived effectiveness of power interact within the situational

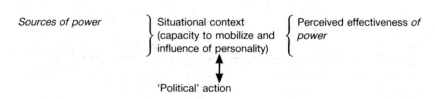

Figure 4.5 Model of power and effectiveness

context to produce 'political' activity (see Figure 4.5). One of the purposes of political activity is to influence the situational context, in order to make better use of the power source, and to increase the perceived effectiveness of power.

A HUMAN RELATIONSHIPS QUESTIONNAIRE

Notes

In a different version, this questionnaire is also known as 'The Machiavelli Test' and is used to measure machiavellian tendencies. It was developed by Richard Christie in New York, and considerable research has been done using the test. It is surprisingly effective in predicting whether a person becomes emotionally involved with other people, or simply uses them for his own ends.

Men are generally more machiavellian than women, despite popular belief to the contrary! People in the 'manipulative' professions, such as lawyers, teachers and nurses, score more highly than those in the passive professions, like accountancy or science. People with high Mach scores are better at coping with uncertainty.

Machiavellianism does not appear to be related to other psychological traits, such as intelligence or extroversion. People with high intelligence are not thereby any more or less machiavellian than their less bright colleagues.

However, if they are machiavellian, their intelligence helps. Some British research reported by John Touhey in the *British Journal of Social and Clinical Psychology* seems to show that the right mixture of intelligence and machiavellianism can be important in ensuring that you get on in life. Touhey looked at a group of 120 men who, compared with their fathers, has either risen or gone down in the world. He found that those who had gone up, with better-paid, socially more desirable jobs, had high scores on both IQ and Mach test; whereas those who had gone down had equally high Mach scores, but much lower IQ scores.

So a high score on this test will give you a high machiavellian tendency – but beware you don't overstrain your intelligence!

Power and politics

The questions

The following questions ask you about how you behave at work, what you believe about human relationships, and what value you place on them.

Each question is presented as a statement; you are asked to choose one of five possible responses:

Strongly agree : Agree : Don't know : Disagree : Strongly disagree

There are no right answers, and no wrong answers; so please be as honest as you can. (See Table 4.2 for the scoring key.)

	Strongly agree	Agree	Don't know	Disagree	Strongly disagree
1. You should only tell someone the real reason for doing something if it serves a successful purpose.	[ ]	[ ]	[ ]	[ ]	[ ]
2. People who lead upright and respectable lives will get on in the world.	[ ]	[ ]	[ ]	[ ]	[ ]
3. Braveness is inherent in most people.	[ ]	[ ]	[ ]	[ ]	[ ]
4. You should always assume that people can be villainous and that this will appeal if given a chance.	[ ]	[ ]	[ ]	[ ]	[ ]
5. Telling people what they want to hear is the best way to deal with them.	[ ]	[ ]	[ ]	[ ]	[ ]
6. The old saying that 'there's one born every minute', is not true.	[ ]	[ ]	[ ]	[ ]	[ ]
7. Lying to other people cannot be forgiven.	[ ]	[ ]	[ ]	[ ]	[ ]
8. Giving the actual reason rather than ones which may carry more weight is the way to behave when asking someone to do something for you.	[ ]	[ ]	[ ]	[ ]	[ ]
9. It is sensible to pander to important people.	[ ]	[ ]	[ ]	[ ]	[ ]
10. It is hard to be successful in an organization without cutting corners.	[ ]	[ ]	[ ]	[ ]	[ ]
11. What differentiates criminals from other people is that they are foolish enough to get caught.	[ ]	[ ]	[ ]	[ ]	[ ]
12. Euthanasia should be a choice for those having an incurable disease.	[ ]	[ ]	[ ]	[ ]	[ ]

	Strongly agree	Agree	Don't know	Disagree	Strongly disagree
13. In the final analysis, most people are good and well meaning.	[ ]	[ ]	[ ]	[ ]	[ ]
14. You should only act when it is morally defensible.	[ ]	[ ]	[ ]	[ ]	[ ]
15. Humility coupled with honesty is a better combination than dishonesty and self importance.	[ ]	[ ]	[ ]	[ ]	[ ]
16. Unless forced to work hard, most people will not stretch themselves.	[ ]	[ ]	[ ]	[ ]	[ ]
17. Being good in all respects is quite possible.	[ ]	[ ]	[ ]	[ ]	[ ]
18. The death of a parent is more easily forgotten by most people than the loss of a piece of property.	[ ]	[ ]	[ ]	[ ]	[ ]
19. It is simply asking for trouble to completely trust someone else.	[ ]	[ ]	[ ]	[ ]	[ ]
20. It is best always to be honest.	[ ]	[ ]	[ ]	[ ]	[ ]

Table 4.2 Scoring key for human relationships questionnaire

Question No	Strongly agree	Agree	Don't know	Disagree	Strongly disagree
1	5	4	3	2	1
2	1	2	3	4	5
3	1	2	3	4	5
4	5	4	3	2	1
5	5	4	3	2	1
6	1	2	3	4	5
7	1	2	3	4	5
8	1	2	3	4	5
9	5	4	3	2	1
10	5	4	3	2	1
11	5	4	3	2	1
12	5	4	3	2	1
13	1	2	3	4	5
14	1	2	3	4	5
15	1	2	3	4	5
16	5	4	3	2	1
17	1	2	3	4	5
18	5	4	3	2	1
19	5	4	3	2	1
20	1	2	3	4	5

Calculate your overall total score:

Score = ____

Analysis

Score	Comment
20–38	Goodness shines through you. How do you survive?
39–54	No is not an impossible word to say, you only think it is.
55–69	An honest cynic; at least relatively honest.
70–85	Congratulations – you could be an honorary member of the Borgia family.
85–100	You might even be able to teach Machiavelli something ('Never give a sucker an even break' – W.C. Fields).

References

Adler, A. (1929), *The Practice and Theory of Individual Psychology* (London: Routledge and Kegan Paul).

Baddeley, S. and James, K. (1990), 'Political management: developing the management portfolio', *Journal of Management Development*, vol. 9, no. 3, pp. 42–59.

Cadbury, Sir A. (1987), 'Ethical managers make their own rules', *Harvard Business Review*, September–October.

Cavanaugh, M.S. (1984), 'A typology of social power', in A. Kakabadse and C. Parker (eds), *Power, Politics and Organizations* (Chichester: John Wiley).

Crozier, M. (1964), *The Bureaucratic Phenomenon* (Chicago: University of Chicago Press).

Dixon, N.F. (1976), *On the Psychology of Military Incompetence* (London: Jonathan Cape).

French, J.R.P. and Raven, B. (1959), 'The bases of social power', in L. Cartwright and A. Zander (eds), *Group Dynamics, Research and Theory* (London: Tavistock).

Hartley, J.F. (1980), 'Personality of unemployed managers: myths and measurement', *Personnel Review*, vol. 9, no. 3, pp. 121–6.

Heller, F., Drenth, P., Koopman, P. and Rus, V. (1988), *Decisions in Organisations. A three-country comparative study* (London: Sage).

Hickson, D.J., Hinings, C.R., Lee, C.A., Schneck, R.E. and Pennings, J.M. (1971), 'A strategic contingencies' theory of intraorganizational power', *Administrative Science Quarterly*, June, pp. 216–28.

Kakabadse, A.C. (1983), *The Politics of Management* (Aldershot: Gower).

McClelland, D. and Burnham, D.H. (1976), 'Power is the great motivator', *Harvard Business Review*, vol. 54, pp. 100–10.

Machiavelli, N. (1981), *The Prince and other Political Writings*, selected and translated by Bruce Penman (London: Everyman).

March, J.G. (1955), 'An introduction to the theory and measurement of influence', *American Political Science Review*, vol. 49, pp. 431–51.

Mulder, M. (1977), *The Daily Power Game* (Leiden: Martinus Nijhoff).

Pettigrew, A. (1974), 'The influence process between specialists and executives', *Personnel Review*, vol. 3, no. 1, pp. 24–30.

Plato (1971), *Gorgias*, translated by W. Hamilton (Harmondsworth: Penguin Books).

Raven, B. (1965), 'Social influence and power', in I.D. Steiner and M. Fishbein (eds), *Current Studies in Social Psychology* (New York: Holt, Rinehart and Winston).

Sayles, L.R. (1958), *The Behaviour of Industrial Work Groups* (New York: Wiley).

Tyson, S., Barclay, C. and Handyside, J. (1986), *The N Factor in Executive Survival* (Cranfield: HRRC, Monograph No. 1).

Walton, R.E. and Dutton, J.M. (1969), 'The management of interdepartmental conflict: a model and review', *Administrative Science Quarterly*, March, pp. 73–84.

5

Careers and transitions

Definitions

We can differentiate occupation from the notion of career in a fairly simple and straightforward way: an occupation is a work activity in which people engage. The activity itself has a market value and people are therefore paid to engage in it; the work activity itself may be a single task or a group of similar tasks organized in similar ways in various establishments. The performance of these tasks or work activities requires certain skills, knowledge, aptitudes and interests and brings with it certain rewards. A career, on the other hand, is a sequence of occupations, jobs or positions engaged in, or occupied throughout, the lifetime of the person. The choice of and success within these roles are determined in part by the aptitudes, interests, values, needs, prior experiences and expectations of the person in question. There may be occasions where the two words are indeed synonymous; occasionally, as can be the case in skilled trades, e.g. bricklayer, plumber, etc. The same is equally true of the professional classes, where the examples would include people such as doctors, physicians, lawyers, etc. Skilled tradesmen and professionals have one thing in common: both invest heavily in terms of time and money in preparation for their occupation. Moreover, by and large, the financial and social rewards for remaining within their chosen field are great enough to maintain people in it throughout their working lives.

Perhaps the most pragmatic and simplest of the definitions was that coined by Wilensky (1961, p. 523). He defined 'career' as a succession of related jobs, arranged in a hierarchy or prestige, through which people move in an ordered (more or less predictable) sequence. Modern career theory and common parlance inevitably frame careers in terms of advancement along some kind of hierarchy of power or prestige. We talk easily today of career ladders, plateauing, promotion, demotion and even sideways or lateral transfers, but until relatively recently this was not the case.

The basic difference between an occupation and a career is the longitudinal, sequential character of the latter as opposed to the static nature of the former. An occupation is what you do to earn a living at a particular time. A career, on the other hand, is a sequence of positions occupied over a period of time. Until the late 1960s to early 1970s organizational behaviour focused on occupations. The attempt was made to match individual traits and characteristics with those of people currently engaged in a particular occupation. The career model changed that focus to one of viewing the characteristics of people pursuing different sequences of educational and occupational positions, and on the nature of these sequences.

A career therefore, is a sequence of positions; in a sense it is the course of continued progress in the life of a person. Clearly this concept involves the notion of development, with positions leading from one to another either vertically or laterally within one or more organizations. The movement may be systematic or haphazard. For the majority of people, whatever move is made at one point in a career is at least to some degree an outcome of the positions which they have occupied earlier. Indeed, it can well be argued that careers begin before employment for we are at least to some extent shaped by parental background and by our peer group whilst at school and in other levels of education. Moreover, careers extend beyond there into retirement. As the 'death following retirement time span' increases so people need more and more to find things to do in order both to structure life and give it meaning. In these terms we might argue that career is not simply defined in terms of the roles which people have assumed over a period of time but rather in terms of the preparation for different roles, of actually playing them and then relinquishing them.

The original work on careers and career development took as its starting point the life stages of individuals. Whilst Shakespeare was concerned with the Seven Ages of Man, today five life stages tend to be implicated in the analysis of people at work. Respectively, these are childhood, adolescence, young adulthood, maturity and old age. This original conceptualization by Super and Bohn (1971) was revised into nine stages by Schein (1978). His stages were: growth, fantasy and exploration as stage 1; entry into the world of work stage 2; basic training stage 3; full membership in early career stage 4; full membership mid career stage 5; mid-career crisis stage 6; late career in non-leadership or leadership role stage 7; decline and disengagement stage 8 and retirement stage 9.

Development of life stages

Although Schein gives a great deal of detail about the different life stages and career stages for individuals (Schein 1978, pp. 40–6) we offer here a very brief résumé of his analysis.

1. **Growth** – this is the age in which people take on such roles as students, and applicant. At this stage of their career development people attempt to develop a basis for making realistic vocational choices. This may well necessitate the obtaining of appropriate education or training. People do this in many different ways either by discovering role models from which they can learn about occupations, or by developing and discovering their own values, motives and ambitions and linking those into their own career choices.

2. **Entry into the world of work** – here the roles have changed from aspirant into becoming a recruit or indeed an entrant into the organization. At this stage the individual enters the labour market and gets a first job which may well be the basis of a career. It is at this stage that a first rite of passage becomes evident (see below).

3. **Basic training** – the roles here include those of trainee and novice. The individual is concerned to deal with the reality of the shock of what work and group membership are really like. It demands that he or she overcomes the insecurity and inexperience and begins to develop a sense of confidence in what they have to do.

4. **Full membership in early career** – the roles here include full membership of the organization. Typically, the age range would be from 17 to 30. At this point in their career individuals accept responsibilities and successfully discharge the duties associated with their first formal assignments. This period involves not only

performing effectively but also learning how things are done and how to improve both themselves and the rest of the organization. They begin to accept partial responsibility both for themselves and for other people within the organization. Organizationally, what is looked for at this stage is full commitment.

5. **Full membership mid-career** – the roles here include full member in some way or tenured member. It would indicate such work as supervisor or manager. Some people may remain at this stage of their career, which can occur at any time from the age of 25 and beyond. For many people it involves remaining technically competent and continuing to learn in their chosen area of specialization. It may also involve them in accepting higher levels of responsibility, including that of the work of other people. There will also be times when they have to deal with failure. Such failure may be because of poor performance or when tenure is actually denied to them.

6. **Mid-career crisis** – as such this occurs, so theorists would have us believe, between the ages of 35 and 45. It could be said that the mid-life crisis commences at the age of 21 and ceases around the age of 65 and 70. It simply peaks in the mid-years. At this stage people make a major reassessment of their progress relative to their ambitions. This may force decisions on them, such as to level off their career track or to change careers or indeed, perhaps, to forge ahead to new, higher and perhaps different challenges. It involves the realistic assessment by the person of their talents, motives and values.

7. **Late career** – Schein actually differentiates two forms here, that of non-leadership and leadership. In both cases the age range is from 40 to retirement. In the case of non-leadership the individual is envisaged as having a contribution to make within the organization, either as a member of the management or simply as a member who is close to the decision-making process itself. It may even be that at this stage the individual is considered to be dead wood. Despite this, he or she may still be maintained within the organization. If the decision is made to maintain their technical or functional career track then quite often more time is spent deepening the skills which are already there. Quite often this is also the time when they begin to be more interested in developing interpersonal and group skills, especially if the organization utilizes group work to any extent. In the case of the leadership roles the types of job being envisaged are those of general manager, senior partner, entre-

preneur, and so on. At this level the skills of the individual are used for the long-term welfare of the organization. The task is to integrate the efforts of other people and to influence broadly rather than on a day-to-day basis. In both cases, at this age, people have to learn how to deal with factors outside the work situation which can often have quite important implications for the way they actually work.

8. **Decline and disengagement** – the age at which this begins to occur is from 40 until retirement. Different people simply begin these processes at quite different ages. It may involve the individual in learning to accept reduced levels of power and responsibility. It might also involve, especially for those who are not in senior management positions, learning how to manage a life which is less dominated by work.

9. **Retirement** – as with the other rite of passage into the world of work this transition also requires a major adjustment on the part of many people. They enter the retirement stakes with little or no preparation for the quite major changes which occur. One of the greatest problems is not just to maintain a sense of identity but also to maintain a sense of worth. Often it is difficult to find ways of using the accumulated wisdom and experience of the individual.

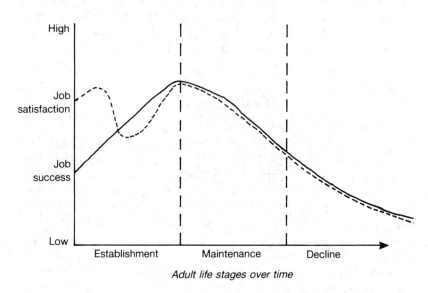

Adult life stages over time

Figure 5.1 Adult life stages (Source: Cytrynbaum and Crites 1989, p. 68)

There are arguments suggesting that there are relationships between adult life stages, as hypothesized by Super and Bohn (1971), and job satisfaction and job success. Figure 5.1, taken from Cytrynbaum and Crites (1989), shows this. Their argument is that there appears to be considerable documentation evidencing that career satisfaction follows a cyclical curve. Starting at a high level (on occupational entry), it dips heavily during the establishment stage when initial expectations of advancement are delayed or thwarted. Recovery occurs, though not to the previous high level, reaching a peak at about the age of 40. On the other hand, career success begins at a lower ebb but increases linearly from occupational entry to mid-life. Thereafter, for the majority, a decline sets in. The overall implication for career counselling and employee development work is that either of these could be oriented towards assisting those having an adjustment problem. In other words, if the individual has just entered the world of work then they experience a high level of job satisfaction but may be frustrated by slow advancement. Many of their problems will centre, possibly, upon job success. Those at the height of the career development curve, at the beginning of the maintenance stage, might have the mid-career crisis question as to whether to change jobs. The issues for them here are, having attained high levels of satisfaction and success, should they stay with that and revise their aspirations and expectations, or should they change jobs. As with many of these theories, until recently the work was inevitably undertaken on men; when looking at women, as Reinke *et al.* (1985) have shown, the importance of the family life cycle cannot be ignored.

Trait theories

These theories are concerned to show that optimal career outcomes for the individual and the organization can best be derived through a congruence between the individual's characteristics and the demands and requirements of the organizational environment. The concern therefore was to find ways of studying and measuring individual differences as well as matching people to the jobs. By and large, these approaches relied on the use of tests of one kind or another as well as counselling. What was then sought was a correlation between the measures derived from the individual and successful job performance. The emphasis overall, however, has been on describing and measuring individual characteristics rather than organizational variables, which is an important distinction between this theory and other theories concerning careers in organizations. Traditionally, vocational psychology has overlooked the effects of organizational variables and the dynamic quality of people and the environment in which they work. The variables which have been looked at in large measure are concerned with abilities. Beyond that, the vocational interests, needs and values of individuals have also been dealt with.

New approaches to career theories

The static nature of these theories has already been mentioned. However, there is a further issue to do with tests, especially tests of ability. It is now well recognized that many tests disadvantage minority groups in various ways. In part this is because of their socioeconomic disadvantage. The question is not one of test validity but, rather, how selection decisions should be made. In the early stages of trait factor theories this particular issue worked against being able to derive more generalizable theories across working populations.

But there is more than this, for the self-concept that people carry includes such things as self-esteem, stereotypes, perceptions of social environments, and so on. Moreover, background variables such as gender, socio-economic status and race have received insufficient attention. What we do know is that our interests can be modified in adulthood given appropriate learning experiences. Because we assume that such things as our values and interests are dynamic over time it leaves us in a quandary when we begin to look at trait theories concerning career development. The evidence from the study of personality and abilities generally is that there are fixed elements within the individual. If this evidence were to be followed through it would lead to a static idea about careers in organizations. Fortunately, the evidence, in overall terms, indicates that these variables are themselves dynamic.

One of the most renowned trait factor theories in the area of careers on the trait factor side of things is that of Holland (1973, 1985). Central to Holland's theory is that vocational satisfaction and stability, and indeed achievement, depend on the congruence between the personality type and the environment. The personality types alluded to also characterize environments. Six personality types were hypothesized as follows:

1. **Realistic** – related to outdoor and technical interests.

2. **Investigative** – intellectual and scientific interests.

3. **Artistic** – creative, expressive, literary, artistic, musical and other areas.

4. **Social** – interested in working with people.

5. **Enterprising** – interest in persuasion and leadership.

6. **Conventional** – enjoyment of detail, computational activity, high degree of structure.

Typically, questionnaires or inventories were used to measure people on these various dimensions. Using them, two important predictions were then made. The first was that congruent individuals, i.e. individuals whose interests and demands were congruent, would be more satisfied and less likely to change their environment than would those where there was incongruence between these aspects. The evidence accruing over the years indicates that this hypothesis seems to hold. The second hypothesis was that incongruent people would be influenced by the dominant environment (in other words, their employment) towards congruence. The evidence here is inconclusive. Few studies have done the necessary longitudinal work to see whether this is in fact the case. What studies have shown is that people who are congruent, in terms of their employment, are a very small proportion of a given population. For example, in the case of accountants in a study undertaken in 1981 only 27 per cent of these accountants had Holland code types congruent with their occupational choice. The implication here is that some 73 per cent of those who were reviewed in the research had traits or characteristics which were incongruent with the work that they were actually undertaking. It is this group who present an extremely important and interesting challenge to career theorists and practitioners.

Trait factor theories

Much of the work in this area has been dealt with in static terms. What is now required, and what is beginning to happen, is that people look at how incongruence begins to change towards congruence over time. It is important to look at what effects the process of organizational socialization has on incongruence itself. Plainly, this has important implications for maximizing organizational commitment and productivity, and it also has implications in terms of adult career changes. Trait factor theorists have limited views of the range of important individual variables since insufficient attention has been paid to sex, race and socio-economic status.

However, there is research which is beginning to work in this area. It can be categorized under three major headings. First, job characteristics theory is concerned with the fit between the characteristic of the job and the needs of the job holder. Secondly, biodata is also being used to see what relationships exist between life history experiences and vocational interests. There is some indication that family background experiences are influential in developing particular types of people, i.e. types in the Holland sense of that word. Thirdly, and perhaps most importantly, whereas trait factor theories emphasize the structure of personalities, current theories are looking more towards the process of social negotiation by which individuals and organizations adjust their expectations of each other. It is only in this way that a workable level of congruence can be achieved.

Career development programmes are not only now widely accepted but are also seen as critical to individuals and organizations. Programmes such as these cover a wide range of issues from individual careers and work/family adjustment, to policy and strategic concerns such as the ageing of the work force, adaptation to new technology and organization productivity. In essence, a career is defined as the evolving sequence of a person's work experiences over time. Careers reflect the relationships between people and the providers of official position, that is institutions or organizations. Career theory, therefore, is concerned *inter alia* with how these relationships fluctuate over time. In a sense we could view careers as both the study of individual and organizational change. In looking at the things which affect career choices, then, the range of factors involved is quite large: we can look at careers at the psychological level of analysis in which the career is seen either as a vocation or as a vehicle for self-realization; it may also be viewed in psychological terms as a component of the individual life structure; and in the social psychology field, a career may be viewed as a response to external role messages.

Sociologically speaking, the career can be seen simply as the unfolding of social roles or alternatively, as an indicator of social mobility. Anthropologically, a career can be seen as a set of status passages and views taken about rites and ceremonies which occur in careers all the time. Economically, of course, a career can be seen as a response to market forces and leading from that we have the notion of political science in which a career is seen as a way of gathering prestige, and so on. Two other aspects can be viewed in terms of the career: initially, it might be viewed from a historical perspective in which the influence of prominent people and specific events are reviewed; secondly, geographically, careers can be viewed simply as a response to particular geographic circumstances. In this instance the focus would be on such things as the availability of raw materials, natural harbours, etc. Of all these the concentration will be on the psychological and sociological perspectives.

The family

Careers and career development cannot be looked at in the isolated arena of the world of work; other factors plainly contribute. One of the major factors is the world outside work and, specifically, the family. As we pass through the various life stages so the family places different and increasingly complex demands upon us. The commitments which are engendered when people enter marriage go far beyond those imposed by a job or career. The resolution of potential conflicts between work and family, because they are external to work, requires insight and adaptive capacity, not just on the part of the individual concerned but also by the organization which employs him or her. Conflicts which are not dealt with are quite likely to lead to reduced performances.

At one level it is easy to differentiate relationships between work and family life. Thus some people have an extended work/home environment in which the overlap between the two is often great and sometimes total. The role, then, between the spouses is one of collaboration. This is quite different from the position where the relationship between the two situations is minimal, home becomes an alternative to work and the spouse is then placed very much in a supportive role.

The third category is where work and home are in opposition and may even compete. In these circumstances, especially where the work itself is physically or psychologically exhausting, home becomes somewhere for recuperation and the spouse has little if anything to do with the career progression of the worker. Plainly, there are other features which will impact: these would include such things as the hours of work and their distribution as well as things like the geographical locale of the job, and the amount and difficulty of travel involved.

Some of these conflicts are enhanced greatly in the case of the dual-career family. One basic option is for the couple to reach a consensus on which partner will be more work-involved and which will be more family-involved. Such a decision could be permanent or renegotiated as needs change. Alternatively of course, they may share responsibilities and maintain sharing throughout the life cycle. Quite often people who make these sorts of decisions have to turn to external resources to help them cope with day-to-day living.

The whole subject area of careers is dynamic. Or, rather, the individual's career takes place in a dynamic environment. As individuals we may have both on an individual level and within our organization role, a long-term developmental process. However, it should never be forgotten that this process has to interact with short-term group and inter-group dynamics within an organization. In other words, organizational, group and individual variables will affect a particular person's career progression.

Learning how to cope is inevitably a major life task, especially when we review careers. Schein refers to this as constructive coping. It involves the diagnosis of the real problem by the particular individual and then looking more closely at the reactions to that problem and the feelings in the face of it. Having done that, he argues that an appropriate coping response has to be selected and followed through by not just assessing the consequences but also by diagnosing the consequences of that coping effort. Nor is this coping merely about working through the life stages that we all go through. On the contrary, it is also concerned in the world of work. The evidence suggests that people who think in these terms don't just do so for themselves and the particular problems and issues which face them at this time, but rather, they look at the issues in terms of the organization and how other people are acting. What we become increasingly aware of is that relationships with other people are especially relevant to effective coping. We often need and require the ideas, perspective and emotional support of other people. It is for this reason that we often require to establish meaningful relationships either within the world of work or externally from it into which we can tap. It is a prime skill for those people whose careers will be spent within organizational contexts. Interpersonal competence is vital for career advancement.

It is perfectly possible to conceptualize both vertical and horizontal career tracks. Vertical careers are those which would trace increments in formal authority; in this instance the movement would be to successively higher levels of stratification and perhaps entry into more élite social networks. On the other hand, horizontal careers are more likely to show increments in prestige or expertise. The movement here could be specified as being towards a more central position in some social network located at a specific level of a strata. However, to fully understand the process of career development it is necessary to attend to the dynamics of life; the process of development and adjustment.

Schein's three-dimensional model of careers is a most interesting one combining a series of different aspects within the context of the world of work. What we can differentiate are movements up a hierarchy during the course of careers, i.e. as individuals we achieve a certain number of promotions. At the same time, most people move along a functional or technical dimension which describes their area of special expertise or skill. The combination of these gives us two quite different movements within the organization. We may move hierarchically within a particular specialism such as production or sales, in which case the movement is of a vertical kind; alternatively, there are people who switch areas or disciplines and whose movement therefore can be seen as being horizontal, switching between departments. What Schein so cleverly adds to this is the more subtle dimension of movement towards the centre, or as he says, 'toward the inner circle'. By this is meant the core of the occupation or organization. Movement in this inward direction is earned through acquiring responsibility and the trust of those people at the more senior levels of the organization. In a sense, it might be thought of as a political dimension. It may well be, indeed, that this dimension is particularly important for those people who have reached their final resting point hierarchically within the organization. For such people a shift towards the centre in essence has elements of growth attached to it. Schein depicts this three-dimensional concept as a cone (see Figure 5.2).

Having entered into the organization, the transition stage itself and the period directly following it can be categorized in three dimensions. The entry stage includes the period of preparation and training directly following the hiring decision. The second stage, and often the most important, is the socialization stage which includes all the early processes of learning the ropes and how the organization itself works. This includes ideas on how to get along with other people and how to undertake the work. In a sense it is the same process that is often experienced by parents of adolescents, for it is a period of mutual testing by the individual and the organization in order to derive a more detailed contract psychologically. The third stage is that of mutual acceptance. This point includes not only the various processes of formal granting of membership of the organization but

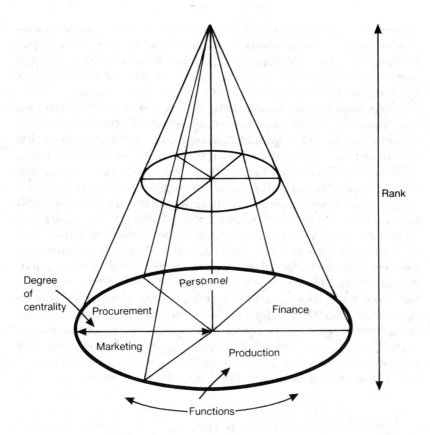

Figure 5.2 Three-dimensional career structure (Source: Schein 1978, p. 39)

also the informal aspects. At this stage, all that has been established is that there is a match between the individual's needs and those of the organization.

During the early stages of the individual's time within an organization there are some potential negative outcomes both from the viewpoint of the individual and of the organization. Organizationally it is important to avoid the turnover of high potential new hires as well as the antitheses of this, i.e. the failure to discover incompetence at an early enough stage. Further, organizationally, we must beware of the problems of demotivation and even the learning of complacency. For the individual the major negative outcome is the lack of opportunity to test him or herself and to determine precisely what their limitations are. If the opportunity for self-tests is not provided by the organization then sensible people seek these out for themselves. Organizationally, it is important for the employee to learn how to work with people, to deal with them, to manage resistance to change and, perhaps most importantly, to deal with their own boss and peer group. Beyond that it is vital, if the career choices are to be made within that organization, to ensure that a sense of identity within the organization is created, maintained and even enhanced.

During the period of mutual acceptance, the gravest danger is that insufficient information is generated for either the organization or the individual to determine whether the other should be accepted. For the employee, the early career track must generate opportunities for testing to see whether there is a potential match of the individual and organization. Quite often people complain that they do not know where they stand within the organization. Strangely, and in the same way, the managers will often complain that they do not know how the new employees feel about the organization and their own jobs despite the fact that there is evidence to show how these people do feel about these issues. In these sort of circumstances it comes as no surprise to find each party begins to second guess the other and create thereby some nasty surprises, perhaps in the form of resignations or sackings. Career planning, therefore, demands that both line managers and staff specialists within the organization work to create better systems and procedures for integrating employees.

Rites

Status passages were how the rites of passage were originally conceived. Career transitions may occur imperceptibly, as when a physician suddenly realizes that administration has taken over from being a doctor. Some turning points, on the other hand, are unpredictable, as for example with the intercession of war or some other catastrophe. However, the notion that careers unfold in stages is one which is well presented in the literature. Indeed, the rites of passage notion often denotes a fundamental change in an individual's identity. These 'rites' represent the change in status symbolically. For example, titles such as 'Doctor' or 'Queen's Counsel' are conferred at ceremonies when individuals have achieved certain qualifications. Organizations also provide clear indicators of their acceptance of people into particular status groupings, such as the award of a reserved car parking space for senior managers. This change is not just so far as the external world is concerned but often takes place in the person's conception of self. Typically, careers were pieced together from a string of alternatives. On to this a set of interpretive resources were offered to individuals by the collectives to which they belonged. Interestingly, consistent with this thinking is the idea that career lines can exist only when a number of individuals have followed the same path. It is for this reason that the idea of creating career tracks within newly formed organizations such as investment banks gives us such difficulties.

Models

There are other models which have been postulated in this area. One which links many of the life span models to that of Schein is Driver's (1982) career concepts which he describes as underlying a person's thinking about his or her career. This is a directional pattern model. Four types were hypothesized as follows:

1. **Transitory** – one in which no set job or field is ever permanently chosen. There is no pattern of movement from job to job. Often seen among semi-skilled workers.

2. **Steady state** – one in which the individual stays in one work role for life. It was commonly seen (no less so today) among established professions, doctors, lawyers, etc.

3. **Linear** – a chosen field is adopted early in life and plans for upward movement developed and executed. This is often to be found among corporate managers.

4. **Spiral** – a view that one develops in a given field for a period of time then moves to a related or even a new area on some kind of cyclical basis.

Nor can we simply look at careers in terms of individuals. The form of organization will plainly affect the career structure within it. If, for example, there is strong competition for the product as well as a high degree of openness of the organization to employment at all levels then this has direct implications for the extent to which careers within that organization are structured. Indeed, looking at these two dimensions of competition and openness to the outside labour market at least four different forms of organization can be defined (see Figure 5.3) (Sonnenfeld, 1989). Thus we would have one definition for low

117

		ACADEMY	BASEBALL TEAMS
Competition	High	IBM HP	Consultants Public Relations
	Low	CLUBS Government agencies Utilities	FORTRESS Retailers Airlines
		Low	High

Openness

Figure 5.3 Classification of organizations (Source: Sonnenfeld 1989, p. 215)

competition and relatively closed, i.e. low openness, being club-type organizations, which would include government agencies and utilities. Organizations having high competition but low openness would include such organizations as IBM and Hewlett Packard; the classification for these (Sonnenfeld 1989) is that of academy. Those organizations having high openness but low competition would include retail businesses, publishing, and so on – even perhaps such organizations as airlines – and they would be classed under the fortress format. High competition and high openness is, by Sonnenfeld's classification, called the baseball team and would include organizations specializing in such things as public relations, consultancy, bio research, and so on.

The rationale for these different labels is that the baseball team format relies on individual performance. Individuals who have transferable talents are important. What is therefore created is an infrastructure of head hunters to find those people who are readily exchangeable. The academy, on the other hand, is a more stable institution with an objective of developing the knowledge of its highly committed members. The club, or fraternal order, is oriented towards the rules of fair treatment of its members with loyalty shown through seniority. The fortress is simply an institution under siege with low commitment to individuals. The larger goal is institutional survival even at the cost of individual members. The strategic orientation of a firm shapes the supply and assignment flows for its workforce, which in turn leads to a different emphasis on various career system activities. Nor is this system a static one. For inherent in it is the notion of dynamism, i.e. that an organization can shift from one cell into another. A classic example of this is investment banking during the late 1980s to early 1990s which shifted from high openness of its internal labour market with high competition to a low openness while still maintaining high competition. In this way, such organizations move from the baseball team category towards the fortress category.

Career anchors

Kakabadse has made a great deal of use of people's value-systems as a way of determining the likely effects of groups of people coming together to work as a team at senior management levels. Schein talks about career anchors, one of the three major components of which are the attitudes and value systems as perceived by the individual. To this are added motives and needs, as well as talents and abilities. All of them are dealt with in a self-perception form.

Until the individual's talents are tested in real-life situations they may not even understand what they bring to the organization. It is only as a result of early interactions between the individual and the work environment that these career anchors come into existence. The anchors themselves give an indication as to the career options which become available to the individual. If these career anchors are incompatible with the form of work which is being undertaken then there are direct implications both for performance and for the psychological well-being of the individual.

Career anchors may take the form of technical or functional competence, managerial competence or emotional competence. Whilst the first two are self-explanatory the third needs a brief explanation. Emotional competence is the capacity to be stimulated by emotional and interpersonal crises rather than to be exhausted by them. It involves the capacity to bear high levels of responsibility without becoming paralysed. It also involves the ability to exercise power without guilt or shame. This third competency is probably most important in identifying the kind of person who will succeed in high-level managerial roles. As an aside, technical people tend to be more concerned about the content of the work; managerially anchored people are more concerned about the size of task and the challenge. In many ways, it might be argued that management people are highly dependent on large organizations within which they can shift to senior levels, deriving much of their own identity from the fortune of the organization itself. Such people often introduce themselves in

119

terms of jobs, company names and the size and scope of the organization.

Three other career anchors are described by Schein. The first is security and stability; people with these attributes make good organization men and women and are more willing than most to accept an organizational definition of their careers. Secondly, creativity may be seen as a career anchor. It is crucial to the understanding of the career of the entrepreneur and is found in those people who wish to be autonomous, managerially competent, and yet able to exercise their special talents rather than simply to build some kind of money base for security. It is interesting to note from the works of Schein and Greiner an agreement that these creative talents, which lead to the initial building of new organizations, can be dysfunctional when the organization they have built needs to stabilize and develop effective routines. What tends to happen is that the entrepreneur shifts from the organization allowing others to run it whilst he or she sets up a new enterprise, or this transition is forced on that individual by the under managers or the board of directors. There are occasions when the individual devises or develops a special role in the organization in order to maintain the creative demands, but few shift their orientation towards learning how to play a senior management role.

Autonomy and independence is the final career anchor. Such people find organizational life restrictive and even irrational; by and large they are less concerned about missed opportunities for promotion and have few aspirations to higher management levels generally. For them the major aspect of autonomy is to be able to set their own pace, schedules, life styles and, perhaps most importantly, work habits.

Career anchors clearly reflect the underlying needs and motives which people bring into the world of work, the individual's values and their discovered talents. It is the process 'of integrating into the total self concept what one sees one's self to be more or less competent at, wanting out of life, one's value system, and the kind of person one is that begins to determine the major life and occupational choices throughout adulthood' (Schein 1978, p. 125). In other words, the career anchor itself is learned: but it is a learning which combines self-perceived motives, values and talents.

There are many other ways of categorizing people at different stages of their careers and, indeed, of categorizing organizations. It is quite possible to see people over time progressing from being impulsive at the initial stages through to being opportunistic and diplomatic, becoming a technical expert and perhaps an achiever to finally ending as a strategist. Nor does this final stage necessarily take a length of time to achieve; some people are at the strategic level of analysis from a very early age.

Mentoring

The mentoring role within the organization can be quite crucial in terms of careers. The concept itself is not such a simple notion; there is a wide range of possible work assignments which involve different forms of mentoring. For a start, the mentor can take the role of teacher, coach or trainer – the sort of person who teaches others a great deal about how things work. Alternatively, the mentor may be seen as a positive role model. This is the sort of person who sets a good example of how to get things done. On a different footing there are people who give quite specific pieces of guidance or help to individuals as they travel the career track. The mentor roles involved here are those of talent developers, and door openers. A talent developer is the sort of person who gives others challenging work from which they can learn. A door opener is one who gives opportunities for growth, producing assignments whilst at the same time ensuring that the battles at more senior levels are successfully won.

Changing the emphasis once more, we can see the mentor as some kind of parental figure. In this case the mentoring may take the form of protection in which the mentor allows mistakes to be made by the individual in the interest of learning without risk to the job itself. The alternate form is the one which most people treat as the main mentoring role, that of sponsor. In this case the mentor will give visibility to his or her protégé to make sure that they have a good press within the organization, especially with higher level people so that they will be remembered when new opportunities come along. The final format is one which is rarely thought of in terms of mentoring yet is plainly vital within some organizations. This is where the mentor him or herself may be the successful leader of the organization. In this case the individual supporters ride along with the leader, their loyalty being to the individual rather than the organization.

Mid-life

The problem of mid-life is often one of growth. Because of the pressures people are often strongly tempted towards complacency, and in a sense become resigned to their fate. This is the case even when clear options for development may be available. These aspects are made more poignant by the fact that four major variables impinge more heavily on us at that mid-life point than possibly at any other time in our careers. The first of these is the simple emotional realization of our own mortality, that time is finite, and this leads to potential stresses for some individuals. There is also a rekindling of adolescent impulses and the resurfacing of adolescent conflicts. In part this is engendered by the third element, that of the changing relationship to the individual's spouse and children, especially as those children become adult. Finally, there is an anxiety which comes from the realization that there are limited organizational opportunities. As we grow older there is, for the majority of us, a decreasing number of career options and opportunities. In any case, as we move up the organization the narrowing of that organizational pyramid simply implies fewer and fewer opportunities. And, although there is a slight change occurring in today's environment there are societal norms and stereotypes which militate against older people.

Gender

Much has recently been written in the area of gender issues concerning all aspects of work, but when it comes to career, the work of Gallos (1985) is particularly interesting. She argues that the time has now come to move beyond the debate of whether women and men are developmentally different. The focus now should be on understanding more clearly the differences and their implications. Women construct their conceptions of themselves, their lives and the world around them differently from men. By definition, therefore, it is implicit in women's different vision of reality that there is a potential for questioning present beliefs about what is essential for a creative and productive society, how a successful course should be charted to manage life's critical adult challenges, the balance between work and other things. Despite the fact that women who work now constitute almost half of the total work force there is no theory of women's career development. Much of the research on them is fragmented and only at the exploratory level.

Women in managerial occupations would appear to be better adapted to the increasing uncertainty of labour markets and opportunity structures by virtue of their more value-driven orientation towards career development. This is in marked contrast to the characteristically rationalistic orientation of male managers. What appears to be a consequence of this is that men have most of their radical transitions early in their careers. Women, on the other hand, maintain a higher rate of divergent mobility throughout their careers.

The issues about racism, women and even dual career relationships are of primary interest to those looking at careers. However, it should always be borne in mind that almost everyone is concerned about juggling a work life, a personal life, a family life, a leisure life, a home and even other facets of living. These things are not just relevant to minority groups within society. This fact needs greater emphasis in theories of careers. However, in looking at people who do have dual careers, Hall and Hall (1980) identified the following four different types:

1. **Accommodators**   – where each was highly involved in different spheres.

2. **Allies**   – both involved in the same sphere but unconcerned with the other's progress.

3. **Adversaries**   – each highly involved in their own work and wanting the other to do the home tasks.

4. **Acrobats**   – each highly involved in both home and work.

The argument was put that accommodators and allies would have lower stress levels than adversaries and acrobats. However, it is not just between the individuals themselves that problems can occur; organizational practices also create issues and problems for dual-career partners. Action areas which have been looked at by many organizations now include such things as spouse relocation assistance, child care assistance, flexible work scheduling and even two-career recruiting.

Stress

By and large, job stress literature reflects a bias towards individual action and responsibility. The concern is to try to enable people (and train them) to cope. Yet there is little doubt that there are organizational influences and economic constraints on careers which begin to emphasize the shared responsibility between the organization and

123

the individual, not just for fostering career development but also because of the implications for stress on the individual. The link then goes beyond simple individual coping strategies and organizational interventions towards career management strategies which have stress alleviating potential. In other words, models of career stress should not assume that it is the individual's responsibility to cope. On the contrary, they should consider intervention at the organizational level as well.

There is a series of questions which is raised in terms of the necessary research on careers and its implications for stress for the individual. Initially, we may be concerned whether certain types of career transitions may be more inherently stressful than others, which leads to the question of whether coping strategies vary by type of transition. In essence this leads on to further questioning concerned with both the individual and situational factors which may contribute to the stress experienced during a particular type of transition. Indeed, when we remove our blinkers and look at the individual level of analysis then we may be concerned with whether individual coping strategies vary by sex, race, type of transition, career or life stage, career motivation, or other non-work variables. All this leads us to consider the effectiveness of coping strategies (for different career stresses and stress reactions) and social support, to see whether they have any effect on career stress or whether such strategies moderate the impact of career stress or stress for the individual. Although these questions are of interest, none can be seen to have been answered in any degree within the current literature.

In the main studies cast job stress as a problem and there is a basic assumption that it should be reduced. However, there are positive, developmental aspects of stress which are often referred to by some writers as 'power'. There are arguments, therefore, for preserving such aspects. Indeed, it may even be that what is at the time considered to be an extremely stressful career transition may, in retrospect, be viewed as a positive experience in the context of resulting career development. The problem is in the definition of such transitions, which brings home the point, quite markedly, that the concept of duration of time is vital both to the study of careers and to transactional process models of stress and coping.

Transitions

There are many theories which are concerned with the transitions

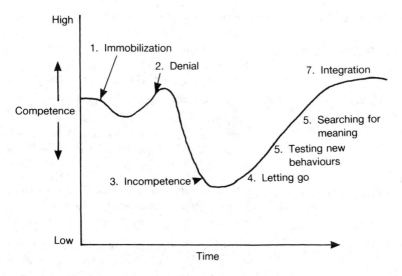

Figure 5.4 The transition curve

side of career theory. Nicholson (1986) has a five-stage model involving the following aspects.

1. **Preparation** – processes of expectation and anticipation before change.

2. **Encounter** – affect and sense-making during the days or weeks of job tenure.

3. **Adjustment** – subsequent personal and role development to reduce person/job misfit.

4. **Stabilization** – settled connection between person and role.

5. **Preparation** – the renewal of the cycle.

   Possibly the most utilized theory is the one shown in Figure 5.4, which is useful in most transition states from organizational change (see Chapter 8, below) and culture change interventions, through to individually oriented changes. Its great strength lies in the fact that, by enabling people to derive a better understanding of their current position as well as what may shortly be happening to them, they are able to create more appropriate coping strategies. By this means the transition process may be speeded up.

The seven phases from the diagram are as follows:

1. **Immobilization**: the individual is overwhelmed with what is about to occur. There is a mismatch between high expectations and reality.

2. **Denial**: there are often two separate issues at this stage of denial of the need for change. They are a retreat into old ways, often at a high level of performance, and/or, an emerging, but fake, competence in the new.

3. **Incompetence**: a highly frustrating period in which there is a recognition that the change is necessary, yet the coping ability is not yet available.

4. **Letting go**: probably the most uncomfortable, yet exciting, time in which there is an acceptance of the new reality and the individual lets go of past (and comfortable) attitudes and behaviours.

5. **Testing**: here is where anger and frustration really grip. The individual tests out new approaches and behaviour (perhaps leaning towards stereotyping 'the way things should be done') and begins to deal appropriately with the new reality.

6. **Search for meaning**: by searching for underlying meanings in order to gain understanding, the individual is better placed to begin the internalization process. Why things are, and have to be, difficult is an important aspect for the individual to grasp.

7. **Integration**: the meanings and reality are incorporated into new behaviours. These now form a basic part of the individual's repertory of behaviour.

There are alternate ways of even viewing transition stages. Rather than seeing them as stages we could look at the dimensions which underpin these stages; things which Nicholson calls 'transition cycles'. The dimensions which he hypothesizes are as follows:

- **Speed** – how rapid is transit through one or more cycles.

- **Amplitude** – how novel or how radical are the demands of the transition.

- **Symmetry** – how much relative time is spent in different stages of the cycle.

- **Continuity** – how interlinked are cycles and the extent to which they follow any logical sequence.

- **Discretion** – how much control the mover has over passage through the stages of the cycle.

- **Complexity** – how clearly or easily can the tasks of the transition cycle be defined.

- **Propulsion** – the extent to which the cycle was initiated by the person or by external events and forces.

- **Facilitation** – what supports and resources are available to aid the person's passage through the stages of the cycle.

- **Significance** – how personally or organizationally important are the outcomes of transition.

What these dimensions allow is the description of careers in terms of sequences of particular types of transition cycles. This will allow for a more flexible account of careers as well as, potentially, the definition of different career stages. It might even be that it will allow the characterization of different forms of organizational environments and cultures.

Synchronization

Arguments have been put forward to show that for the majority of people there are quite specific times during their life development when certain things happen, e.g. having a family. What has been found is that there is generally more support for people who are in synchronization with these notional patterns. For those who are not in synchronization, the support of organizations and other people is less apparent. This particular issue is aggravated for the dual-career couple. Almost inevitably, at least one of them is not in synchronization either with the other or with the rest of society. This creates stresses both for the individual and the couple which can lead to deleterious performance. If the organization is to ensure high productivity, survival and continued growth, then one of the implications of this is that organizations need to design innovative career development patterns to integrate the preferred career path of individuals. In a sense, the argument is that by helping people to facilitate the integration of work and home life into a more meaningful array, employee motivation will be enhanced as will their involvement and potentially their productivity.

It is only in relatively recent times that career paths have come to be looked upon as the products of individual–organization negotiation. Whilst we today accept that such negotiation is part and parcel of the relationship with the organization this was not always the case. In previous times and indeed still in many organizations, career paths were preordained by high-level 'human resource planners', which meant that individual employees could not take a particularly proactive part in determining their career.

There is an argument in career theory which states that because many organizational contexts are weak or ambiguous they allow personal dispositions to shine through. In other words, people shape their environments as much or more than they are shaped by those environments. The hypothesis is that it is personal control which is the primary mechanism which people use to express themselves within organization settings. Such a view would reopen the arguments about the helplessness of individuals within organizations to affect outcomes so far as their own careers are concerned.

Personal control

Personal control has been hypothesized as one of the means by which individuals influence work outcomes. Personal control refers to the proactive regulation which people take in their work lives. Of course people are much more likely to initiate action when they believe that they have personal control to the extent that they may affect a change in a particular direction. Bell and Staw (1989) hypothesized that there are certain individual characteristics which indicate the capacity to take control in these terms. These characteristics include self-monitoring, which is a characteristic to be seen in those people whose behaviour is regulated by situational contingencies, i.e. their behaviour tends to be situation specific. For this reason, because low self-monitors are resistant to situational pressures they are more likely to initiate attempts at personal control.

The other characteristics are, in the main, those which common sense would indicate as being important. They include risk-seeking, dominance and power needs, a history of control and even work as a central life interest. Schein's career anchors are also included in this. People whose career anchors would be centred on stability and security plainly would not be expected to grasp the potential to alter the direction or take control generally of their career. Finally, the individual's history of control will also affect their future influence attempts.

On top of that there is a second batch of modifiers of behaviour under the heading of personal control. Personal control would include control over outcomes, control over behaviour and the ability to predict outcomes and behaviour. It is at the third stage of this particular model that the interest must focus. The hypothesis is that if people fail to take control, in personal terms, then one of two outcomes become possible – either withdrawal from the organization itself or from the particular chosen career at that point of time and secondly, potentially, a learned helplessness. Moreover, this feeling of helplessness is likely to spiral, for as they are perceived to fail so they will receive fewer and fewer opportunities for control. On the other hand, if the individual feels and has other controls over the work behaviour and inputs then the result should be greater satisfaction with his or her career and perhaps even greater career involvement.

Career development

It has also been hypothesized that career development is most easily undertaken by people who have the capacity to cultivate so called spiral career concepts. The implication of this spiral career orientation is that the individual makes extensive use of information and develops a complex career plan that changes often and is affected by both work and non-work experience. Trial and error is, for this person, an important source of information. Furthermore, the individual's capacity to decouple or segregate his or her own identity from the job itself is an important consideration; the more the individual's identity is inter-twined with their job the more reluctant they are to change jobs. If this career flexibility takes the form of preparing for learning and exploration throughout their career, then the individual's tendency is to become attached to processes rather than structures.

Work history

An alternative view of careers is proposed by Nicholson and West (1989). Theirs is both a cynical and interesting viewpoint. They counsel against the use of the word 'careers' to describe what they believe is better termed 'work history'. The arguments they put forward are quite powerful: for the majority of people the forward plans that they make are often delusory; indeed, few people have control over their options, opportunities and the influences which will come to bear. Nicholson and West do not actually say, but it is inherent in what they write that work history is more often than not a series of fortuitous circumstance. There is a sting to the argument which they propose, i.e. that the whole notion of career and career development justifies the existence and employment of many groups of professionals such as career advisers, counsellors, vocational analysts, and so on. Within the organization, they argue, the myth is perpetuated: it is the recruiters and other agents of the organization who inform recruits about the optimistic future that their lives may take within the organization. There is some evidence that what they say is right. Within many organizations it is extremely difficult to progress people's careers in the way that would best fit that career and the organization. However, there is another sense in which they are wrong. If the planning and preparation have not taken place, then when the opportunity does present itself the individual is unable to take advantage of it. The old adage that one has to work hard to be lucky is no less true in this area than in any other. However, this does not gainsay the fact that many people's career tracks are not orderly patterns of choice and development; any continuity for them often resides in their own selves rather than in their work histories.

As a result of the changes which are occurring within organizations, especially that of a shift from vertical to horizontal relationships and networks, career development is becoming less intelligible and visible. Moreover, as people become more specialized in their work there is a move towards working for multi-employers rather than a single one. There is more casual, temporary and part-time work; with the increasing number of consultancies, this change has become more apparent to management. It may be that independent consultants

(a) Add the major component of your current job.

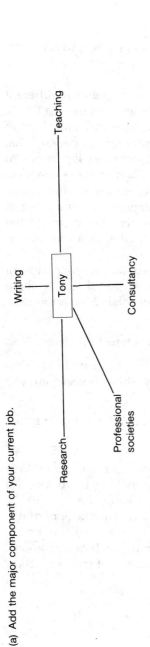

(b) This may take a little time, but it is important to write out as many elements as you can recall.

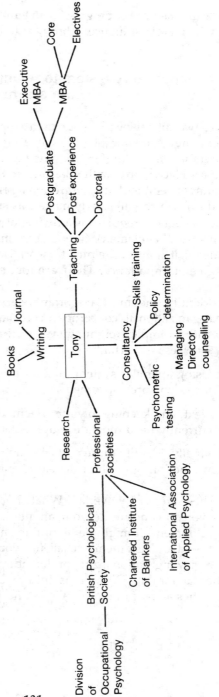

Figure 5.5 Job mapping

measure their career progression in terms of the level of the organization at which their influence is brought to bear.

Job mapping: A system to review careers and current job opportunities

One way of reviewing your own career is to diagram the different components of your job. This can easily be undertaken using a Buzan diagram (see Figure 5.5). Essentially you begin with blank sheet of paper. Place a box, with you in it, in the centre of that paper. What you now need to do is go through a series of steps (see Figure 5.5 (a) and (b)) which will slowly make this simple diagram more complex.

What is now required is a review of these elements. In the review, some of the elements are placed into categories of importance. Indeed, it may be helpful to work out a system to determine the degree of importance. There are four steps to take, as follows:

1. Identify the most important elements so far as your current organization is concerned. You may find it useful to rate these with a simple weighting system, e.g. 1 for vital, 2 for important, 3 for less important.

2. Using a similar system identify the most interesting elements so far as you are concerned.

3. Next, and keeping to your system identify, these areas where you currently need most development.

4. Finally, identify these parts needing most attention for your future promotion, growth or development.

These areas may overlap. What should show up is an area or areas for you to concentrate your attention on in looking to your career development. It might be helpful to share this with a close colleague or friend and ask them to challenge you, allowing you the opportunity of reviewing, rationalizing or defending what you have diagrammed. The diagram may also be useful preparation for such organizational activities as performance reviews and the analysis of training needs.

References

Arthur, M.B., Hall, D.T. and Lawrence, B.S. (eds) (1989), *Handbook of Career Theory* (Cambridge: Cambridge University Press).

Bell, Nancy E. and Staw, B.M. (1989), 'People as sculptors versus sculpture: the roles of personality and personnel control in organisations', in Arthur *et al., op. cit.*

Cytrynbaum, S. and Crites, J.O. (1989), 'The utility of adult development theory in understanding career adjustment process', in Arthur *et al. op. cit.*

Driver, M.J. (1982), 'Career concepts: a new approach to career research', in R. Katz (ed.), *Career Issues in Human Resource Management* (Englewood Cliffs: Prentice Hall).

Gallos, J. (1985), *Power and Competition in Dual Career Marriage: An exploration* (Boston: Harvard Graduate School of Education).

Hall, D.T. and Hall, F.S. (1980), 'Stress and the two career couple', in C. Cooper and R. Payne (eds), *Current Concerns in Occupational Stress* (New York: Wiley).

Holland, J.L. (1973) (2nd edition 1985), *Making Vocational Choices: A theory of causes* (Englewood Cliffs: Prentice Hall).

Nicholson, N. (1986), 'Turning points, traps and tunnels: the significance of work role transitions in the lives of individuals and organisation', in H.W. Schroiff and G. Debus (eds), *Proceedings of the West European Conference on Work and Organisation* (Amsterdam: North-Holland).

Nicholson, N. and West, M. (1989), *Transitions, Work Histories and Careers*, in Arthur *et al., op. cit.*

Reinke, B.J., Holmes, D.S. and Harris, R.L. (1985), 'The timing of psychological changes in women's lives: the years 25–45', *Journal of Personality and Social Psychology*, vol. 48, no. 5, pp. 1353–64.

Schein, E.H. (1978), *Career Dynamics* (London: Addison-Wesley).

Sonnenfeld, J.A. (1989), *Career System Profiles and Strategic Staffing*, in Arthur *et al., op. cit.*

Super, D.E. and Bohn, M.J. (1971), *Occupational Psychology* (London: Tavistock).

Wilensky, H.L. (1961), 'Orderly careers and social participation: the impact of work history on social integration in the Middel Mass', *American Sociological Review*, vol. 26, pp. 521–39.

6

Organizational theory

The organization of people into effective working groups has always been at the heart of the management process. 'Organizations', that is 'formal' organizations have 'objectives which are explicit, limited and announced' (Udy 1965, p. 678). They are formed with a common, formal purpose and require people to enter into formal relationships which have some contractual basis. The extension of the 'organization' into a collection of linked formal groupings under the direction of a hierarchy of leaders creates a structure of relationships.

Commentators have for many years tried to explain the formal and informal relationships produced within organizations. Their 'theories' of organizations result from diverse assumptions about the purpose of work organizations, the reasons why people work and the consequences for relationships, and for social action which stem from formal organization structures. These organizational theories address particular questions. For example, how is business strategy linked to organization structure? How do organizations adapt and survive? What impact does organization structure have upon the effectiveness of a business? In recent years new organization structures have emerged, such as those found in franchise operations, in 'divisionalization' with separate business units, in smaller, flatter structures, and in loose federations of sub-units.

Managers are often impatient with 'theories'. They seek prescriptive answers to the issues they raise about what will work for their particular organization. Impatience which results in simplistic generalized solutions is the enemy of thought and knowledge. 'Theories' are the only practical means of transferring learning from one situation to another. 'Organizational theory' should therefore be seen as a guide for decisions, a set of explanations and statements, based on research and experience, which describe different kinds of working relationships and their consequences.

Classical theories

It may be comforting to know we are not the first to contemplate questions about how best to organize people and tasks. Rulers and the administrators of powerful states have always needed to adopt some organizing principles in order to accomplish their aims.

Organization under the Persian, Macedonian, Roman, Arab, Turkish, Spanish, Portuguese, British and Russian empires was each sophisticated according to its own time. For example, bureaucracy as an organizational form was an outstanding feature of the Chinese state. The official bureaucratic hierarchy which China developed over the centuries was sustained by the shared values promulgated by Confucius. It was legitimated by competitive examination systems and formal promotion schemes which helped to maintain the formal hierarchy of reporting relationships. Even under such dynasties as the Sung and the Ming, China was larger than Western Europe, and the population governed through the political structure was greater than that of any one government since, with the exception of the British Empire (Latourette 1959).

The 'classical' theories in modern times had their foundations in sociological explanations of economic phenomena. These were attempts at describing how the organizing principles long applied by · political and military rulers were adapted to organizations with economic purposes.

Adam Smith's *The Wealth of Nations* published in 1776 described how efficiency could be improved by adopting the division of labour as the axiom for design. The division of labour, he believed, is effective where there is the following:

1. A **unity of control**: there should be a hierarchical pyramid with a centre of authority, and a specific span of control at each level.

2. **Specialization**: according to the purpose of the task, the 'process' or the client or customer.

3. **Geographical unity**: people should be located in physical proximity according to their specialization.

It is perhaps not surprising that in the age of reason Adam Smith emphasized logic and rationality. What is more noteworthy is that the division of labour remains a maxim in organization design today. Early writers on organizations were mainly concerned with accountability, expertness and economy. By the early part of the twentieth century commercial organizations had grown to the proportion of a government bureaucracy, were equally impersonal and required compliance with the rules of work which grew from the division of labour.

The realization that bureaucracy is a recognizable organizational form which has sociological consequences, created an interest in organizational theory. Max Weber outlined the features of bureaucratic organizations which were efficient. As he described them bureaucracies are as follows:

- A continuous organization of official functions bound by rules.
- Organized with a specified area of competence, for each unit.
- Organized so the offices follow the principles of a hierarchy.
- Set up with rules which are technical (related to the task) and normative (related to conduct).
- Employ staff as officials. They hold and discharge their offices according to impersonal criteria.
- Legally constituted so that positions are not held as of right, and ownership is separated from control.

We must remember that in the nineteenth century, nepotism and jobbery were normal. Bureaucracies offered an organizational system which was less subject to personal bias, and which used non-ascriptive criteria; as a consequence, people were selected and trained more efficiently. Weber went further than this. He pointed to the way bureaucracies helped to legitimate the authority exercised in a legal/rational way by officials. If the legitimacy of managers is questioned, they refer to the rules. The fact that the rules exist is sufficient. Rarely is the right of the organization to create rules challenged.

The progress of rationalist thought found its parallel in the managerialist philosophy which emerged at the beginning of the twentieth century. In the United Kingdom, engineers and general managers wrote about organizations and the role of the manager for the first time (for example Slater-Lewis 1896; Liversedge 1912). Henri Fayol in France was a general manager of a large mining business, who wrote a paper in 1908, entitled 'Administration industriale et générale' in which he formulated the idea that management consisted of five elements: planning, organization, command, coordination and control. These categories, with the addition of 'motivation' are often used even now to describe managerial work.

The notion of 'scientific management' which is associated with F.W. Taylor in the United States embodies the belief in workers as rational beings who seek to maximize their earnings, and a management whose task is to install procedures and techniques which produce maximum effort and efficiency. 'Taylorism' is more a management philosophy than an organization theory. Nevertheless, it can be seen how the elaboration of techniques such as 'time and motion study' and incentive payment systems were a natural development from managerialism and the belief in a rational, ordered structure.

The 'human relations approach'

By the 1930s and 1940s the prevailing ideas of 'scientific management' were discredited by many in the West, where there was a growing awareness of the non-rational factors which govern relationships stemming from the work of Freud and Pareto. During this time the complex psychological processes revealed by Freud were reaching the popular imagination, and Pareto had come to the conclusion that economic theory could never explain human behaviour in the real world, which he saw required an understanding of non-rational conduct.

Informal relationships at work were seen to have a significant influence on work output in the 'Hawthorne' studies, as we described in Chapter 2. The prescriptions for these three studies at Western Electric's Hawthorne works near Chicago was to find the conditions most conducive to productivity. In this Taylor-like search, the first experiment was to change the lighting. However, changes in illumination produced no noticeable change to productivity. In the relay assembly room study, six women were put in an observation room to assemble electronic relays. A series of experimental variables were used such as rest periods, but the research showed that regardless of these variables, productivity tended to rise during the two-year research period. This has been accounted for by the 'Halo' or 'Hawthorne' effect – the effect when a phenomenon under study changes *because* it is being studied.

The 'bank-wiring room' study was an attempt to overcome the Hawthorne effect, by using the method of participant observation. The researcher was accepted eventually as a member of the work group. In this experiment, wage rates were varied according to output. Instead of a steady increase in production, there was a reduction. The informal groups had developed their own norms. The norms suggested that output should not vary with wages – there should be 'no rate busters', 'no chislers' and 'no squealers' (no one should tell management about the norms). The groups imposed controls through peer pressure, and sometimes through physical means.

In the second study, the researchers had altered the women's definition of the situation, the worker felt more important, more informed. In the third study the workers tried to protect the independence of their own group.

The rewards of belonging to a primary, face-to-face group were more important than the rewards offered by management. Management should therefore operate in a social rather than an economic climate, it is argued. There was a deep distrust of management, and the restrictions on output seemed to show symbolically workers' independence. The question remains, whether the behaviour of the work group was rational. The answer to this depends upon their definition of the situation. It could be said to be rational because of the following:

1. It reduced competitive conflict between the members of the group.

2. It increased job security. Higher output levels would have resulted in job losses, as targets were achieved more quickly.

3. Information is an important resource in controlling other people. Restrictions in output increased the group's control over their own environment, and reduced management's capacity to predict their behaviour.

One might conclude therefore that the worker's behaviour was rational, within the bounds of their definition of the situation. Following on from Hawthorne and the human relations approach, organizational psychologists such as Argyris, J.A.C. Brown and Zaleznick proposed a 'social' 'self-actualizing' model of mankind rather than the economic rational creature of the classical theorists. The vision of motivation contained within their theories emphasized the personality needs and the informal processes of work groups.

The tendency is for such writers to argue that organizational life can and should provide opportunities for 'self-actualization' through changes to the organization structure in order to resolve the inherent conflict between organizational and individual goals. This prescriptive approach leaves them open to the charge that they too readily describe what ought to happen rather than what does happen (Silverman 1970).

In *The Human Side of Enterprise* Douglas McGregor puts forward the famous formulation of 'Theory X' and 'Theory Y' – polar opposite assumptions about people held by managers in organizations:

> The central principle of organisations which derives from Theory X is that of direction and control through the exercise of authority. The central principle which derives from Theory Y is that of integration: the creation of conditions such that members of the organisation can achieve their own goals best by directing their efforts towards the success of the enterprise. (McGregor 1960, Ch. 3)

From this quotation we may see the essentially unitary frame of reference adopted by those following the human relations approach. In fact, the significance of the informal organization structure, and the divergent interests found between management and workers makes the pluralist frame of reference an equally justifiable position (Fox 1966). Instead of seeing organizations as teams, working towards a common goal, it is more accurate to describe them as groupings engaged in a political struggle to satisfy their own interests. Politics is about access to power, and the alliances and cliques which may form at work in attempting to influence events are just as real as those found in the House of Commons, where there is a plurality of interests to be experienced.

The two different approaches to human relations may be illustrated by two studies which look at office cliques. Both these research studies used a common definition of cliques which are described as informal organizations composed of representatives of differential work segments – that is, either horizontal or vertical groupings with cross-cutting alliances.

Where the researchers' conclusions differ, however, is in that in the work of Gross (1965) cliques are seen to help to give meaning to otherwise meaningless office work, by offering congeniality and as a consequence they served an important communication function for the organization. Dalton's (1959) study of managerial cliques shows how in vertical cliques a 'symbiotic' relationship emerges where a top manager offers patronage to a junior in return for information; or a 'parasitic' relationship between junior and senior managers occurs, where through friendship a senior manager supports a more junior. To Gross, therefore, cliques are an adaptive mechanism, which helps the organization to function. To Dalton, cliques follow strategies which are political in purpose, as individuals form alliances to vie for power.

Systems theories

One of the most beneficial analytical tools consultants can use is the representation of organizations as 'systems'. There are many applications of systems theories, but they all draw on the following two main ideas:

1. Organizations are described as possessing the qualities of a biological organism. They are said to have 'survival' needs, like plants and animals. This analogy with organisms results in a belief that organizations 'behave' rather as people and animals act. Much attention is given therefore to the way organizations adapt to their environment.

2. The main ideas are imported from general systems theory: in particular the notion that there is an interdependence between the elements – the input, throughput and output. The logical, rational relationship between the parts is built on feedback loops, the output from one sub-system being the input to another. For example, the whole transportation of people and goods around London could be described as an overall system, which comprises sub-systems of trains, overground and underground, road vehicles, roads and pedestrians, all interacting. The whole transport system is itself a part of the wider economic system in London, which by moving goods and services about enables economic transactions to occur. This in turn enables the social system of relationships, social groupings and social norms to flourish.

From these ideas we can see that there are linkages between sub-systems and systems. A breakdown in one part of the system might lead to a collapse in other parts of the wider system. A public transport strike would ultimately affect the whole social system of London, for example.

In a work context, we can think of highly critical parts of work systems where problems can cause chaos. This is well known to militant trade unionists who can target computer installations or mail deliveries, for example, which quickly puts pressure on management to settle their claim, whilst only involving a small number of union activists. On a more positive note, this shows how even the humble post clerk fulfils a function as vital as the sales team for the survival of the business.

The idea that one can judge the extent to which activities or subsystems assist an organization meet its needs for survival and growth was developed by Talcott Parsons who argued that the extent to which an organization, activity or sub-system performs certain key functions will determine its survival. His test of functionality is that systems or sub-systems should perform the functions of the following:

- Adaptation to the environment.
- Goal attainment for the organization.
- Integration within the organization.
- 'Latency' or pattern maintenance (the maintenance of roles and patterns of social relationships).

The extent to which these elements are found in an organization will determine its survival (Parsons 1951).

These functional prerequisites are a valuable test of how an organization can survive by paying attention to the way the systems interact within the organization, and with the outside environment. Organizations are 'open' systems in that they must adapt to wider social systems.

However, critics of systems theorists point to the weakness of accepting as unequivocal 'givens' such notions as 'organizational goals'. Goal displacement is after all common, where leaders or other members are able to influence the actual aims of an organization. The covert aim of those in power is frequently to remain there, whatever the objectives or what is best for the business. Subversion of goals through goal displacement is therefore to be expected, and there are well documented cases of goal succession, where the organization, having achieved its original explicit purpose, then finds another goal, in order to stay in being. A current example is NATO, originally created as a military alliance opposing the Warsaw Pact, now seeking a political goal, in a Europe much changed by the collapse of the Soviet empire.

One contribution from system studies has been to put the question – what is the function of this organization or unit? – regularly on the agenda. Open systems remind us that the boundaries and the social environment within which the organization exists are significant aspects of its relationship with its clientele. Blau and Scott (1963) have tried to clarify this relationship by categorizing organizations according to their clients as follows:

- **Mutual benefit associations**: these exist to service their own members (for example trade unions, professional associations).

- **Business organizations**: the main purpose is to serve the shareholders' interests and the general public.

- **Service organizations**: these are schools, hospitals and the like which have particular client groups.

- **Common weal organizations**: which serve the public at large, such as the police, welfare services and government departments.

The discussion of systems theories so far takes us to the point where we can see that they have a prescriptive tone, explaining what is functional, and placing adaptation to the environment as a central issue for organizational survival. This leaves two major problems which have to be addressed: first, the question of how to incorporate the informal processes such as those which result in goal displacement or goal succession; and secondly, the issue of how different internal formal processes, such as the technical and task systems in use react to the environment.

A number of researchers have tackled these issues from both the direction of the impact made by technology on the work groups and by looking at the informal processes which are behaviourally so significant. Here, although accepting that organizations may be regarded as 'systems', the view is taken that there is also a separate social system in the informal groupings of people which the Human Relations school have suggested we ignore at our peril. The problem is then to match the 'task' system embodied in the formal structure and technology with the informal 'system' of people's perceptions.

The difficulties arise when the two are in opposition. Conflict occurs when there is a breakdown in stable work groups due to the technical system in operation. Writers in what is now called the 'socio-technical' system school have typically examined technical systems in detail to show the social consequences.

One of the best examples is the coal mining study by Trist and Bamforth (1951) on the social and psychological consequences of the longwall method of coal-getting. Three quotations explain the study:

the outstanding feature of the social pattern with which the pre mechanized equilibrium was associated is its emphasis on small group organizations at the coal-face.

With the advent of coal-cutters and mechanical conveyors, the degree of technological complexity of the coal-getting task was raised to a different level.

The associated characteristics of mechanized complexity, and of largeness as regards the scale of the primary production unit created a situation in which it was impossible for the method to develop as a technological system without bringing into existence a work relationship structure radically different from that associated with hand-got procedures. . . . It seems to the present writers, however, that a qualitative change will have to be effected in the general character of the [technical] method, so that a social as well as a technological whole can come into existence.

The argument put forward by researchers such as Miller, Rice, Trist and Bamforth is that improved performance may result from the following:

- Small work groups, internally led.
- Technical systems which take into account both the formal and the informal processes of work groups.
- Taking into account organizational and extra-organizational needs in the environment.
- Some form of regulation between the task and the informal system – such as work group problem-solving, team-building and the use of communication techniques.
- Creating commitment among the workers to the task which should satisfy both the needs of the organization and the social needs of the workers.

Arising from these ideas have come the approaches to work and job design which are discussed in Chapter 2. It should be noted that practical management techniques have arisen from the socio-technical systems approach. Equally important has been the notion that a manager's role as a leader is to reduce conflict and to respond to the technical and social contingencies in the organization. The early research into these issues has resulted in a broad set of ideas on what happens in organizations and why.

Contingency theory

Contingency theory shares a common ancestry with socio-technical systems theories. The early beginnings of what we now call contingency theory can be found in those studies which examine what happens to the behaviour of organization members as a consequence of technological change. For example, Burns and Stalker (1961) researched the UK electronics industry at the end of the Second World War. They saw industrialism as the product of two technologies: social and material. In order to explain the current industrial system, they believed a thorough understanding of the past to be essential as well as an appreciation of the market circumstances facing particular industries.

They put forward two 'ideal types' of work organizations to explain the different organizational forms, which they dubbed 'mechanistic' and 'organismic', or 'organic'. Mechanistic systems were ordered societies, where work was precisely defined, with strong vertical interaction through a bureaucratic structure, with its centralized command structure where decisions flowed downwards.

This stable, ordered, rational framework contrasted with those organizations which had to adapt to unstable conditions – as faced by the electronics industry which passes through rapid technical and

Table 6.1 Two ideal types of organizations

Mechanistic	Organic
Specialized differentiation	Contributive approach to tasks
Abstract tasks	Realistic tasks
Immediate superiors coordinate	Continuous redefinition of tasks
Precise definition of jobs	Personal responsibility for problem-solving
Hierarchical structure	Commitment to the concern
Information and decisions downwards	Commitment to the technology
Vertical interaction	Network structure of control
Strict rules of work/conduct	Lateral communications
Loyalty essential	Knowledge at all levels
Local knowledge emphasized	Prestige attached to general expertise

market changes. In 'organic' systems, responsibilities and functions change continuously to cope with unfamiliar problems. The key to success according to Burns and Stalker was for people working in organic systems to have a broad vision of organizational goals, and to be able to communicate easily via lateral channels.

The two ideal types of organizations can be contrasted (see Table 6.1).

The important lessons from Burns and Stalker are first that different approaches to organization structures suit different industries. Mass production systems and stable work patterns are best served by a mechanistic approach. Technically innovative industries, and those facing volatile markets are better suited to an organic approach. Secondly, managers should recognize when organizations are required to move from a mechanistic to an organic approach.

Burns and Stalker point out that mechanistic organizations often are unable to adapt, but instead enter various pathological states such as the 'ambiguous figure' system whereby decision-making moves to the top, with the chief executive by-passing the normal line, and making deals with various subordinates because he or she is over-worked. The focus then shifts to 'political' action, and ways of controlling access to the chief executive.

A famous series of studies by Joan Woodward (1958) conducted between 1953 and 1957 in Essex showed that technical complexity and the type of production system were significant determinants of organization structure, decision-making and management style. She researched the three main types of manufacturing systems: unit production, mass production and process production methods (see Table 6.2).

To quote Woodward: 'The widely accepted assumption that there

Table 6.2 Technical systems and organization structure

Organizational variables	Unit	Mass	Process
No. of levels in hierarchy	3	4	6–8
Span of control	21–30	41–50	11–20
Wage costs:			
% of total costs	36	34	14
Flexibility	+	−	+
Specialization in management function	−	+	+
Quality of industrial relations*	Moderate	Poor	Good

* Note: Measured by pressure on people, ratio of supervision to operators and size of work group.

are principles of management valid for all types of production systems seemed doubtful – a conclusion with wide implications for the teaching of this subject' (p. 4).

From these studies we can see that what happens in organizations is contingent upon markets, history, production system and technical complexity. Although Woodward did not find a relationship between size of the firm and technical complexity, the size is likely to influence the decision-making processes and the lines of communication.

It may also be argued that size influences the extent to which rules are utilized, and therefore the degree of formality. Pugh *et al.* (1969) have shown that what happens outside the organization, its 'context' of history, ownership pattern, as well as internal factors such as size, the products and services, the technology in use, location and interdependencies with other organizations, determine the appropriateness of organization structure.

This reliance on contextual factors to explain organizational behaviour supports the theories of situational leadership described in detail in Chapter 3 (Fiedler 1967; Hersey and Blanchard 1976). Management style is clearly related to organizational context. The question remains concerning the way organization structure is influenced by the company's markets, and the environment in which it operates. Organizations are open systems, and whilst technology has been proved to be one key to the nature of the organizational context, it is the interaction between markets and technology which is most likely to reveal the relationship between strategy and organization structure.

From the study of organizations in the plastics, food and container industries, Lawrence and Lorsch (1967) attempt to explain the internal states and processes in an organization according to their external environments. They take an essentially pluralistic viewpoint and show how the various departments within an organization become differentiated, because of their own technology, time horizons and objectives, and that this is caused by the interaction necessary between the various sub-units and their external contacts.

Thus a finance department may operate on a financial planning cycle which is in tune with banking, investment and taxation requirements, whilst the production department becomes attuned to the technical requirement of the production system, and of the suppliers of raw materials. Marketing departments as well as production departments subdivide, for example into product groups as companies differentiate their products. As these organizational sub-units begin to differ more and more, so there becomes a need for greater integration. Lawrence and Lorsch argue that the most effective organizations are those which have managed this differentiation and integration process through internal conflict-reducing activities (e.g. cross functional committees, and by appointing people to integrator roles).

A new research tradition within organizational theory has been promulgated by Williamson (1973) who writes as an economist, concerned to explain organizational efficiency. The 'markets and hierarchies' approach takes the issue of the impact of environment on organizational design to a broader position where organization structure decisions are taken on the measurement of transaction costs. It is thought these are crucial to the efficient running of organizations, because differential transaction costs are responsible for the decisions on how to organize the business.

It is argued that there are markets and internal modes of contracting in which these costs may be used to decide where the transactions will most efficiently occur – within a hierarchy (an internal market) or an external market. Williamson goes beyond these 'make or buy'-type decisions, however. Markets and hierarchies theory relies on the twin assumptions that people are both opportunistic and are also rational within the bounds of their own situation. Given the desire to economize on transaction costs, Williamson and Ouchi (1983) summarize their approach to organizational design:

> The basic organisational design issue essentially reduces to this: organise transactions in such a way as to economise on bounded rationality whilst simultaneously safeguarding those transactions against the hazards of opportunism. (p. 17)

In the same article, the above authors argue that there are two optional forms of contracting within organizations: soft and hard contracting. Soft contracts are found where there is a 'class' identity, people contract on a relational basis, trust is high and there is mutual support. Hard contracting parties to an agreement remain autonomous, take care of their own interests with formal contractual relations and job specific duties.

The advantages of this theory are that the organization is seen to be interdependent with its economic environment, and given the pursuit of efficiencies, business can take a variety of organizational forms, dependent upon the transaction costs, from the traditional bureaucratic hierarchy to a franchise operation or collaboration between confederations; organizations are seen as dynamic in form not static. The internal contracting within organizations determines the internal structure of relationships.

The research into this approach is continuing, and there is scope for more applications. As a means of explanation of the divisional and business unit form it has advantages. Transaction costs are now a key factor for public and private sector organizations. For example, Unilever's research establishment in the United Kingdom is funded through contracts (not always renewable) from its operating companies. The National Health Service, as another example, is setting up an internal market for health care where hospitals will be able to compete for patients, and doctors have new and relatively hard contracts to govern their working relationships.

The limitations to this approach have promoted a controversy over the use of an economics language to describe and analyse sociological phenomena – issues of power and group behaviour are swept aside by the assumption of a prevailing motivation to economic, if bounded, rationality. Willman (1983) has successfully shown how Williamson's model is really normative, since Williamson assumes only workers (not managers) are opportunistic and managers (not workers) are subject to bounded rationality. If the managers are seen more realistically as opportunists, the notion that the organization is run for efficiency purposes is called into question. Perhaps another problem is the stance on technology which although expressly included in the theory's emphasis on the continuous process of reorganizing for efficiency, is not thought to have any implications for organizational design.

Conclusions

Much of the debate since 1945 has been about which paradigm best describes organizations as sociological phenomena. A variety of theories have been presented here to assist the reader to obtain new insights into organizational problems and issues. These notions about organizations present different images, or metaphors of organizational life (Morgan 1986).

Comparing and contrasting different images or theories helps to define the characteristics of organizations, and their causes. Organizational culture, leadership, the legitimacy of authority, rationality, informal processes and group behaviour, survival behaviour, survival capabilities, the impact of technology and efficiency have all been discussed in the context of these theories. Managers are often concerned about the design implications of any given 'theory', and each of the theories presented here has a design corollary. It is to these design issues we should now turn.

Case study

Relating job design and socio-technical systems: The case of Clerical and Medical Insurance Group

Clerical and Medical Insurance is a mutual Life Assurance business with 2,000 employees, 1,200 of whom are employed at HQ in Bristol. The company markets life, pension and investment products, which are sold through Independent Financial Advisers (IFA).

Business strategy

The group offers products at the upper end of the market and has sought to position itself with a highly professional image and a strong focus on customer care. A significant issue for the new strategy was improvements to the information technology systems to support the quality improvements required in the field.

New technology

In the past, the introduction of computers had resulted in an element of 'de-skilling'. All the work was heavily proceduralized, with staff employed in a 'factory' process to input the data.

However, an increasing proportion of data input, quotations, basic underwriting and output was being done on-line at the branches, at the time of customer contact. The plan was for all the IFAs to have their own on-line computers so that routine work was pushed back towards those who interfaced with the customers. The result was that there were more opportunities for Head Office staff to be involved in problem-solving.

Management problems

In the past a number of organizational problems had surfaced:

1. There were small spans of control – too many supervisors and a perception was held that people were under utilized.

2. The most interesting work had tended to be kept back by the supervisors for their own use.

3. There was considerable specialization at the clerical level, with little flexibility or variety, and little meaningful feedback.

4. Customer service problems had arisen because clerks could only deal with routine matters and tended to pass up for solution more complex problems.

5. There was vertical rather than lateral communication.

6. An element of status consciousness had entered the organization with unnecessary controls imposed from the top.

Job design

With the change in strategy and the introduction of new technology, an opportunity was created to redesign the jobs – to match the social with the technical systems. This came when two policy servicing divisions – the New Business and the Records Divisions (which deals with traditional individual business) and the Unit-Linked Division were reorganized. Together they employed around 400 people.

The divisional managers therefore were formed into a project group with the human resource specialists to examine and redesign jobs at the clerical and supervisory levels. The brief for the project group was:

To examine the organization of tasks, working networks and job relationships to achieve the most effective match between the requirements of the business and its technology and the needs and capabilities of job holders.

The classic job design issues were addressed so that there was greater autonomy, with more responsibility pushed down to the clerical level, fewer supervisors and more lateral communication, the clerks were reorganized into teams and there was an increase in the problem-solving capabilities of the clerical and supervisory levels.

From this came the capacity to match the technical system with a working approach which integrated customer service for both divisions. The introduction of the new computer system was supported with more effective human resource systems. A unified service was thus offered to IFAs and policy holders for both product ranges. The variation in volumes between the two different kinds of business provided a more even work flow when they were amalgamated.

As a consequence, service standards were maintained, staff morale and motivation was increased and there was improved retention of staff against strong local labour market competition.

(Drawn from a case prepared by Glenys Emam of Clerical and Medical Insurance Group. To be published in S. Tyson and A. Kakabadse, *Cases in European Strategic Human Resource Management*, forthcoming, Routledge.)

References

Blau, P. and Scott, W. (1963), *Formal Organisations: A comparative approach* (London: Routledge and Kegan Paul).

Brech, E.F. (1953), *The Principles and Practice of Management* (London: Longmans).

Burns, T. and Stalker, G.M. (1961), *The Management of Innovation* (London: Tavistock).

Dalton, M. (1959), *Men Who Manage* (New York: Wiley).

Fayol, H. (1908), 'Administration industriale et générale', in the *Bulletin of Metallurgical Society* (published by Pitman under the title of *Industrial and General Management* in 1948).

Fiedler, F.E. (1967), *A Theory of Leadership Effectiveness* (New York: McGraw Hill).

Fox, A. (1966), 'Industrial sociology and industrial relations', *Research Paper 3* (London: HMSO).

Francis, A., Turk, J. and Willman, P. (eds) (1983), *Power, Efficiency and Institutions* (London: Heinemann Educational Books).

Gross, E. (1965), 'Characteristics of cliques in office organizations', research quoted in N.J. Smelsner (ed.), *Readings in Economic Sociology* (Englewood Cliffs: Prentice Hall), p. 96.

Hersey, P. and Blanchard, K. (1976), *Situational Leadership* (Greensboro, NC: Center for Creative Leadership).

Latourette, K.S. (1959), *The Chinese: Their history and culture* (New York: Macmillan).

Lawrence, P.R. and Lorsch, J.W. (1967), *Organization and Environment: Managing differentiation and integration* (Boston: Harvard).

Liversedge, A.J. (1912), *Commercial Engineering*, summarized in E.F. Brech (1953), *The Principles and Practice of Management* (London: Longmans).

McGregor, D. (1960), *The Human Side of Enterprise* (New York: McGraw-Hill).

Morgan, G. (1986), *Images of Organizations* (Beverly Hills: Sage Publications).

Parsons, T. (1951), *The Social System* (Glencoe, Ill.: Free Press).

Pugh, D.S., Hickson, D.J., Hinings, C.R. and Turner, C. (1969), 'The context of organisation structures', *Administrative Science Quarterly*, March, pp. 91–114.

Silverman, D. (1970), *The Theory of Organisations* (London: Heinemann).

Slater-Lewis, J. (1896), *The Commercial Organisation of Factories*, summarized in E.F. Brech, *op. cit.*

Taylor, F.W. (1911), *The Principles of Scientific Management* (London: Harper and Row).

Trist, E.A. and Bamforth, K.W. (1951), 'Some social and psychological consequences of the long wall method of coal getting', *Human Relations*, vol. 4., no. 1., pp. 6–24.

Udy, S.H. (1965), 'The comparative analysis of organizations' in J. March (ed.), *Handbook of Organizations* (McNally: Chicago), pp. 678–709.

Weber, Max (1947), *The Theory of Social and Economic Organisation* (Oxford: OUP).

Williamson, O.E. (1973), 'Markets and hierarchies. Some elementary considerations', *American Economic Review*, vol. LXIII, pp. 316–25.

Williamson, O.E. and Ouchi, W.G. (1983), 'The markets and hierarchies programme of research', in A. Francis, J. Turk and P. Willman (eds), *op. cit.*

Willman, P. (1983), 'The organisational failures, framework and industrial sociology: in A. Francis, J. Turk and P. Willman (eds), *op. cit.*

Woodward, J. (1958), *Management and Technology* (London: HMSO).

7

Organization structure

The all-pervasive presence of bureaucracies in our everyday life might lead us to think that this is the only organization structure which should be studied. It is true that most organizations, whether in public or private ownership resemble the bureaucratic form set out by Max Weber and the classical theorists. This is a consequence partly of the growth of large organizations, and of the separation of ownership from control. There are now many variants on the bureaucratic form, and different sizes and shapes of organizations.

In this chapter we will discuss the design issues facing managers and look in turn at the strategy/structure interface, the principles of organizational design, organizational forms and the implications for behaviour now and in the future.

Strategy and structure

Strategies can be followed at a corporate, division or business unit level. Alfred Chandler's axiom 'structure follows strategy' was based on the evidence that as companies diversified their product range, so their structures moved from a simple to a more complex functional and divisional form. Burns and Stalker (1961) successfully demonstrated how different industries and markets influenced structure, and Miles and Snow (1978) have developed a fourfold strategic typology based on the match between the strategy, the market environment and the organizational goals which influence the control systems (see Figure 7.1).

	Mechanistic	Organic structure
Stability in product markets	Defender	Analyser
Dynamic/unstable product markets	Reactor	Prospector

Figure 7.1 Strategy and structure (a combination of Burnes and Stalker, and Miles and Snow)

This fourfold typology produces the following analysis:

- Defensive strategies are operated by companies with a limited product range which they defend in a simple bureaucracy.

- Prospector strategies are adopted by companies which seek out and exploit new products quickly, moving in and out quickly after making profits. This requires highly flexible structures and competencies in many different technologies. There is little formalization therefore.

- Analysers move into new markets or products only after prospectors have broken new ground for them, and proved the market exists. This is a 'me too' product strategy ideal for mass marketing of cheaper consumer goods. The organization will therefore have certain stable elements, for example its financial control systems, but will be able to set up new business units quickly.

- Reactors are those organizations which do not have a consistent strategy and which are slow to move to new positions in spite of the dynamic opportunities available.

Michael Porter's taxonomy of competitive strategies is based on the imperative that managements must follow a strategy of maximizing on the organization's strengths. This can be achieved by seeking cost leadership; that is, being most competitive on cost at a quality equivalent to competitors, or by differentiating the product or service sufficiently to justify a price premium. Differentiation might also be achieved through focusing on a particular niche – exploiting a narrow aspect and gaining advantage with either lower costs or filling a particular niche competitors have neglected.

The organization structure implications are really on the same dimension as Burns and Stalker: cost leadership comes through tight controls and formal mechanistic centralized-type organizations, whereas differentiation strategies require flexibility and a more organic approach.

The problem with all attempts at classifying strategies and expecting particular structural outcomes is the contingent nature of organizations. The interaction between structure and strategy cannot be isolated from other influences, such as the history, size, markets and technology of the organization. Even the personality of the founder, for example Watson of IBM, is likely to affect the strategy and structure equally.

A simplistic causative chain:

Markets – Strategy – Structure

could better be redesigned as shown in Figure 7.2. In short, they are intervening variables which influence structure and which are likely to influence the particular structure which emerges. Structures are not in fact designated explicitly in every case. They are, like strategies, often emergent and often controversial.

Organization strategies and structures are dynamic not static. Changes to the many variables which influence both mutually require a response. In the strategy literature, most of the disapproval is loaded on to organizations which are slow to respond to change, or which are uncertain about the strategic changes they should follow.

The way organizations grow and change is described by Greiner (1972) as a process of evolution and revolution. We examine this in Chapter 8. Greiner argues that structure can determine strategy.

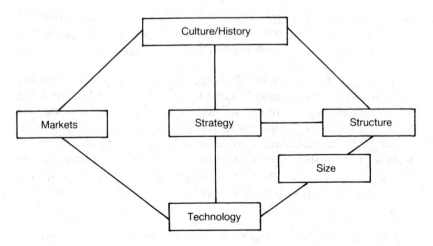

Figure 7.2 Strategy and contingency

Taking a contingency view, he suggests that as an organization's size and age increase there is prolonged evolutionary growth. These evolutionary periods are interspersed with turbulent changes, when traditional management practices have to be revolutionized. One of the lessons from Greiner's study is that yesterday's solutions are tomorrow's problems. Organization structures are not static, but change in response to internal and external pressures.

Structure does not always follow strategy therefore, and there are often tensions between what people in the company believe should be the strategy and the structural constraints. What is seen as an appropriate strategy is also conditioned by the management style and the prevailing culture, which are reinforced by structure. The organizational context can itself be a valuable guide to future strategies.

For example, a large company with 1,000 television servicing technicians faced a sudden fall in the demand for rented television receivers. In thinking out the future strategy, the organization structure of branches and depots and the skilled technicians were seen as a major resource which resulted in a change of mission, redefined as providing home entertainment and security. The company repositioned itself to exploit the opportunities for installing and servicing computers and security equipment, along with videos, television receivers, satellite aerials, etc.

Centralization versus decentralization

From the debate on strategy we can see there are often good reasons for centralizing control. There also seems to be a cyclical process by which centralization is followed in time by a need to delegate and decentralize, as Greiner's model explains.

The practical question of what role should a 'head office' play in an organization was recently researched by Cresap consultancy (1987). They researched forty-five leading British companies to discover how head offices are organized, what functions were included and why. They conclude that there are four types of head office as follows:

1. **Targeting**: defines fundamental objectives and sets and monitors financial targets. Delegates operating decisions. Provision of service to operating units is not a head office role. Staff act as advisers.

2. **Guiding**: coordinates business strategies, set and monitor financial and business objectives; provide inputs to major operating decisions.

Some services are provided on an as-needed basis. Staff act as coordinators.

3. **Directing**: participates in development of business strategies and their implementation; participate in major operating decisions. On-going service and support is an integral role of head office. Staff are sellers of ideas and policies.

4. **Running**: plans, policies and guidelines developed and monitored from head office; takes major operating decisions. Support activities are predominantly undertaken at head office. Staff are 'tellers': they tell units what to do. The number of staff at HOs therefore varies with the role. Staff act as advisers, sellers of ideas, policies, 'tellers'. The number of staff at HOs therefore varies with the role.

All HO carried out certain 'core' tasks – that is, they defined the mission, set and monitored financial targets, conducted external relationships, dealt with statutory requirements and managed senior executive resources. It is those tasks through which the company manages its external environments (for example, capital markets, the media, government), and those which relate to the future of the business as a whole (the mission, corporate planning, etc.) which were regarded by all companies as core head office activities. Thus, finance departments, strategic and business planning, company law offices, and public relations were always included irrespective of the size of head offices. Many companies had others as well. For example, 95 per cent had personnel functions, 80 per cent had internal audit departments and 70 per cent had property services. This study reports on the depth of involvement of head offices with their subsidiaries.

The arguments about centralization or decentralization depend upon what kind of central or regional/divisional authority is proposed. In practice, most large organizations must delegate everyday running to local management, or the centre becomes immobilized with too much information, and too many decisions requiring local knowledge. However, what is delegated and the kinds of structural relationships which emerge are questions for the Board or top team to decide.

Chandler (1962) noted how the multidivisional structure, the 'M' form, had developed in organizations such as General Motors, Du Pont, Standard Oil and Sears. The four main levels found in the 'M' form were said to be as follows:

- The **field unit** (i.e. the plant level, or branch office).

- **Departmental headquarters** (this coordinates the work of the field units).

- **Divisional central office** (this plans and has a responsibility for a whole area of business).

- **Corporate office** level (this oversees all the divisions).

In this way large organizations can provide flexibility and a strong customer focus at the level of the field unit or the business unit, whilst simultaneously moving the whole 'group' or company in a coordinated way towards strategic objectives, through the links between division and corporate levels.

Organization design

There are three main issues to consider when designing an organization in a bureaucratic form:

- The size of the hierarchy.
- Spans of control.
- The grouping together of activities.

Hierarchy size

The size of the hierarchy of necessity varies according to the size of the organization. As the size increases the number of levels increase from four, typical of small organizations, to six levels when the number of employees reaches 1,000. As the number of employees rises, the increase in the number of levels in the hierarchy slows down, so that at 10,000 employees the norm is around seven to eight levels. The choice when designing an organization is between increasing the number of levels or of increasing the span of control at each level. The 'span of control' is the number of subordinates a manager can supervise effectively.

Spans of control

The arguments for and against large spans of control can be summarized as follows:

For large spans of control

- There is a saving on management salaries, and large spans are therefore more economic.

- With fewer levels we might assume information will flow more quickly, upwards and downwards.

- There is less risk of too many overlaps in authority and account-ability.

- If the same work has to pass through too many hands, there is a lack of motivation and work is delayed.

Against large spans of control

- Large spans make control difficult. Most researchers suggest 3–6 subordinates as a maximum. There are problems otherwise of attention, memory, etc.

- Where the work interlocks, it is difficult to manage large numbers of people. The interdependence between subordinates increases, with the combination of reciprocal interrelations increasing from 6 relationships with 2 subordinates per manager, and then exponentially to 18 relationships with 3 subordinates, to 44 relationships with 4 subordinates and up to 100 relationships with 5 subordinates.

This is illustrated in Figure 7.3.

Manager with two subordinates (relationships numbered)

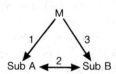

Plus the relationships [4] M + Sub A: Sub B [5] M + Sub B: Sub A and [6] M: Sub A + Sub B

Figure 7.3 Span of control and the number of relationships

Lockheed method

A more 'scientific' method was devised to discover appropriate spans of control by the Lockheed Missiles and Space Division. A technique reminiscent of job evaluation was used, where supervisory roles were examined against a list of elements, to which points values were attributed, according to the degree of supervisory burden these elements imposed.

The elements were as follows:

● Similarity of functions.
● Geographical contiguity.
● Complexity of functions.
● Direction and control required.
● Coordination required.
● Planning required.

Against these, definitions of the degree of supervisory burden were given, with a points weighting or value for each definition. For example, coordination required the following:

● Minimum relationships with others (2)
● Relationships limited to defined courses (4)
● Moderate relationships easily controlled (6)
● Considerable close relationships (8)
● Extensive mutual non-recurring relationships (10)

The points values were then added together and compared with points values and spans of control for benchmark jobs. These benchmark jobs were selected from units which were effectively managed. From the points values on the benchmark jobs a 'supervisory index' was created, this being a range of points against which the span of control of the benchmark jobs were plotted – thus creating a list of points values associated with specific spans of control with which any supervisory job, having been evaluated on the degree of supervisory burden, could be compared (Child 1984).

One should beware of assuming that this is a 'scientific' method, but it does offer a rational approach, even though considerable judgement is required.

The number of subordinates that a manager might expect to deal with successfully therefore depends upon the following:

● The degree of interaction between the people being supervised.

- The extent to which the activities are dissimilar. Relatively large spans of control are possible where there are specialists or experts each working with a high degree of autonomy.

- The incidence of new problems, systems and new staff under the manager. In start-up situations, or at a time of major change, it is not possible for managers to manage effectively through large spans of control.

- The physical dispersion of the unit. The geographical distance clearly results in management difficulties. For example, a sales manager in London might have twenty sales representatives reporting. For the same number of representatives covering Scotland, the North of England, Yorkshire and Lancashire, two or three managers might be necessary.

- The extent of a manager's other activities is also significant. If he or she is expected, for example, to carry a portfolio of clients as a professional, then the time left for supervision of other staff is reduced.

The grouping together of activities

When considering which activities should be grouped together within the organization, there are six points of comparison between tasks. These are the following:

1. Functional similarities, e.g. personnel department, finance department.

2. Process similarities, e.g. typing pool, word processor operators.

3. According to service or output, e.g. type of client – retail outlets for example.

4. Geographical, e.g. factory manager and immediate reports.

5. Timescale, e.g. corporate planners.

6. Complementary process, e.g. foundation-laying and concrete-mixing.

Although the functional organization is most common in bureaucratic forms, as a basis for the division of labour, the other organizing principles are becoming more acceptable. For example, in some of the big clearing banks word processing is now sometimes located away from expensive localities, in areas of cheaper employment costs, which is made possible by the automatic transmission of data between London offices and offices in the provinces.

The organization of companies around these products and services is also more frequently the case. In order to operate effectively in Europe, ICL reorganized its structure around its product groupings, or missions. Geographical reasons and complementarity are often associated – for example, a manager and secretary require geographical proximity, and work as a team with complementary activities. Similarly, projects are often handled by teams working together towards particular deadlines, so the complementary process also has a similar time-scale.

For large, complex businesses, the divisional form is a way of creating groupings of organizations which have sufficient similarity in their missions for services and management across the division to have a shared strategic purpose. The decision on what should be grouped together is based on a mixture of reasons. A mixture of mission or service to customer, geographical proximity (making economies of scale possible) and some complementarity of process are the most likely to be useful.

When organizing units and deciding which parts should be associated under different managerial controls there are three major considerations as follows:

1. How does the work flow relate to the structure?

2. What are the information-sharing needs of departments and of job units?

3. What are the communication needs of managers and groups?

One of the difficult problems to solve in organization design, is how to cope with both the work flow and the informal social needs, whilst maintaining a rational set of formal relationships which allows for the efficient use of resources and for managers to be accountable.

Those who adopt a socio-technical systems approach have attempted to do this by trying to match the task (or formal) system with the human, social needs through job design and job enrichment schemes offering sustaining, interesting work which is inherently motivating, with as much autonomy as possible and with task-oriented groupings.

New technology and organization design

When new technologies are applied there are opportunities for job redesign and for organization restructuring. In manufacturing, the use of robots, computer numerical control (CNC) machines and knowledge-based systems has resulted in more integrated structures. Widening consumer choice and competitive pressures produce shorter product life cycles, and designs for different markets. These demands can only be met by greater flexibility in design, and in the manufacturing and distribution processes. CAD/CAM systems mean a flexible manufacturing system can be used. With the integration of computer systems increased automation reduces the need for human physical effort, but increases the need for intellectual ability, for management coordination and for maintenance skills.

There are choices about how new technology is applied. These resolve into either 'technocentric' or 'anthroprocentric' approaches. Technocentric approaches attempt to create the unmanned factory. The design processes are broken down into simple choices. This approach relies on the use of technology to make all the main choices, and to carry out the production. A common database is required, together with a 'data highway' and a set of data exchange interfaces. The human element is reduced to a minimalist role, i.e. of maintenance and external relations.

Alternatively, the anthroprocentric approach leaves most of the decisions in human hands:

> Instead of incorporating almost all knowledge and the sequence of work as far as possible in the computer system, in this case the computer serves as a general and consistent information system, also performing routine operations but leaves the planning of working actions to the workers' and designers' skill. (Brödner 1990, p. 107)

Anthroprocentric approaches do leave room for job redesign, and give scope for job enrichment or job enlargement (Corbett 1990). We discuss these concepts in detail in Chapter 8 on organizational development, but here we should note that the upgrading of skill requirements, and the shift towards more responsible work – often requiring the employee to handle ambiguous and complex systems – means that whichever of the two approaches is adopted, the manufacturing organization of the future is likely to be a diamond rather than a pyramid shape (see Figure 7.4).

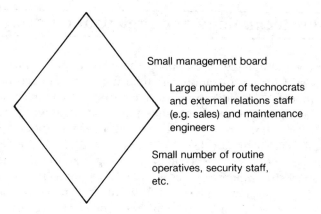

Small management board

Large number of technocrats
and external relations staff
(e.g. sales) and maintenance
engineers

Small number of routine
operatives, security staff,
etc.

Figure 7.4 The future manufacturing organization

The possibilities, even in low-tech businesses such as garment manufacturing, for restructuring work around small, semi-autonomous work groups suggest that multiskilling will remove the need for large numbers of unskilled operatives at the bottom of the organization. The consequences for payment systems, training, development and for management control when staff are organized as teams with considerable personal autonomy are beyond the scope of this chapter, but we can see there are implications for all these policies (for example, a move from piece-work to group bonus in rewards) and for management style.

Matrix organizations

An approach to organization structure which attempts to make the best use of the organization's resources, and to preserve a balance between work flow requirements and functional management, is the matrix form.

A matrix organization is one which operates on both a mission or project and on a functional or unit basis. Most typically, people deliver a service, or work from a base of expertise or organizational power, into a project or activity which draws on numerous skills, expertise or power bases.

Figure 7.5 shows a typical structure where the projects, or missions, draw on a range of functional staff as and when necessary. The essential characteristic of all matrix forms is that staff work *both* as

	Projects 1	2	3	4	etc.
Project leader					
Functional staff					
Marketing					
Finance					
Personnel					
Public relations					
Production engineer					
Computer staff					
etc.					

Figure 7.5 A typical matrix structure

members of a functional group or unit *and* as members of a project or mission team. They are therefore likely to have two different managers, as there are project team leaders with different responsibilities from the functional manager.

Because there is a widespread dislike of 'working for two masters', matrix structures are often criticized. One way to avoid confusion and ambiguity is to differentiate the various kinds of matrix organization, so that we are clear of their purpose, and clear about the power relationships (Knight 1976), as follows:

- **The overlay matrix**: the project or mission team leader has reporting responsibility for the team. He or she has power over the team members' everyday tasks, and overall responsibility for the project. The functional manager retains long-term career control and responsibility for the quality of the specialists' work.

- **The coordination matrix**: a project coordinator is appointed. He or she has responsibility for the project, but not for the team. The project coordinator only coordinates the team's activity, chairs meetings, produces reports and the like, but has no direct power over the team, who remain under the day-by-day control of their functional managers.

- **The either/or matrix**: the employee is *either* on the project *or* working in the functional specialism. In this case, the resources

165

are assigned to a project on a temporary basis, for short-term periods, when the employee is entirely under the control of the project/mission leader, before the employee returns to the functional group.

Matrix structures of the overlay type formalize the informal lateral communications which would normally exist between departments. This is an attempt to apply resources to different organizational outputs so that the organization can respond flexibly to varying demands. One further benefit for the specialists deployed in this way is that they may be exposed to situations which will give them an appreciation of the wider implication of their work. In general, matrix structures open up communication within organizations.

Conflicts do arise, however. The power of a functional manager is reduced, and the role becomes supportive or reactive. Unplanned demands for staff by mission heads who do not have the responsibility for finding or training the specialists can be difficult to meet. Without the ability to plan and develop people through a range of tasks the functional manager may feel unable to deliver adequate resources. This frustration is matched by project leaders who have little control over the resources allocated to them. There is also sometimes a threat to the specialists' occupational identity, and feelings of stress may emerge as the individual is asked to respond to demands from two different sources simultaneously.

Organization structure – the dominance of sub-units

Henry Mintzberg (1983) takes the view that every organization has the following five parts which are contained within a prevailing ideology (see Figure 7.6):

1. The technical core – for routine activities.

2. Middle management.

3. Top management.

4. Technical support.

5. Administrative support.

These five parts can be brought together in six different configurations

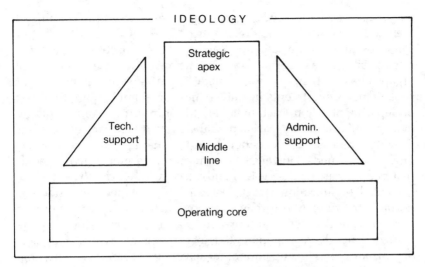

Figure 7.6 Mintzberg's organization parts

according to which part needs to be dominant for the organization to function. He describes these as follows:

1. Simple structures: small entrepreneurial companies; top manager and workers.

2. Machine bureaucracy: large mass production operations; 'mechanistic'.

3. Professional bureaucracy: production core comprises professionals, e.g. hospital, university.

4. Divisionalized form: large organizations sub-divided according to market needs.

5. 'Adhocracy': designed to survive in a complex environment; 'soft' structures supported by strong values/cultures; matrix form.

6. Missionary: virtually all operating core; shared values; loose division of labour; little job specialization.

Participative approaches to organization structure

To avoid the dysfunctions of organizational conflict, and to make the best use of the ideas and talents of employees, various approaches exist which also serve the need to give employees a say in the running of their unit, or of the whole organization.

For example, collegiate approaches can be used to rotate the responsibility for a department among the members. Small professional organizations, such as law or medical partnerships, management consultants, departments in universities for example, pass the head of department role to each member, either in turn, or on a seniority or sapiential authority basis, perhaps every two years or so. This provides management experience and a sharing of power for the group concerned. However, a continuing administrative base is required to manage the system and procedures efficiently.

Parallel organization structures can be developed alongside the normal structure, which may draw on each level of employees to work on questions of long-term importance. General Motors in the United States have experimented in this regard, where a parallel organization was set up to look at questions of strategic planning. This consisted of a committee on business strategy which had ten observers, who in turn headed up ten business planning councils. In these councils there were further observers who were members of support councils, leading on down to support teams. Each level had a specific research responsibility or area to investigate, and members of the councils and teams were selected by management on ability. They were appraised and rewarded both for their normal organizational role, and separately for their work in the parallel structure.

Management style and organizational culture

Questions about how work is organized cannot easily be distinguished from questions of management style and organizational culture. We can differentiate between participative, authoritarian and *laissez-faire* styles for example; the appropriateness of each being in accordance with the organization's traditions, the expectations of the employees, the tasks in hand and the characteristics of the people with whom the manager is dealing.

Certain kinds of organization structure lend themselves to certain styles of management and are often found in particular organizational cultures (Harrison 1972; Handy 1976). Bureaucratic forms often house authoritarian managers who establish a role culture, where status and role are the source of power. By contrast, matrix structures are task-oriented cultures where one might find participative styles.

Small organizations and entrepreneurial business might utilize a range of styles, but will probably be based on a 'power culture', where a possibly benevolent authoritarianism is the norm. Here the power stems from one person and he or she calls the shots. Formal authority is thus less important than the boss's word. Professional organizations, where there are large numbers of specialists are more likely to encourage a person culture, where relationships are the most significant determining power factor and a *laissez-faire* style may develop because it is a highly individualized culture.

Organic versus bureaucratic forms

The future for organizations is more likely to require an organic response to organizational design issues. We examined the origin of this term 'organic' in Chapter 6 where we described an organic approach as one in which the management adapt and change the structure quickly in response to market and technological changes.

It is becoming clearer now that there are a number of different organic forms. Some of these have been described as 'adhocracy', because they emerge and change so flexibly. William Ouchi uses the term 'Theory Z' organization to describe American companies which had developed a modified form of organization, similar to the Japanese approach to management – companies such as IBM, Proctor and Gamble, and Hewlett-Packard where people join a 'clan' culture – with non-specialized career paths, long-term employment and slow promotion. Here, the decision-making is based on consensus, there is a belief in collective responsibility and a concern for the people in the business (Ouchi and Jaeger 1978).

Collateral organization forms are also being developed as loosely structured small teams or separate business units who can solve the more unusual, unforeseen and therefore unplanned problems and changes faced by most organizations today. They are not unlike the parallel organization form described above. They can take risks, be creative and innovative whilst the main work of the business continues without disruption. They can draw on whatever level of management or experts are necessary from the main organization, thus using expertise not normally available to a small business. Such a collateral form is ideal for product development, or for examining acquisition or divestment problems. The possibilities for 'intrapreneurship' and change are therefore considerable (Kanter 1983).

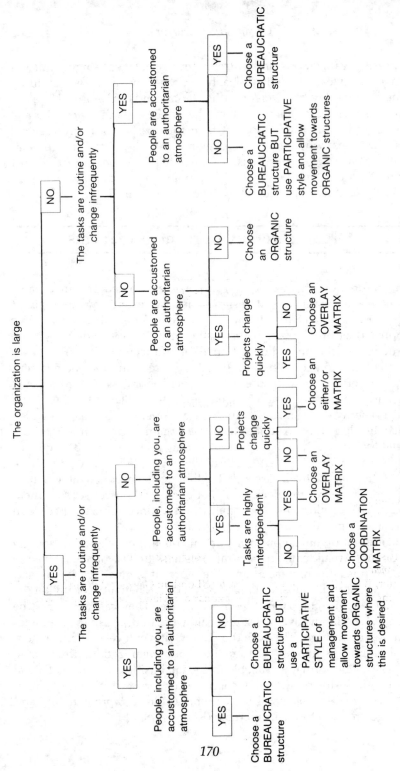

Figure 7.7 Choosing an organization structure

Conclusions

The selection of particular organization forms and structures is therefore dependent upon the degree of change, size, the culture of the current organization and the expectations of its members, the interdependencies of tasks, the types of missions or projects and the organization strategy concerning growth and the importance placed upon accountability and control. In Figure 7.7 these choices are set out in a decision tree which aims to simplify the choice, and in so doing to identify the key points in organization design.

References

Brödner, P. (1990), 'Technocentric–anthroprocentric approaches: towards skill based manufacturing', in M. Warner, W. Wobbe and P. Brödner (eds), *New Technology and Manufacturing Management* (Chichester: John Wiley).

Burns, T. and Stalker, G.M. (1961), *The Management of Innovation* (London: Tavistock).

Chandler, A. (1962), 'Strategy' and 'Structure', in *History of the Industrial Enterprise* (Cambridge, Mass.: MIT Press).

Child, J. (1984), *Organisation. A Guide to Problems and Practice* (London: Harper and Row).

Corbett, J.M. (1990), 'Design for human–machine interfaces', in M. Warner, W. Wobbe and P. Brödner (eds), *see* Brödner.

Cresap/IBM (1987), *The Effective Head Office* report published jointly.

Greiner, L.E. (1972), 'Evolution and revolution as organizations grow', *Harvard Business Review*, July/August.

Handy, C. (1976), *Understanding Organisations* (Harmondsworth: Penguin Education Series).

Harrison, R. (1972), 'How to describe your organization', *Harvard Business Review*.

Kanter, R.M. (1983), *The Change Masters* (London: George Allen and Unwin).

Knight, K. (1976), 'Matrix organisations: a review', *Journal of Management Studies*, May, pp. 111–30.

Miles, R.E. and Snow, C.C. (1978), *Organisational Strategy, Structure and Process* (New York: McGraw Hill).

Mintzberg, H. (1983), *Structure in fives: Designing Effective Organizations* (Englewood Cliffs: Prentice Hall).

Ouchi, W.G. and Jaeger, A.M. (1978), 'Type 2 organisations stability in the midst of mobility', *Academy of Management Review*, April, p. 3111.

Porter, Michael, E. (1980) *Competitive Strategy: Techniques for analysing industries and competitors* (New York: Free Press).

8

Organizational development and organizational change

Definitions

Organizational Development (OD) tends to mean different things to different people. The range of views, interests and practices is very diverse.

Originally, organizational development was defined as the current effort of behavioural scientists, that is, all those from psychologists, through sociologists, to anthropologists, who applied their knowledge with the aim of improving business organizations. Maintaining the generality, their concern would be with the effectiveness of the organization or sub-units within it. As the educative process begins to have its effects within organizations, this definition broadens to include the endeavours of general managers. Additionally, it may often be found that people undertaking either a training, management development, or personnel, function will operate as developers of the organization in these terms.

An alternative definition, borrowed from the psychological definition of intelligence, is that OD is what organizational development people do!

Aims

The concern within OD is to generate sufficient valid information from within the organization to be able to help it, and its members, to make free choices. These choices are concerned with assisting the members of the organization to reach some kind of solution to problems or issues which currently face them. OD does have a further concern, which is strengthening the problem-solving abilities of the organization. In other words, organizational developers seek to make themselves redundant.

It should also be noticed that OD is concerned with the development of the whole organization. Its orientation is not simply with individual managers or other employees of the organization. Having said this, however, there is some evidence (see below) that, whilst organization developers might have that as an aim, the reality of their actions shows a greater concern at the individual level of analysis.

The distinction between OD and organizational change is a 'fuzzy' area. One argument is that OD is also concerned with planned change. Certainly, until recent years, this planned change has been purely centred around interpersonal issues and problems. This orientation is, however, slowly changing. The brief now in OD is much wider and encompasses many of the issues that, some years ago, would have been classified purely as organizational change.

By its very definition, OD is client-centred. This has two implications. The first is that the problem, or issue, has to be perceived as such by the client. Secondly, and perhaps more importantly, the client actually generates his or her own solution. Moreover, because it is a change process, it is, by definition, process-oriented. Originally, the concern was merely with attitudes and relationships within the organization but OD has now moved on towards structure and procedural changes. It is also noticeable that OD is not a concept in the scientific sense of the phrase. It is not precisely defined, nor is it reducible to specific uniform and observable behaviours. But it is big business.

OD is further used as a term to describe the processes of reviewing and improving the effectiveness of an enterprise and its organization. Originally emanating from the behavioural sciences, it has tended to concentrate on actions and interactions between individuals in the working groups and with relationships between groups. In this case, most practitioners are behavioural scientists, or have derived their concepts and skills from the behavioural sciences. Beckhard (1969) defined OD as

> a planned effort, organisation wide and managed from the top, to increase organisation effectiveness and health through planned interventions in the organisation's processes using behavioural science knowledge. (p. 12)

Thus, OD may be considered from four points of view as follows:

1. An objective to be achieved.

2. A body of knowledge concerned with the managing of the development of the organization.

3. The strategies and policies for reviewing and seeking to improve the effectiveness of an enterprise or part of it.

4. Activities to implement the strategies and policies.

OD, therefore, involves the following:

- Making a diagnosis of what is needed to improve the effectiveness of an enterprise and establishing objectives from these.
- Developing a strategy to obtain these objectives.
- Developing activities to implement the strategy.
- Ensuring feedback to monitor and evaluate progress.

It is, thus, a long-term and continuing process.

Historical approach

OD developed out of management development. It took what was happening during the 1950s and enlarged upon it. It is also a direct descendant of training (T) groups. Dealing with each of those in turn, we can see the roots of management training both within the armed forces in the United Kingdom and in the so-called 'J program' (job instruction training) in the United States. Both of these led to management training as we have understood it for the last two or three decades. In the United States the early work was concerned with convincing foremen that they were actually managers. Roethlisberger's (1947) work on the foreman is a classic in this regard. In the United Kingdom it took a slightly different direction towards the now mainly defunct training boards and the increasingly sophisticated management colleges offering independent and general management training to a wide range of different organizations and cultures. Moreover, during the period of the last forty years, we have seen an increasing sophistication in techniques and devices to inculcate what are considered to be the necessary behaviour changes and attitudinal changes. These techniques have included lectures, guided discussions, case studies and business games, role playing, participant observation, distance learning and, with increasingly complex technologies, things like interactive videos, etc. Interestingly, almost all of these devices are very much trainer-oriented. That reality is now changing within organizations.

In the initial stages, what was being done in the arena of management development was seen to have limited impact. It was for this reason that organizations turned to the T group system as a way of undertaking OD to obtain faster and more permanent results. The foundations of T groups is to be found in the work of Lewin and Moreno during the decades of the 1940s and 1950s. The concentration in the early years was very much on the training of chairmen and members of groups and concern, more specifically, was with group rather than individual factors.

However, during the 1950s the co-founders of this movement split their orientation: Lewin moved more towards the research end of the spectrum whereas Moreno shifted his concern towards national training. Initially, clients were people, who it was felt, first, had a need for this training and secondly, could act as influencers within organization settings. For that reason these early clients included people such as educators, social workers and, within the organization setting, personnel. The movement grew rapidly up until the mid–late 1960s, with particularly rapid growth within organizations in the Western world. It led to the professionalization of trainers and also to the notion of encounter groups, which have variously been defined as a 'poor man's do it yourself'.

T group methods and assumptions

The basic assumption underpinning T groups is that the individual could learn through current experience – so-called experiential learning. Its orientation was very much at the non-rational or emotional level of analysis. Underpinning all the work was the assumption that people had the power to grow, which is an assumption that underlies much management training and development work today.

However, one major change we have seen over the intervening years is that one basic assumption of T groups was that people would have a positive response to negative criticism or feedback. From the behavioural school of thinking, from G.B. Watson onward, we know that that assumption was badly placed. The major concern with such training was to free people's emotional responses. This was achieved by emphasizing people's sensitivities to other people's attitudes and belief systems, as well as varying emotional responses. In fact, it might be argued that although the concern was with attitudes, of its three components emotion stood in first place. The skills being emphasized were those involved in dealing with other people within the organization. However, T group work was rarely carried on within the organization setting and this led to a further assumption that there would be some carry over from the training situation to the real-life situation.

T group forms

The training itself used many different forms of groups. The basic classifications of these groups were stranger, cousin, family and diagonal. Stranger groups were literally, as the title suggests, people who had had no previous contact. Often they would come, not just from different parts of the same organization, but actually from different organizations. Cousin groups, on the other hand, were people who came from the same organization and, indeed, often from the same level within the organization, but who had little contact with one another in the work situation. Family groups, as the name again implies, comprise the boss and his or her subordinates.

Diagonal groups comprise a slice across the organization both in terms of levels and departments. Where T group work differed with different individuals was in the extent to which training was actually structured.

Furthermore, different trainers were more or less concerned to emphasize rational versus emotional training. In some instances, the depth of intervention, especially at the emotional level, was profound. From all this, we saw the emergence of two different themes. First, organizational and job-centred problems could be solved by family groups. The second theme of encounter groups was quite different. This is the so-called 'touchy feely' which is concerned with personal growth and attitudinal or, indeed, personality change, and emphasizes the expression of emotion rather than understanding.

T group criticism

The tenor of some of the foregoing comments implies that there is some criticism of T groups. This would be the correct view. The criticism reached a crescendo in the mid–late 1960s when it became increasingly apparent that the very process to which people were being subjected was, in fact, extremely stressful. In many ways, the process was perceived as a violation of the personal privacy of individuals. It certainly created tensions and, in some cases, actually led to mental breakdowns. To a large extent, many of the problems were created because trainers were insufficiently well prepared or trained to cope with the powers which they were unleashing within groups. So concerned did some organizations become during this time that policies were created forbidding people to go on sensitivity or T group training sessions.

It was also argued that the training itself was unrealistic. There was little carry over into the job and any skills which had been created were very quickly extinguished in the organizational setting. This, of course, has been a besetting problem for all training interventions in all organizations. However, one major criticism, without any doubt, was that the wrong lessons were being taught. The concern was with emotional freedom and sensitivity to other people, whereas organizations themselves were concerned with logical analysis, decisiveness and, most importantly, political skills.

Finally, the concern was with changing attitudes and personality. Two aspects are worthy of note here. First, the argument has been put forward that alternatives are actually better; that is, that we should look to structural or system changes rather than attitudinal and personality ones. Secondly, there is a moral and ethical dilemma. People are actually paid for their behaviour; that is, for their performance. What they are not paid for is to have specific attitudes or personality variables inherent in their make-up. For example, it is not so much whether somebody is racially prejudiced but rather whether there is a manifestation of it within the organization setting. At that level of analysis, we are concerned with the behaviour not the attitude. The counter argument, that any change of behaviour will lead dramatically to a change in attitude, is acknowledged. However, the attempt to change behaviour is quite overt and the direction of that change is also made clear. The individual, therefore, can choose whether he or she pursues that change or not.

Because of the concerns with T group, and the number of consultants undertaking T group work, a change in orientation occurred. What was found during the 1960s and 1970s was the emergence of the so-called change agent. Until this point, the T group had been concerned with attitudes, and perhaps behaviour, although only in terms of single facets of behaviour, rather than being concerned with situations.

By and large, organizational development (OD), as it had then become known, was much more concerned with planned and managed organizational change. Moreover, there is now a concern with the environment as it impacts on a specific organization.

None the less, some similarities remain. Emotional change is still one of the priorities, at least in part, in OD. This is often encapsulated in the concept of 'values' and, in addition, the intervention is usually based at the individual level. In both cases, there is a great need for interpersonal trust in order to confront interpersonal issues and problems. The focus of OD programmes shifts as the development begins to take place, from the individual level of analysis in the initial stages, through that person's relationships with others, and through departmental interactions and team building towards relations between groups and within the organization generally. If the orientation is specifically and exclusively to do with the individual, then what we are talking about is training not OD.

Depth of intervention

OD has shifted dramatically from a concern with individual attitudes and interpersonal relationships, through the impact the individual's work has on other people, into such arenas as the reward system and the structure of the organization. 'Rewards' encompasses much more than the notion of money or bonuses. Rather, the concern is to manipulate people, in the most positive sense of that word, via procedures such as management by objectives, appraisal, and so on. In other words, 'reward' here is meant in the very widest sense.

In terms of structure, the concern is with role relationships, reporting relationships and even such aspects as job descriptions and the organization structure itself. Depending upon the form of OD intervention, some, or all, of these may be combined at any one time. What is central to OD is feedback as a change mechanism, in both a positive and negative form, that is, both critical comment and praise are sought. Inevitably, the concern is with the behaviour and its effects as perceived by other people, i.e. peers, subordinates, etc. Different organizations have used different systems to undertake this kind of work; such systems include, for example, management activity profiling. What is being attempted is to differentiate the ideal from the actual behaviours or styles of individuals or groups. People are made to face problems directly, either in a face-to-face situation, or by thinking about the implications of other people's ideas, and so on.

Issues

Perhaps one of the most important issues is the degree of consultant control. This is combined with the degree of isolation, i.e. from the realities of the job, as well as the perceived purpose of the intervention. What we know is that while psychological safety is paramount, there are times during the intervention when we actually wish to create a feeling of discomfort within the clients so far as the status quo is concerned. There are occasions when we require high degrees of isolation from the organization. Yet, at the same time, it is recognized that the greater this degree of isolation, then the less transferable may be the resulting behaviour changes back into the organization.

There is another concern. When dealing with personal unfreezing and values, there is a danger that the people concerned may become overly dependent upon the consultant. In essence, the greater the divorce from the job, the greater is the psychological safety so far as the individual is concerned, and the less transferable are the behaviours. In any event, there is a major difference between the intention to change and the actual implementation of any agreed change. In these situations, the climate of the organization is vital in order to ensure that change is maintained. For this reason, the development of sustaining mechanisms must occur within the organization. Thus, the change itself, in a sense, needs to be fully negotiated with all the implications which underpin the concept of negotiation.

One part of the concern, at this stage, has to be with the answers to the questions: Why do organizations engage in OD? Who makes the initial decision? How and when do they decide to call in the consultant (assuming it is an external individual)? The answers are crucial to the success or otherwise of the intervention, and the motives and expectations of all parties, as well as ownership, both for the problem and its solution, are critical issues. In all this, the initial period, during which both the organization, and therefore its members, and the consultant or consultants, are sizing one another up, is critical to the success of the intervention.

The motives which people bring as reasons for interventions are numerous. A few are listed here. It may well be that some individual, usually a powerful manager within the organization, has undergone a so-called 'conversion', i.e. he or she has experienced or heard about

OD and has 'seen the light'. Occasionally, OD is concerned with raising morale and sometimes the consultant is brought in as a 'handyman'. In this case, the concern is with a specific problem which the consultant is called in to fix. There are other motives which are perhaps a little less wholesome, such as the dubbed 'Mafia' connection where the consultant is actually brought in to 'fix' an individual within the organization!

Change agent

There are several important specialist roles in OD. These include the following:

- Helping with the diagnosis of the need.
- Planning and conducting training activities.
- Acting as a catalyst in the management of internal change.
- Contributing knowledge of the art and science of managing the development of the organization.

These roles are usually referred to as those of the change agent. This may be someone, either inside or external to the organization, who provides technical, specialist or consulting assistance in the management of a change effort. An aspect of the change agent's role, which is often overlooked, is that of helping to maintain the momentum of development which often flags after initial enthusiasm.

The effectiveness of any enterprise is the concern of all those who work within it. The development of the organization can only be successful if operating managers, at all levels, understand, and are committed to and involved in, the processes by which improvements can be achieved. They plainly need to be able to see the benefits of any such process in terms of practical results. Any programme obviously requires commitment and support from the top. However, there are numerous examples of particular pieces of work in small units which have been undertaken on the initiative of individual managers, and which have achieved worthwhile results. Quite often this form of experimental work will help both to develop experience and establish credibility for such processes within the organization. For example, the introduction of team briefings as a way of disseminating managerial decisions and information down the organization, and listening to issues from lower parts of the hierarchy, may well begin in one section or department. Once any problems have been solved and the benefits are being seen by other sections, then the utilization of such briefings can be quickly widened.

Other issues

Almost, but not quite inevitably, the degree of top management involvement can be crucial. Minimally, management need to be seen to be supportive of the intervention; at the other extreme, they need to participate fully. In many ways, it depends upon the goal being sought, but, without the visible support of management, the chances of success are vastly reduced. Even the client him/her self may change during the intervention. There may well be an initial contact but then the intervention itself shifts into the department or section of the organization which is requesting the intervention. The difficulty this creates for the interventionist becomes the question of who precisely is the client. The interventionist is often concerned as to whether he or she is dealing with the whole or part of the organization, for there are many implications in dealing with just a part.

Another element is whether the climate is such as to enable the intervention to be successful, and, again, whether the intervention occurs during a crisis or during some slack period within the organization. Although many other parts of the organization would argue that their own capacity to undertake change is vastly increased in slack times, it is a far-seeing, and frankly unusually bold, organization that maintains the intervention even when times are strained.

Possibly because the values inherent in OD are of a theory-wide typology, power and conflict within organizational life are often ignored, or, at least, they were ignored. More and more these issues are coming to the fore. There is now a preparedness to acknowledge the importance these factors play in organizational effectiveness. Thus, in looking at the effectiveness of a management team it is not enough to look at leader–subordinate relations or the team roles each will adapt. On the contrary, the politics of those relationships also need to be confronted at some stage if the team is to be enabled to move to its next level.

Research in this area has been hampered by a series of problems. The criterion problem is inevitably an issue, but the dynamic reality within which organizations have to exist makes the development and measurement of criteria difficult. Measurement can be undertaken at very different levels, from the immediate, i.e. as soon as the

181

intervention has finished, through to the ultimate level, i.e. some considerable time later when all the learning has been internalized. In other words, are we concerned at the reactions level of analysis or are we concerned with the longer term issues which emanate from any kind of intervention? As soon as we become concerned with the ultimate level of analysis, then the number of uncontrollable variables becomes a major concern to the organization and to the ethics of the intervention itself. In any case, there will often be effects of the kind noted in the original Hawthorne studies, the now well-named 'Hawthorne effect'. Finally, the bottom line has to be a concern with cash generation for the future viability of the organization.

There was a view, some twenty years ago, that OD needed not only to take more account of the impact on managers of the formal organization, but also that before concentrating on styles of behaviour it was necessary to assess what problems with organization tasks had to be solved. The argument then was that there should first be more concentration on task than on process issues. The emphasis is changing once more and has been doing so over the last decade and the shift is back towards styles and skills of behaviour.

Individual level

With some notable exceptions, there has been a quite major shift in the arena of training towards a form of 'sheep dip' approach, in which the individual, and his or her needs, are no longer considered fully. However, OD demands that we do not lose sight of the importance of developing and training autonomous individuals. We need to ensure that, within the organization, we have people who are able to initiate and implement, as well as to be members of an effective working group or network. One of the implications of this is that some attention might be paid to the development of inventories of specially skilled people within the organization.

Simmons (1989) puts forward the argument for self-management teams. These self-managing teams (SMT) are a linear descendant of the semi-autonomous work groups of the 1970s. The planning for such teams does not simply involve touring the plant and having meetings to determine whether SMTs could make some significant improvement; rather, what is required is a review both of customers' needs and how the current work systems operate. Only then can a shift be made, if at all, towards the delegation to the teams of authority and responsibility for meeting customer needs. This change in emphasis, from one organizational culture to another, demands a well thought through managerial philosophy and strategy. In these terms, we have to turn to the model clarified by Carnall (1990) to look at how change and OD can both be initiated and maintained within organization settings.

To summarize, OD seeks to create high performance and high commitment work cultures. The characteristics of such organizations, which give them their competitive advantage, are: competence, caring and flexibility. Within such organizations, it has been argued, management views people as both resources and collaborators in the competitive market. For this reason, it is more likely to seek ways in which people's commitment, competence and intelligence can be aligned behind the goals of the organization. By definition, therefore, the organization undertakes to use delegation, team work across boundaries, empowered people, technology integrated with people and a shared sense of purpose. Within such environments, it is no longer simply the task of the senior management team to be primary keepers of the vision. Instead, it is shared through the organization. Moreover, managers manage not just the environment, but attempt to anticipate and manage the future. The argument then becomes whether competitive advantage is gained from the dual orientation of both satisfying the customer and developing people within the organization.

The goal of improvement is ostensibly to achieve some equilibrium within a system. The process itself involves using external realities as motivators for change and improvement. The whole implication of improvement is that people understand those aspects which will aid or create difficulties in reaching a goal. At one level, this notion of continuous improvement places its emphasis on the process of reaching a goal. However, processes involve people and we must, therefore, learn to appreciate how to manage the people side of things when looking at aspects of OD.

Diagnosis

The task of diagnosis is to establish facts and to identify problems, and perhaps even to make comparisons and evaluations. There are many methods which may be used and these are becoming both more prolific and more complex. They include such things as attitude surveys, interviews, questionnaires, data from easily available sources – i.e. manpower turnover, analysis of the working of systems, and of critical incidents, analysis of group and inter-group meetings, etc.

Any diagnosis must combine the experience of operating managers at several levels with the skills and perceptions of those who are driving the actual change or development. In this way, operating managers are involved from the start and, therefore, are encouraged to take responsibility for their own problems. The basis is thereby laid for commitment to objectives, for change and for the activities to achieve the objectives.

When we look at some of the rationalizations which underpin the bringing in of an external consultant, then what often faces organizations is the advent of some new fad or buzz word. Whether in fact it works is a moot point. However, because managers are very solution-oriented, and because they are faced with enormously difficult tasks, something which proffers an easy solution is to be welcomed. However, perhaps what we need to do is to focus people on gradual steps in their movement towards a goal. Grounded in the notion of reinforcement contained in the behavioural sciences, the effect of the positive reinforcement of small gains is often out of proportion to the amount of effort which is expended. As their successes become visible, employees may well be able to create and attract allies and thereby lower resistance to subsequent changes. It is in this arena that we can see the development from OD into organizational change, the notion of discrete versus discontinuous change. OD is concerned, by and large, with evolutional or discrete change, often extended over many months or years. As a gross generality, organizational change is concerned with revolutionary or relatively sharp and sudden changes to which the organization must swiftly adapt.

What is often not recognized in undertaking any kind of OD initiative is the amount of time which is required before results actually begin to occur. Quite often, communication within organizations is endangered by a number of different managerial prerogatives. Fear of relinquishing absolute control, and information filtering, might well be argued to be part of this, as is so-called 'muddle in the middle'. This latter characteristic is often symptomatic of organizations in which information filtering, especially by middle managers, is the status quo. What is required is an analysis of the situation and a recognition of this specific problem. For example, in a case involving hourly paid workers, they were still complaining after some days about the quality of their shift meetings and their need for consistent information about matters which impinged on their job performance. Although it was readily agreed that two-way communication, participation and improvement in shift meetings were called for, when an attempt was made to create a powerful two-way communication system it was found that it required not only an enormous amount of attention, but also a great deal of flexibility and patience. Results are never immediate.

One of the real questions which now have to be asked by managers within organizations is the part which they play within them. In a sense, the real question is: Why do I exist? It has been argued that this personal crisis is rooted in a loss of an overlap of values and beliefs between the individual and the organization. Current organizational development efforts are now mainly directed to this area, beginning at the very top of the organization in such work as that undertaken by Kakabadse (1991). His concern was to review the effectiveness not just of the top teams in organizations but of the chief executive or leaders of that team, by reviewing their value systems in organizational terms.

One of the problems with OD is the creation of enthusiasm for a project in the initial stages. This is often followed by rapid decay, which is characterized by peaks and troughs of excitement and frustration. This is part of what Sheane (1978) has named 'project interruptus', referring to that feeling which individuals often have of not being able to finish and complete projects which have been started. What OD seeks to do is to allow the decision-making process to become clearer and to acknowledge that any problem may have more than one owner.

Developing the effectiveness of the enterprise is central to the task of all managers. They need to be intimately involved in the process of diagnosis and in the activity of development itself. Not only will they be aware of the needs, but they will also have to live with the consequences of the actions taken to meet those needs. And they must both initiate and energize such actions. The process of diagnosis, establishing strategy and implementing the tactics to deliver that strategy, are the core of a manager's job at whatever level he or she operates. Managers, therefore, need to be at the centre of OD activities. This involves them in both observing, and therefore standing back from, the management process, as well as undertaking actual management work. In a sense, it involves the individual in becoming his or her own critic and consultant. Two problems are inherent in this. First, in order to create an ongoing process of organizational learning, most managers will require some guidance and training. Secondly, and perhaps even more importantly, few managers are allowed the time to undertake these roles, advisable though they may be.

As an element of improving the organization, one orientation which is often taken is that of improving the team. Any OD contract involves at least six different aspects. In essence, these reduce to the following:

- Contracting.
- Explaining and agreeing the process of intervention.
- Data collection.
- Data analysis.
- Data feedback (under which heading is also included diagnosis and action planning).
- Finally, but by no means least importantly, the review.

However, this is OD in a very formal way. There are alternatives which are based heavily on the actual manager working in the organization. Here the concern is to move away from more formal bureaucratic practices into those which are less formal, in order to attempt to discover what is going on within the organization. It is at this stage that the politics of OD begin to rear their head. The whole issue of politics is important and was dealt with in Chapter 4.

It should be mentioned that in any attempt to include key decision-makers and opinion leaders in the OD strategy, different levels, roles or departments, need to be involved meaningfully. Such involvement may be on the basis of expertise or formal role but, more pragmatically, power is also involved. In these terms, power is defined in terms of organized energy or, alternatively, the power to influence outcomes.

OD, as it has been formulated, is reactive. However, current work has to shift from that emphasis to one which is proactive within the organization. The advice here is to confront problems as early as possible. In a sense, what the manager, or OD person, has to do, is to go out and seek the so-called 'bad news'. Having valid and up-to-date information about the state of the system enables interventions to be thought through before the problem becomes too great.

Culture and organizational development

Change, or OD interventions, are often occasioned by the organization's inherent inertia. For this reason, the issue of decline often heralds an organization's entering into an OD or change intervention. Nor can it be said that the problem of declining industries is one which is purely Western: Japan, too, has its share of problems in this area.

There is a classic example in the Japanese brewery industry: Asahi Breweries Limited had been declining over about thirty-five years. The underpinning reasons for the decline could be traced to two major factors: a concentration on the restaurant market and, most importantly, a product which was not perceived to be of the highest quality. What was needed was a major break within the culture itself in order to shift the orientation of the people working within the organization. As is often the case, this was effected by the initiation of a new president in 1982. The change which resulted was a simple one. The emphasis now was placed on manufacturing consumer-oriented products and, at the same time, seeking to create a more positive work environment for the people within the organization. By inserting quality control programmes as well as research campaigns and intensive advertising, a turn-around was effected over a fairly short space of time. Changes also occurred within the organization structure itself which led to the removal of communication gaps between production and marketing departments. The role of central staff functions was reinforced which had the effect of improving research capabilities and introduced product divisions, an essential part of the total change plan. The success of the total strategy also helped the change in the orientation of the employees of the organization.

There is a very thin dividing line between organizational change and OD. OD is, by its very nature, evolutionary: that is, change brought about in small, discrete steps. In this way, OD may be seen to comprise continuities. On the other hand, organizational change is much more likely to take the form of discontinuities. There is, by comparison, a relatively sharp change in direction in some way, shape or form within the organization. Even using this discrimination, there are still broad areas of overlap between the two concepts.

Change itself can come from within: for example, there are parts of even dynamic organizations which tend to stagnate. Such departments or subsidiaries need to change to improve their effectiveness. On the other hand, external change comes from without and is the end result of environmental changes. The healthier organization sees external change as an opportunity which it can therefore exploit. Indeed, it might well be argued that change in the environment has accelerated and, moreover, is likely to continue certainly at the same if not a faster pace. In part this change is reinforced by the explosion of knowledge in science and technology and by the spread of education and the questioning of our traditional education and value systems. More than ever today we are aware of new and often revolutionary methods of production, distribution and speed and range of media communications. Commercial enterprises which do not exploit, or at least adapt to these changes are likely to stagnate or go under. Public service enterprises which fail to do so lose credibility with their public.

There are often conflicts within organizations. The direction which has been decided upon may favour centralized control and militate against delegation. Efficiency may be promoted by specialization but this latter aspect makes coordination much more difficult. Adaptation may require flexibility and that in turn militates against control. Social satisfaction may be highest where working groups are autonomous, posing problems for direction and control. Priorities between such conflicting influences inevitably have to be judged by the needs of the particular enterprise in the specific situation. These priorities plainly change over time. Diagnosis of problems is therefore vital prior to the evolution of a change strategy.

Enterprises are complex. They comprise many different elements: people, tasks, technology, structure, procedures, systems, values and norms, capital, etc. Moreover, they represent a meeting point of a variety of interests which would include such people as suppliers, customers, creditors, debtors, managers, employers, the community at large, and so on. There is a massive interplay between these interests which together comprise the culture of the organization. Of necessity there are interdependencies between them; a change in one will almost certainly have repercussions for some or all of the others. In undertaking change within the organization the attempt is being made to create conditions in which people can behave effectively and efficiently. Actions such as changing structure, or training people, enriching jobs or whatever, if undertaken in isolation without recognizing the impact of each on the others, are likely to end in disappointing results.

Part of the need to look at organizational change within the organization is to shift the emphasis from that basic conception inherent in work which talks about espoused theories versus theories in action. Organizational development is an attempt to shift the emphasis towards action. For example, in discussions, managers will often state that they have a preference for participative systems which they claim will lead to desirable outcomes. In these terms, it might be argued, they would see a general need for organizational change and development. Moreover, they would be quite likely to express a willingness to support such change, especially if it were to lead towards a more participative system.

Their actual actions, however, belie their words. Generally speaking, managers do not install such systems. Collins *et al.* (1989) stated that one of the primary ingredients missing in a managerial evolution towards participative systems is a lack of what they term transformational leadership. In other words, there is a need for a fracturing of the current status quo in some way. This notion of discontinuity is what underpins organizational change. However, in order for the change to be made effective in as many ways and directions as possible, there needs to be a set of developmental stages which we would encapsulate under the generic heading OD. It is in this context that the disruptive effects of organizational change are smoothed over in an effort to make the organization more effective.

Models

A panacea for organizational change is often to be found in the literature. For example, Uhlfelder and Werner (1989) suggest that the process of change demands that the organization should analyse and adapt itself through the use of experts. Experts are defined as the employees doing the work. The design team itself is comprised of a vertical slice through the organization; the team directly reports to the management team. Uhlfelder and Werner's argument is that the design team should follow five basic steps which include, for example, the identification of the processes under study, the development of current state 'technical maps' and the development of ideal state 'technical maps'. Through defining the ideal social system and the development of an implementation plan a team can plainly push forward to the implementation and evaluation stages.

However, as with all recipes in the area of organizational change and development, Uhlfelder and Werner ignore the fact that the elements which have to come together are not always the same. Situations both between and within organizations are rarely identical. Whilst there will be times when the change can be created from within the organization, equally there will be times when changes are actually required either in the management team itself or in the chief executive officer. Beyond that there will also be times when the direct input of an external source is required.

What they do fairly acknowledge is the need for ownership of the

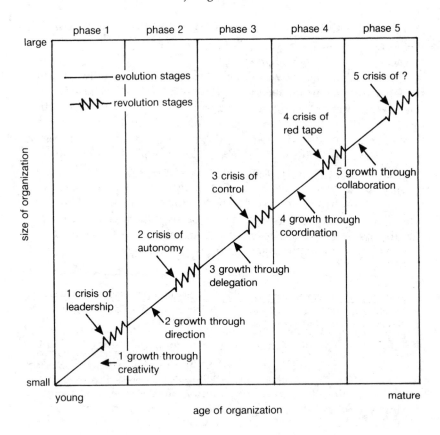

Reproduced with the permission of the President and Fellows of Harvard College, from the *Harvard Business Reviews*, July/August 1972.

Figure 8.1 The five phases of growth (Source: Greiner 1972)

need for change, and the need skilfully to bring about that change. Indeed, a common problem in the change literature is not that there is no attempt to derive a strategic model for change. On the contrary, this is often well done. The tactical or implementation stages are where most of these fall down.

Greiner's (1972) model (see Figure 8.1) is a case in point. It shows various stages through which an organization is likely to go during its growth periods. The potential issues and problems between various stages are highlighted (see also Table 8.1). The major problem, however, should also be seen as one of managerial behaviour: that

Table 8.1 Issues and problems during the five phases of growth

Phase	
1. *Initial creative* Led by the founder entrepreneur(s) with a loose informal organization	Ends in a crisis of leadership: if the initial founders are not able to make the transference to managing larger scale or more complex operations
2. *Direction* Led by a strong business manager with a hierarchical departmental structure, budgeting systems, standards and incentives	Demand for more autonomy by lower level managers
3. *Delegation* Decentralized structure, greater responsibilities given to managers, management by exception, profit centres	Need for control. Increasing problems of coordination
4. *Coordination* Product division, formal planning procedures, strong central services and control of capital expenditures	Revolts against red tape and bureaucracy. Resentment against direction from headquarters staff
5. *Collaboration* Focus on problem-solving, interdisciplinary team performance and remuneration, experimentation, matrix structures, real-time information systems	Psychological saturation resulting from emotional and physical exhaustion after intense team work and pressures for innovative solutions

is, what managers have to do in order to overcome these crises, and what in time span, etc., should be determined.

It should also be noticed that Greiner originally suggested, when first devising the model, that the important element in the strategy of organizational change is for the organization to recognize where it is in the historical pattern of development and, therefore, what the next step should be.

In a recent survey undertaken by Cowling (1989), traditional personnel activities such as communications, pay systems, and so on figured prominently in change processes. However, he found little evidence that the personnel function itself took a lead in initiating change. Almost inevitably the initiative comes from the chief executive. What is different from some years ago is that the personnel function is now providing advice and guidance at the most senior levels within organizations. There is a dawning realization within organizations that paying attention to the people side of the business has a major pay-off. As a result the personnel director, given a high level of professional competence, has now become vital to the organization's capacity to implement change.

The initiation of a new chief executive officer is often a potential precursor to any change which the organization needs to input. Evidence from the world of stockholder reaction to succession indicates that it depends upon the rationale for the new Chief Executive Officer's appearance as to whether that individual will have some impact or not within the organization. Where the previous incumbent is perceived to have performed badly, positive reactions often greet Board-initiated successions. Successions are thus often viewed as an adaptive and a positive occurrence. There is a greater likelihood, therefore, that the succession itself will bring about effective organizational change. On the other hand, where the succession has resulted from, for example, death, the new Chief Executive may well be met with negative reactions regardless of what his or her performance may actually be.

Part of the change process can well be seen in the example of NASA which has had to change from a research and development organization into one which works in an operations environment. The transition strategy which is necessary for the effective facilitation of this shift has to include an analysis of where the organization is currently, where it wishes to be, how it will get there and, perhaps most importantly, the importance which is attached to the new state. It is only when the organization, in the form of the team overviewing the proposed transition, understands the current and future states that it can focus on the planning of the actual movement.

Effectiveness

It is difficult to talk about organizational change without looking in some detail at what is meant be effectiveness. Indeed, part of the issue in organizational change is that if the organization is deemed to be ineffective in some way then plainly there is a need for a change. However, the evidence suggests that quite often ineffectiveness within an organization leads to greater difficulties in creating the possibility for change to occur. Again, when we look at the measures for effectiveness we are often even more confounded, for *money measures* tell us only about the past and trends assume some continuity and sameness. What they do not allow us to talk about is what happens with discontinuities. In one sense effectiveness can be defined as the capacity to adapt to changing environments. One of the cornerstones of effectiveness is that of integration.

Any company's performance comprises a whole series of elements which in some way have to be integrated. Performance is determined by achieving or surpassing business objectives and perhaps, indeed, social objectives and responsibilities. Performance is always assumed from some judging party's perspective and here we come to one of the early problems to do with organizations. The notion of who benefits often gives some indication as to who the judging party may be. However, the interests of the various stakeholders in the business often conflict. For example, the shareholder's interests will be different from those of the senior management team, which may be quite different from those of a particular department's or subsidiary's managing director. Indeed, we might also look at the differences within the organization itself for the aims of the marketing group may be quite different from those of the manufacturing group, and so on.

However, putting that to one side for the moment and returning to the notion of integration, we know that integration is concerned with five major elements of the organization. Specifically, these are as follows:

- Knowledge
- Non-human resources
- Human processes
- Strategic positioning
- Structures

Each of these can be defined in its own terms. Thus, for example, knowledge can comprise technical administrative skills as well as the processes which people use. Non-human resources are such things as equipment, plant, technology, capital, work environment, etc. Strategic positioning, again, is almost self-explanatory and plainly includes such things as business market, social policy, human resource planning, etc. In terms of the people, then, the concern here is with their values, attitudes, norms of behaviour and interactions. Finally, structure comprises the way the organization is actually shaped, the management and information systems which it uses and the flexibility with which these are used.

Figure 8.2 Monitoring effectiveness (Source: Carnall 1990)

Effectiveness – success criteria

The whole notion of success criteria leads us into the same form of debate as that of effectiveness generally. Evaluations depend on the evaluator's frame of reference. For different groups and different strata these frames of reference will be different; in other words, the foundations upon which judgements are being made are not fixed. What we have to be concerned with is performance levels compared with system goals and their social origins. Thus, when Deloittes surveyed organizations in 1988 they found that the major success criteria were such things as investment potential, financial stability, management calibre, product quality, innovation, ability to recruit and motivate key staff and asset management skills.

Carnall (1990) shows this in a simple two-by-two figure (see Figure 8.2). On one dimension he has efficiency and effectiveness, on the other quantitative versus qualitative. When we look at measures of efficiency at the quantitative level of analysis then we have reasonably straightforward judgements – though accountants might argue differently – including such matters as cost and profit. Of much greater difficulty is the qualitative spectrum where, especially when we look towards effectiveness, we have issues like adaptability, corporate culture, management development, and so on.

These things are much less easily dealt with, although some organizations are actually doing a great deal to bring about change in corporate culture through these qualitative means. One thing we know from their work is that it is a highly involved and long-term task. In order to bring about change within a corporate culture we are not looking towards a three- to six-month project but rather a three- to five-year project. For example, a part of a major British communications group is in the throes of a culture change. This has involved determining the current culture, deciding on the change needed, developing a strategic plan, and a tactical methodology, implementing this carefully through the organization maintaining a feedback loop and, when completed, ensuring the targets were met. It is a slow process.

Criteria of effectiveness

The issue of effectiveness criteria is a major one. Even if the criteria which have been suggested so far are regarded as objective in their nature, unlike almost all other experimental work, with organizational change it is difficult, though not always impossible, to have a controlled experiment. The kind of criteria that have been used in the past might be as follows:

- **Direction**: Setting objectives, long- and short-term planning; entrepreneurship and sound investment in commercial enterprises; devising appropriate organization structures; maintaining a favourable image of the enterprise. *Measured or indicated by*: the extent to which objectives are achieved – there is foresight in strategy, successful innovation, profitability and high share value, etc. Reality tells us that many of these indicators may prove favourable or not for reasons that are quite outside the actual control of the organization, and they are not necessarily a consequence of its effectiveness.

- **Delegation**: motivation by encouraging well-judged decisions close to the point of action. This implies that managers have the authority required to discharge their accountabilities. *Measured or indicated by*: the extent to which the authority is delegated and whether this is thought to be adequate by the subordinate; the degree of support by superiors.

- **Accountability**: clear understanding of who is accountable for what without gaps between accountabilities. *Measured or indicated by*: the extent to which superiors judge that accountability is discharged in terms of meeting objectives.

- **Control**: monitoring performance against objectives and standards. *Measured or indicated by*: task-related indices, e.g. resource utilization, rejection rates, quality of service, etc. May also include measures of attitude or morale.

- **Efficiency**: the optimum use of resources and the achievement of planned levels of output with minimum costs. *Measured or indicated by*: input–output ratios.

- **Coordination**: integrating the activities and contributions of different parts of the enterprise. *Measured or indicated by*: supportive relationships between interdependent units; the extent of interruptions of flow of activities. May also include stock levels, deliveries, etc.

- **Adaptation**: ability to respond to a changing environment, capacity to innovate and solve problems. *Measured or indicated by*: changes in market share and rate of development of successful new products. May also include creative solutions to problems or the evolution of improved practices.

- **Social systems and personal expectations**: maintenance of social systems and terms and conditions of employment in order enlist people's commitment. *Measured or indicated by*: appraisal reports, attitude surveys, absence rates, staff turnover, etc.

Politics

As with leadership so with organizational change. These things do not happen in some kind of vacuum. The politics of organizations, dealt with in Chapter 4 in this book, are concerned with the resources, processes and forms within the organization. It is the interaction between these and managers which gives rise to the politics within organizations. Politics may well take the form of control of budget or careers, or of information, or even, at a more pragmatic level, of the reward system based in the appraisal itself. Occasionally the forms may be symbolic.

Coupled to this we also have the process of politics which is concerned with a manager's capacity to negotiate with others and to influence them. This plainly includes the mobilization of support by using emotion, ritual and ceremony in order to bring about what for the manager is a successful conclusion. All this is enhanced by the use of the resources within the organization. Apart from the simple resources like the formal authority which a manager may have there are aspects like the actual control of the resources and information, the agenda and perhaps most important of all, access to key people within the organization.

The gatekeepers in these terms may well be very powerful people in political terms. Once we begin to recognize that the politics of the organization are crucial when we are trying to bring about any kind of change within it then we are making headway in determining how the organization can move towards the new state.

There are misconceptions about managing change which often arise from the notion of resistance. The majority of implications of this word are that people deliberately try to disrupt and damage. There is, of course, a sense in which this is true but the whole definition of resistance has to include anything which keeps the company, department or team from moving ahead and changing. This would include, for example, the idea of detachment, a state in which people view the change as not affecting them and which therefore allows them to criticize without necessarily contributing.

It has been argued that nothing makes us less free and flexible than the authority of the past. In many ways, both people and organizations become imprisoned by their achievements and traditions: nothing makes them fail like past success. The implication of this is that progress can only be made if people are prepared to face reality. What is then required is the development of confidence and optimism to tackle that reality.

In some way there has to be a dissatisfaction with the current status. Without this, there is no felt need for change. Secondly, there needs to be a shared vision. Almost inevitably, people will not move as a group until they agree on where they wish to go. Thirdly, they need to understand what the first practical steps are. The fourth, and probably most important variable, is the cost of changing. Even this can be broken down into two different types of cost, that is, economic and psychological.

Readiness to change

What we know about people's readiness to change is that there are two quite distinct forces which act on people. Firstly, there are the forces within the individual him or herself. These forces include his or her knowledge and skills base, the person's own self-awareness and perhaps even their tolerance for ambiguity. There is even evidence that their motivational levels and most importantly their self-esteem, play important parts in their readiness for change. Secondly, there are forces within the system, which include the culture and climate of the organization and the perceived consequences of success or failure within the organization. The combination of these factors gives a description of something which may be called the degree of felt security.

Carnall (1990) argues that if the degree of felt security is either high or low then the response to change will very much be that of rejection, suppression or distortion. People will procrastinate and delay bringing in the change. And in a sense this is understandable: If I feel secure in my current work and situation then what need is there for me to change? On the other hand, if my degree of felt security is very low then anything you do to disturb even that low state of security will be seen to be highly threatening. What Carnall argues is that only in the middle ranges of this degree of felt security is the response to change likely to be very positive. In this case, the positive response will comprise behaviour such as listening, clarifying, exploring alternatives and final the evaluation and incorporation of new data into the way people perceive what is going on.

Within the context of change, we can learn a great deal from studies conducted in psychology. We know that the more people have to say about the form and direction which the change has to take, and the more they are involved with the decision-making process, then the more likely they are to be committed to that process. But there are other issues. First, the goal itself must be specific; the more specific the better. People are unlikely to work for things such as justice but they may well work to erect a new building for the community. Secondly, these goals should be realizable; in other words, whilst there may not be a 100 per cent chance of success, there should exist the possibility of achieving success. Finally, the notion of immediacy is vital; people need to feel they can do something effective immediately.

Stress

Since the early work of Yerkes and Dodson in 1907 and their work with anxiety and performance, we have come to know a great deal more about stress and the way it affects people within organizations. What we do know now is that there is a large number of sources of stress which affect different people differentially. And, moreover, these hold across many distinct populations and indeed across cultures. Within the work situation we know that both change and role strain affect people's performance in a negative direction. In non-work terms, the three highest factors creating stress for people are death and divorce and house movement. Interestingly, moving house is third only in England and Wales; in the rest of the world it goes down to to seventh place.

The argument on stress is very simple and straightforward. The relationship between stress and performance is a curvilinear one (see Figure 8.3). As has been said, this relationship holds across cultures and different individuals. We know, too, that change leads to stress. There are other things illustrated by the figure: first, the movement is left to right; that is, for increasing levels of stress we get firstly increasing, then level, then decreasing levels of performance. Clearly, the implication of this is that we should avoid going too far to the right. A further implication of this is that in order to reduce ambiguity within the work situation communication becomes important. Of course, one might add that the real problem is that we do not know where particular individuals are on the curve itself.

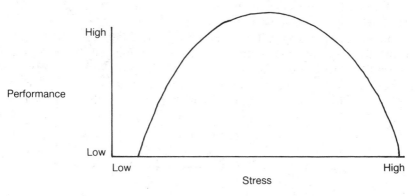

Figure 8.3 Stress and performance (Source: Yerkes and Dodson 1907)

Individual performance

Ket de Vries and Miller (1984) suggested a coping strategy for people within organizations. Their approach works equally well within the change situation. We know that any change creates uncertainty, anxiety and stress. Moreover, changes which impact on people at work will also affect their self-esteem. One aspect of self-esteem of course is that of performance: if people have a low felt self-esteem then performance degenerates. The relationship is not as simple as this would imply, but we do know that the direction of performance and self-esteem are highly correlated. After Ket de Vries and Miller, Carnall (1990) argues that there are the following five major stages which are concerned with performance, self-esteem and people's reaction to change (see also Figure 8.4).

Stage 1: is that of denial – a self-explanatory term. It leads to such reactions as 'we have always done things this way', etc. When people are faced with the possibility of change they will often place a high value on their present circumstance, even when that situation is one about which they have complained bitterly previously.

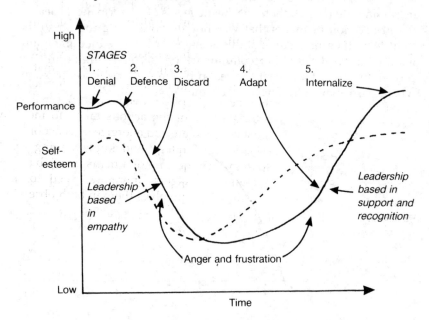

Figure 8.4 The transition curve and empathy (Source: Carnall 1990)

Stage 2: is that of defence. As people appreciate that change is going to occur and indeed has begun to occur they themselves become depressed and frustrated with their inability to cope with this change. Their frustration is often characterized by defensive behaviour. (It has always struck the authors as strange that people who use typewriter keyboards insist on maintaining the 'qwerty' format even though we know it is one of the least efficient keyboards for use with word-processing facilities on a computer. Yet to try and bring about change even at this simple level would be a major undertaking. People will defend the keyboard with vigour.)

Stage 3: is the stage where old habits are discarded. The new behaviours begin to seem to have value. Optimism begins to occur. People often start talking openly and constructively about new systems at this stage. On some occasions the phraseology may be highly pragmatic but it is the first sign that people are beginning to get committed to the change itself. It is a process which begins with perceptive recognition of what is going on around them.

Stage 4: is that of adaptation. Here the process of adaptation occurs, in which individuals test the new situation in detail for the first time. This does not simply involve a change of behaviour on the individual's part, but may often involve the same individual's trying out and technically altering and modifying the new systems which may be being imposed in the change.

Stage 5: is that of internalization. Systems, processes and organizations have now been changed and adapted. New relations have been tried and modified. All of this is incorporated into the new work situation. The organization is set to move to the next stage or the next change itself. Plainly what is vital is that people recognize that they have been effective in this change. This is a crucial aspect to any form of organizational change.

Management style

Part of the problem with organizational change so far as performance is concerned is that there is an anger and frustration in both the second and fourth stages in the model. At the second stage the anger and frustration is based on a future orientation. People at this stage are concerned about what the future will bring. There are new jobs to learn; there are old ways of doing and thinking to discard; there are systems that may not work first time: progress is inevitably slower than expected. By and large, people tend to work longer hours and more days and management becomes much more directive. That same anger and frustration occurs during the third and fourth stages. Here, whilst the issues are based on too short a time horizon, they are almost the same as those seen at the second stage.

As a result, there are implications for management style, and we have seen from the chapter on leadership that there are many different forms of leadership behaviour. In dealing with change, specifically in the second and fourth stages, the forms of leadership which are required are those of empathy (Stage 2) and support and recognition (Stage 4). Inevitably, at the early stages, the manager needs to reinforce the need for change and to reinforce the actions arising from that change. If this does not occur, what we find happening within the group of people involved is that they resist the change itself. It is no good simply being committed internally to the need for change; managers need continually to reinforce why the change should occur, i.e. the need has to be clarified explicitly. That should happen at all levels within the organization.

In the later stages, as described in the model, the notion of support and recognition becomes crucial. As people take on new behaviours they need to be told that these behaviours are appropriate. Moreover, they need to be reassured that the time it takes them to take on these new behaviours is not untoward. For many of us, taking on new ways of working, new machinery, new technologies, takes time. Nor is this time dimension one which is solely aimed at the old: age does not appear to have a major effect in this area. As a gross generalization, we may say that young people are better able by and large to pick up new systems. The rationale here is simply that they have not grown so accustomed to the old methods of working and thinking. Yet there are still major exceptions in this age range which lead us towards thinking that it is difficult to make such generalizations.

Coping with the change framework

In many ways the best framework to cope with change is concerned with the individual and the analysis of their own situation, both in terms of the individual and the situation itself.

We need to be able to answer questions: about ourselves, we need to know whether we would choose whatever is going to occur and we need to be able to accept it; we also need to look at what is the worst and best that can occur. Indeed, it can be quite helpful to look back at our past organizational experiences to discover whether we have been through similar exercises in the past.

There are other questions to do with taking the initiative and in terms of determining what the individual actually wants from what is going on. All of us, too, will have an idea about our capacity to deal with stress and avoid conflict. We need also to be able to hold off blaming ourselves for negative things which occur; especially those which are outside our own control. We also need to be able to analyse the situation itself. We thus need to be able to describe the changes and to be able to describe the behaviours which will be expected of us. It helps, too, if individuals within the organization can try out the new situation in advance.

We can also determine whether the organization is likely to be ready for change. There are a series of aspects which need to be addressed. The first of these is whether the company itself has some kind of track record of change, and if so, what form that takes. It is plainly inordinately helpful if that track record has been successful in the past. Secondly, we need to note what those who are involved in the change, expect from it. The realism of those expectations is plainly crucial. Thirdly, we need to be concerned with the ownership of the idea for change.

This leads us into a debate about the politics of change once more, for ownership must go beyond the single individual. The need for change needs to be owned by all those people who are involved in it if that change is to be successful. Of course, without top management support it is unlikely that the change itself can occur. Yet there are examples where people have actually put organizational change into the middle strata of an organization with some degree of success; but such occasions are rare. Finally, we have to acknowledge that the change itself must be acceptable in terms of the current organizational climate.

There will be times when major change is not needed but rather a change that requires simple fine tuning, that is making something that already works well, work better. Continuous process of this kind can avert the need for major changes. It leads us to what Greiner (1972) called 'habit structures'. Sometimes such structures inhibit adaptation to change. By and large, habit structures are the formal structure and operating mechanism of the organization. They include such things as the following:

- Reward systems.
- Control systems, e.g. plan, budgets.
- Communication systems, e.g. committees.
- Development systems, e.g. selection, training, manpower selection.
- Physical systems, e.g. location, assembly lines, offices, etc.

Problems often arise because of contradictions between the structure and operating mechanisms. For example, it may well be that there are requirements for team work in a matrix system that are counter to the individually based remuneration system. The lesson in many ways is that these systems tend to be run by highly competent and powerful professionals. As a result, those who are concerned with developing organizations and bringing about change within them, need to be familiar with the systems and work closely with such professionals.

When we examine the implementation of change (as opposed to the organization's readiness for change) there is a further series of statements which need to be clarified. For instance, we need to ensure that new practices and procedures are integrated into the organization. We also need to ensure that plans are clarified at all levels, at all times. If necessary, training and support should be worked out well in advance and should be undertaken in such a way as to feed into the organizational change itself. Ownership and commitment have been mentioned many times; it is vital that these are maintained during the implementation stages.

But of all things, the most important is to provide feedback to the individuals undertaking the work itself. Without useful feedback the change process may well still be broadly effective but will certainly take a longer period of time to accomplish. Feedback is one particular aspect of managerial behaviour that is possibly least well done, especially during a change implementation.

Change and discontinuities

Greiner's work looks at the development of an organization as it grows from its early entrepreneurial stages. At the full growth stage of his model, different states for the organization emerge, and at this point, it will be determined whether the organization goes into decline, or stability, or some new form. Perhaps at this stage non-equilibrium theory may be useful in exploring organizational dynamics. The essence of this theory lies in the emergence of a world-view in which instability and disorder are essential elements in the developments of new forms of organizational complexity.

There is no doubt that effective organizations are those which introduce change quickly. They are also characterized as those organizations in which both employees and managers learn about the business as this process proceeds. It is also most helpful if the ways in which change is introduced encourage learning. If this is not the case, then what may happen is that negative attitudes towards change will be encouraged and this will make the process that much more difficult to instigate in future.

The process begins with internal and external pressures for change. These pressures may well include not only declining performance but also declining self-esteem in the work force. What then occurs, hopefully, is the effective management of transitions. This implies that the organization, in the shape of its work force, can deal effectively with changing organizational cultures and with organizational politics. This process involves creative risk-taking and learning, and so far as the people within the organization are concerned, it also involves the rebuilding of self-esteem and deriving new levels of performance and new approaches to behavioural problems.

What is hoped to come out of all this is the achievements not just of organizational change in this instance but also the creation of a pattern for such changes for the future. The whole learning process should be one in which people feel comfortable. They should need to want to learn and by so doing ensure that future changes can be undertaken in an effective way.

Two broad approaches to changing the organization can be identified. The first is through modifying the formal structure, procedures and systems; the second is by influencing more directly the way in which people within the enterprise act and interact. Both approaches are often necessary, and indeed are often complementary. Perhaps what is most important is that people should be able to identify with the objectives of their enterprise and act and interact constructively and efficiently to achieve these. Where this is the case, almost any structure or set of systems can be made to work. However, performance would be particularly enhanced if the structure and systems either positively promote (or do not necessarily militate against) such action.

Even the very nature of managerial work is now undergoing quite radical change. In terms of the politics which are therefore involved, we find today that there are more channels for taking action and exerting influence. In part, this is because relationships of influence are shifting from the vertical to the horizontal. The distinction between managers and those they manage is now decreasing. Perhaps even more importantly, external relationships are increasingly significant sources of internal power and influence. Managers, therefore, need to master change in the critical arenas of power and motivation in order to manage effectively.

As a first step, it is worth identifying the natural forces which are available for change. The concern has to be with those within the organization who are able to effect change. The second stage is the creation of a critical mass through the linking of forces for change to key organizational issues. Quite often, a rationale is required as to why a small group of people should come together in a task force. Following this sort of format, the group itself will not be a committee which will give responses and tell people precisely what they have to do, etc.; on the contrary, it is there to develop thoughts, to stimulate and provide data, and perhaps even produce recommendations. It will act as a resource both to the manager trying to input the change, as well as to the rest of the organization.

Indeed, part of the task force's remit might be to ask for a process plan from the managers. Such a plan would include the capacity to involve colleagues. Often, it can be a useful tactic to create specially designed conferences and workshops, certainly with at least two aims in mind: firstly, to provide understanding and support for the work which has thus far been done; and secondly, to build a sense of commitment and direction to the philosophy which the change implies.

Nor, in undertaking all this, should follow-up be lost sight of. In essence, what you do not want to occur is for the change initiative to begin to lose its impetus, especially where loss of that impetus leads to the negation of the change effort. If that were to happen, then the organization would be worse off than when it started down the track of organizational change. Indeed, in these circumstances, people are likely to suggest that they had tried it but that it didn't work. This reduces the capacity to attempt change next time round.

It has often been argued that change is a long-term and continual process and its measurement is therefore difficult. Substantial organizational change requires at least the following six elements to come together:

1. Pressure from top management for *recognition* of the need for change. This may arise either from environmental circumstances such as lower sales or shareholder discontent and so on or through internal events such as lower productivity, higher costs or inter-departmental conflicts.

2. It may involve *intervention* from a third party at or near the top. Such a person should be able to bring some perspective and help top management to acknowledge their own problems.

3. It is necessary for *diagnosis* and recognition of problem areas involving line managers at various levels.

4. It is necessary to find *creative solutions* as well as commitment to the courses of action which are outlined.

5. There is a need for *experimentation* to establish the viability of the change at various levels by small activities before large-scale changes are introduced. (Although this may not always be the case. Indeed, there are arguments to suggest that sometimes a revolutionary mode of change would be most effective.)

6. *Reinforcement* from positive results is important to the viability of the total change and for subsequent actions. It will lead to an acceptance of new practices as result of the shared effort and positive rewards which have been gained from that effort.

If we follow the Lewin (1947) terminology it is important to go through the process of unfreezing, establishing some model or *modus operandi*, making changes, refreezing and, most importantly, reinforcing the change.

References

Beckhard, R. (1969), *Organisational Developments: Strategies and models* (Reading, Mass.: Adison-Wesley).

Carnall, C.A. (1990), *Managing Change in Organisations* (London: Prentice Hall).

Collins, D., Ross, R.A. and Timothy, L. (1989), 'Who wants participative management? The managerial perspective', *Group and Organisation Studies*, vol. 14, no. 4, pp. 422–45.

Cowling, A. (1989), 'Personnel's strategic role in culture change', *Personnel Management*, vol. 21, no. 12, pp. 10–11.

de Vries, K. and Miller, D. (1984), *The Neurotic Organization* (New York: Jossey-Bass).

Greiner, L.E. (1972), 'Evolution and revolution as organizations grow', *Harvard Business Review*, July/August, pp. 37–46.

Kakabadse, A. (1991), *Wealth Creators* (London: Kogan Page).

Lewin, K. (1947), 'Frontiers in group dynamics: concept, method and reality in social science: social equilibria and social change', *Human Relations*, vol. 1, pp. 5–47.

Moreno, J.L. (1953) *Who Shall Survive* (New York: Beacon House).

Roethlisberger, F.J. (1947), 'Foreman: master and victim of double talk', in G.F.F. Lombard (ed.), *The Elusive Phenomena* (Boston: Harvard Business School, 1977).

Sheane, D. (1978), 'Organisation development in action', *Journal of European Industrial Training*, vol. 2, no. 7, pp. 21–3.

Simmons, J. (1989), 'Starting self managing teams', *Journal for Quality and Participation*, December, pp. 26–31.

Uhlfelder, H.F. and Werner, T.J. (1989), 'To design or not to design', *Journal for Quality and Participation*, December, pp. 38–42.

Yerkes, R.M. and Dodson R. (1907), 'Anxiety drive and performance', in R.M. Yerkes, 'Psychological examining in the US army', *Memoirs of the National Academy and Sciences*, 1921, vol. 15, pp. 819–37.

9

International dimensions

Within the nature of the human animal there seems to be a deep desire to explore distant shores, to find new cultures and to have new experiences. 'Man the Scientist' as George Kelly described him, forever seeks to discover new ways of understanding, and new approaches to life, perhaps motivated by the belief that life can always be improved. From the Vikings to the merchant adventurers, from the voyages of Jason and the Argonauts to the search for the North-West Passage and the exploration of the moon, people have sought romance, profit, wealth, personal advancement and scientific knowledge from foreign lands.

Political and economic linkages have developed over the last hundred years to the point where local disorder or economic turbulence has repercussions world-wide through stock markets, political alliances and international institutions. The move towards European political as well as economic union, the break-up of the Soviet empire, the acceptance that there are global environmental issues, the world-wide reaction to events such as the invasion of Kuwait are all signs of a 'shrinking globe': of our interdependence as people and nations.

As global trends strengthen, then simultaneously there is more assertion of regional identity. In the European Community, South American countries, even in the war-torn Middle East there are signs of common regional ties which transcend national status. The Pacific Rim countries share many common values and in some cases a common history. It would seem likely that regionalism will strengthen as economic blocks become more powerful than countries. There are consequences for all organizations and for labour markets as these trends become more pronounced.

In the modern economic world international sourcing, manufacturing and marketing, the growth of trading blocks, rapid world-wide communications and international competitive pressures have now brought international dimensions into the life of the most traditional national corporation. There is now no real distinction between what is national and what is international. International sourcing and manufacturing have spread where assembly operations can be undertaken in low-cost countries, and where there is a need to meet particular regional market requirements.

New technologies make possible integrated manufacturing and design processes, so that products can be customized and competitive advantages can be found by regional manufacturing which leverages foreign sales. Strong brand names are now marketed globally assisted by rapid communications. Telecommunications networks provide electronic mail, fax and international conferring facilities as well as offer the computing and data transmission capacity for international service and manufacturing operations.

Global corporations are now being formed which have wider spheres of influence than the geographic locations where they do business. Such businesses will require a new 'mind set' among their executives, which Daniels and Frost (1991) have defined as a need to move from what executives perceive in the typical multinational and international companies as geographic boundaries. The business and cognitive style of these global corporations is characterized by a long-term view not bounded by regional or national structures. In global corporations there are networks of trust, economies of scale, strong customer-based values and multiple centres of competence. Even if this vision of the global corporation is only slowly being brought into existence, it does show the way business strategy is heading.

There are four main organizational issues precipitated by increasing internationalism. Cultural differences are significant for managing multinational groups, for decision-making and because of the sensitivities surrounding the religious and cultural differences between customers, suppliers and employees. Secondly, there is evidence of different management philosophies emanating from major trading nations such as Japan and the United States which affect how organizations are run. Thirdly, if these philosophies are pervasive, thereby increasing internationalism, this raises the question of whether there is a convergence occurring between values and beliefs around the world, or whether an underlying diversity persists. Finally, organization structures and careers are changing to accommodate geographical dispersion and because trading blocks such as the European Community have a powerful impact on organization design and on career paths.

Cultural differences

Culture as a topic is central to the study of behaviour in society. Social anthropologists study societies' cultures through ethnographic research in order to show how social systems are manifested. Culture is found in what Lévy-Bruhl described as 'collective representations': the beliefs and values which are the unquestioned basic assumptions upon which rational arguments in that society are founded. That we live in a world of multiple realities should by now be apparent to the reader. From multiple realities come multiple rationalities to explain the perceptions of reality we hold. These explanations are cultural in origin.

The cultural objects in a society are not only the consumer goods, artefacts and personal documents, but also the symbols, myths and legends which are the methods used to explain social reality. Thus 'magic' in one society may be based on religious belief; that is, a supernatural explanation of events may be inherent in the belief system as in Christianity, or these events may be interpreted as signs of some other supernatural power as when the Azande tribe in the Sudan use oracles to predict the success of a journey or an alliance (Evans-Pritchard 1976).

The study of culture should not be confined to research into exotic tribes. Our own reliance on 'rational' processes of decision-making in Western society should not mask the roles played by economists, statisticians and experts of all kinds who perform a similar function to the witch-doctors of the Azande tribe. Economists and corporate planners help to confirm, to advise and to predict about future events even in the knowledge that their predictions may be totally upset in a turbulent world, where a Falklands war, a stock market crash, or a crisis in the Persian Gulf can make all previous trends of prices, interest rates and the like irrelevant to the future. Our 'natural attitude' leads us to believe rational arguments, even when the evidence is missing. The belief in rationality is culturally derived rather than an unquestionable fact of existence.

In practice, many of our most important decisions, such as who to marry, what kind of relationships to have with our parents and children, even our choice of career and interests have not emerged from any sort of rational weighing up means and ends, but are a mixture of emotion and feelings, chance and opportunity. The Azande do not give to the natural world and to the supernatural the meanings which educated Europeans give:

> There is no elaborate and consistent representation of witchcraft that will account in detail for its workings, nor of nature which expounds its conformity to sequences and functional interrelations. The Zande actualizes these beliefs rather than intellectualizes them, and their tenets are expressed in socially controlled behaviour rather than in doctrines. (Evans-Pritchard 1976, pp. 31, 32)

Western attempts to explain all activity in terms of rational and scientific thought would come as just such a shock to the Azande, as their common belief in witchcraft does to Westerners. The utility of the concept of 'culture' is that societies, when examined as anthropologically strange (whether sophisticated or not), reveal the cultural mechanisms by which the underlying belief systems and values are sustained.

Lévi-Strauss has argued that the way we order our environment is to segment space and time, and to try to place the many separate things we see and feel into classes, into an underlying structure. The patterns we use are our cultural interpretations of physical or psychological phenomena, which we come to take for granted. In his work, from *Tristes tropiques* (1955) and *La Pensée sauvage* (1962) to his three volumes on myths, Lévi-Strauss was searching for human universals, using culture as evidence.

By contrast, social anthropologist from the functionalist tradition exemplified by Bronislaw Malinowski have typically used contrasting societies, seeking to describe how the customs, mores and norms of society perform a function for its survival. For example, marriage in most societies serves the function of perpetuating the species within a set of socially agreed norms or rules, whilst providing a system of rights and obligations towards children. However, there are differences in what the marriage contract means, through the varying rights and obligations of the parties towards the spouse and children, and over the goods and wealth of the household. Marriage also links people into an extended family network, through which socially determined relationships arise. Comparisons reveal both the underlying commonalities of marriage, therefore, and also show distinctions: for example, the number of wives, the rights of the in-laws and the differing interpretations of the incest taboo.

The study of national cultures can therefore be from two directions. It can seek to explain behaviour as one manifestation of the underlying structures which are common, because people all over the world face the same problems and have the same needs. Ultimately, this approach becomes a philosophical search for the nature of meaning and knowledge. The other direction is less concerned with epistemological questions, rather it seeks to look at how society is sustained, and tries to control for cultural variables when explaining behaviour.

The most significant organizational research into national cultures is Hofstede's survey of sixty-four national IBM subsidiaries (Hofstede 1984). He defines culture – following Lévy-Bruhl – as 'the collective programming of the mind'. He uses 'values' as conditioning the main underlying societal norms which are the basis of culture. 'Values' he defines as 'a broad tendency to prefer certain states of affairs over others'. He measures culture on four dimensions: power distance, uncertainty avoidance, individualism and masculinity.

Power distance

Inequality is a basic issue in all societies. Hofstede theorizes that bosses try to increase the power distance between themselves and their subordinates, whilst subordinates try to decrease the power distance. He attempts to discover the power distance according to the superior's style of decision-making, colleagues fear to disagree with superiors and the type of decision-making subordinates prefer in their boss. From these answers, he constructs a 'power distance index'.

Lower education, lower status occupations tend to produce high-PDI values, and higher education high-status occupations, low-PDI values. The high-PDI societies use more coercive and referent power

Table 9.1 Managerial behaviour in low- and high-PDI countries

Low PDI	High PDI
Managers make decisions after consultation	Managers make decisions autocratically and paternalistically
Close supervision is negatively evaluated	Close supervision is positively evaluated
Managers see themselves as practical and admit the need for support	Managers see themselves as benevolent decision-makers

whereas low-PDI societies use more legitimate, reward and expert power (see Chapter 4). Managerial behaviour can be distinguished between low- and high-PDI countries shown in Table 9.1.

A number of conclusions come from the power distance indicator: there are different expectations of bosses in different countries; it is more difficult to introduce participation in countries where there is high PDI, than in countries such as Sweden and Norway, where PDI is low. From these conclusions, Hofstede claims that Theory X and Theory Y approaches are cultural phenomena.

Uncertainty avoidance

Different societies adapt to the natural uncertainties in life in different ways. Indicators of uncertainty avoidance are: rule orientation, employment stability and stress.

People in high-uncertainty avoidance indicator countries (UAI) have lower ambition, prefer larger organizations, tend to avoid competition, resist change and dislike working for foreigners as managers. Hofstede could find no occupational or sexual difference in people according to their uncertainty avoidance index.

Individualism (IDV)

This is judged by Hofstede according to the importance attached to personal life and the importance of being trained by the company. In this way, it is assumed there is an individualistic rather than a collectivist approach. A relationship is shown between individualism and power distance whereby high individualism is related to small power distance and vice versa.

Hofstede argues that in stable low-IDV societies, people will transfer part of their extended family or class allegiance to the organization where they work. This helps to explain the approach found in Japanese organizations. There are implications for multi-national organizations, since management style and issues of personal life and training and development policies are related.

Masculinity

People are socialized into sexual roles, and the values associated with

International dimensions

Table 9.2 Sex differences in work goals

More important for men	More important for women
Advancement	Friendly atmosphere
Earnings	Position security
Training	The manager
Modernity	Cooperation in the department

Table 9.3 Calculation of index for certain countries

	PDI	UAI	Indiv.	Masc.
Japan	54	92	46	95
France	68	86	71	43
Germany (W)	35	65	67	66
USA	40	46	91	62
UK	35	35	89	68
Italy	50	75	76	70

Table 9.4 Power distance and uncertainty avoidance

Small power distance, weak uncertainty avoidance	Large power distance, weak uncertainty avoidance
Anglo-Scandinavian	SE Asia
Market model of organizations	Personnel bureaucracy, 'family' type organizations
Small power distance, strong uncertainty avoidance	Large power distance, strong uncertainty avoidance
German-speaking countries	Latin, Mediterranean, Islamic, Japan
Work-flow bureaucracy, 'well oiled' machine	Full bureaucracy, pyramid

these roles predominate in particular societies, for example, male assertiveness, competitiveness and the nature of male/female relationships. Hofstede suggests there are sex differences in work goals (see Table 9.2). It is argued that the humanization of work is associated with femininity, whereas the more competitive and technical aspects of work life are associated with masculinity.

Taking the scores from these four dimensions (power distance,

215

uncertainty avoidance, individualism, masculinity), Table 9.3 shows a selection of countries, where the index was calculated. The method adopted for all the countries was to take a stratified sample of seven occupations at two points in time when questionnaires were completed. With the two measures, power distance and uncertainty avoidance, Hofstede shows there are clusters (see Table 9.4).

Hofstede's work deals in generalizations. There may indeed be national characteristics, but it is likely that there are major variations within societies. For example, Theory X and Theory Y approaches are organization and individual manager specific rather than societally dominant. The notion that all managers have the same vision of power distance or uncertainty avoidance in the United States or United Kingdom, for example, is absurd. The diversity at the organization level means we must only use this research with caution, and not seek to perpetuate stereotypes. There is nevertheless still a benefit in understanding what values underlie each culture, and in acknowledging the impact of culture on work organizations.

This caution over Hofstede's cultural pattern theory is also found in studies on industrial democracy, industrial relations and decision-making (IDE 1981a, 1981b; Heller *et al.* 1988). Heller *et al.*, in their study of decisions in organizations which compared UK, Dutch and Yugoslav organizations show there is no national cultural trend but that the variations such as organization size and organizational culture were more significant. However, differences in formal structure and legal rules about employee participation in decision-making were used by these researchers to explain the differences found in participation in decision-making where British companies consistently had the lowest level of participation and Yugoslav companies the highest level. This finding has implications for the way power and influence is exercised in different countries.

Protagonists of the national cultures argument would probably suggest here that explaining national differences through legal rules rather than cultural influence is a chicken and egg argument – since such an explanation begs the question of why there are different rules and laws in different countries. Cultural influences will always be difficult to discern. Perhaps it is only where extreme differences are found, for example between Japanese and Western organizations, that the significance of national culture appears. As we saw in our previous chapters, organizational contingencies are partial determinants of action, but the importance of cultural pattern theories is that they do help to show the limitations to explanations purely at the organizational level of analysis.

Management philosophies and organization structures

Contingency theorists and open systems proponents have always taken the environment into account, especially perceived uncertainty and the impact of the product and labour markets in which they trade (Duncan 1972; Child 1972).

Comparative studies of different countries frequently focus on the institutional level of analysis. Laws, regulations, state institutions and the process by which economies are regulated are seen as the main determinants of differences between countries. These structural aspects influence which policies, such as recruitment, education, development and career systems, are adopted.

This can be illustrated by the variations in control systems used by different forms of ownership in France, Germany and the United Kingdom. In Germany there are single- and two-tier systems available. In the two-tier there is a supervisory board in control of a management board whose membership is not shared. In the United Kingdom the directors, whether executive or not, sit on the same board; this is also the case with smaller private limited companies in Germany which have the single-tier approach (Lane 1989). German supervisory boards include bankers and directors of suppliers and customers, whilst in France the Conseil d'Administration of the large limited companies is very much the creature of the Président Directeur-Général (who equates to the British Chairman and MD), who has considerable centralized power, being often the only management representative. Family control is also still important in France, even in some of the larger companies, and the hierarchical nature of work relations and the emphasis on functional separation may be greater in French companies than in the United Kingdom (Barsoux and Lawrence 1990).

Differences in industrial relations systems also have a major impact on organizations. For example, the British system is usually described as a voluntary approach. Issues such as trade union recognition and collective agreements are not legally enforceable. There is no system of positive rights; the laws introduced since 1979 have only reduced trade union immunity from liabilities they would suffer under the common law. In Germany, the system of codetermination, whereby workers sit on the supervisory boards and/or on a works council means there is formal participation in major business decisions. The rights and duties of trade unions in Germany, which are industry

217

rather than craft- or occupation-based, are matched by employer obligations in a clear-cut framework which is legally binding on both parties.

The variations in approach to education and training between countries were well documented in the NEDO report (1987) which compared the education and development of British, French, German, Japanese and American managers. Each country has its own system, for example the Japanese preference for the 'slow burn' approach, with promotion and training planned over long periods mostly organized 'on the job', contrasts with the US emphasis on MBA degrees, and the French Grandes Écoles system.

In the institutional approach, we may see the realization of cultural norms through education and training systems and traditions, and through the structuring of the business enterprise as a part of the social and economic system of the country:

> The organisation of a business enterprise and the management and working practices which are a part of it have been created in a complex process of interaction between different institutional structures which mutually reinforce each other. (Lane 1989, p. 292)

The potency of cultural norms seems to depend on how strong are the beliefs and values held by people of influence in a society, and how widespread these beliefs are. Among the many commentators on Japanese economic performance there may be some disagreements on the causes of their success, but there is a consensus about the fundamental values and norms in Japanese society (De Bettingies 1973; Smith 1984): These include the following:

- The strong sense of group or community.
- The strong sense of obligation to parents, to supervisors.
- A willingness to work hard.
- Behaviour which is compulsive, but with strong underlying emotions.

William Ouchi's 'Theory Z' notion was that success comes from a mixture of US and Japanese approaches: a holistic concern for people; long-term employment; non-specialized career paths; a 'clan' approach to participation; decision-making based on shared values; and high trust which allows accountability in the manager's hands because these are well understood common objectives (Ouchi 1981).

It can be argued that Japanese management practices are not

culturally derived, but are part of a deliberate labour market policy similar to those followed by all oligopolistic organizations (Loveridge and Mok 1979; Pascale 1978; Child and Tayeb 1983). A sensitive and thoughtful analysis is provided by Tayeb, who argues from a basis of research into differences and similarities between Indian and British organizations that a multiperspective theory is needed which accounts for the influences of culture, technology, institutional and socio-economic pressures on organizations in order to discover the different causes, and to control for cultural variables (Tayeb 1988).

Since such a 'meta theory' would come close to being a theory to explain all other theories about organizations, this hope may remain unfulfilled.

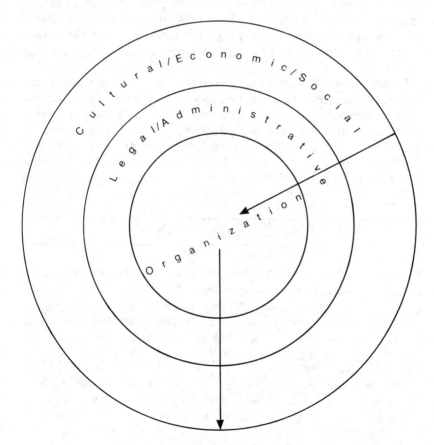

Figure 9.1 The impact of cultural, economic, social and legal forces on organizations

Instead, the intentional nature of organizations should be stressed. Organizations are not just acted upon, they act through their members. In this way economic, social and cultural conditions are changed. The impact of cultural and economic forces on organizations is re-assessed or mitigated by the legal and administrative procedures of the State. Figure 9.1 shows the idea: each outer layer permeates the next layer in a series of concentric circles.

Thus the arrows in the diagram are flows of influence each way. The strength of the influence depends on the power source. Very strong cultural norms as in Japan, are likely to permeate most organizations in that society. By contrast, British society has evolved through a long process with successive migrations producing Celtic, Roman, Norman, American and Commonwealth influences. Cultural and social norms are diffuse, have varying effects on different classes and are bound around notions of individualism and democracy which are in constant tension, with different interest groups seeking power.

Paradoxically, British reliance on informal agreements, conventions and traditions rather than a written constitution, laws and procedures allows flexibility, and encourages investment because there is stability as well as adaptability. There is a price to be paid for this fluid economic and social state. Opposition to strong central control from a politically unified European Community is inevitable. As Sir Winston Churchill commented, the United Kingdom finds itself caught symbolically as well as literally between mainland Europe and the open sea.

The convergence thesis

We began this chapter by describing the trends towards global trading and increasing internationalism. The convergence thesis is a hypothesis which suggests that as organizations face similar problems and opportunities they adopt similar technical solutions, and also common organization strategies and structures. Gradually, the similarities between organizations will be more significant than the differences (Kerr *et al.* 1960). A common range of economic and social conditions were thought to be the consequences of industrialization, common conditions which were driven together by rapid changes in technology and world-wide scientific research.

'Multinationals' or 'international' companies do contribute to the convergence process. Multinationals incorporate staff from the host countries with management cadres from different nationalities, so the common experiences and common socialization processes facilitate the transmission of ideas, and inculcate common values.

Even without international trade, common procedures and techniques have a similar effect. For example, the Hay system of job evaluation can be found in precisely the same form, whether in Hong Kong, Los Angeles, London, Paris, New Delhi or any other major city. This gives the people working within those organizations a common language for describing jobs and responsibilities. The same developments have occurred in other areas of management techniques. The way human resource management has developed internationally bears witness to the validity of the convergence thesis (Brewster and Tyson 1991).

Organizational cultures can be so powerful they outweigh national cultures as determinants of behaviour. Ideas from powerful entrepreneurs travel the globe, and organizational cultures become so strong that an IBM sales representative can be recognized in Berlin or New York (Deal and Kennedy 1982). A Marks & Spencer shop or a McDonald's restaurant has an identity so strong it converts the local territory to become a social space which is independent from its geographic location.

The march of advanced industrial society into the 'developing' world, Eastern Europe's embrace of capitalist values and the Soviet desire for Western economic philosophy can be seen as a collapse of a corrupt and inefficient system, but these trends also offer the frightening prospect of no alternative. The market place is dominant in all aspects of life: in art, in sport, even in education and health. Herbert Marcuse described these conditions where only one way of thinking is perceived as normal, where the rationality of that thinking makes all alternatives unthinkable, as 'one dimensional'. He adapts Karl Marx's ideas on alienation to suggest how technological forces for convergence contain a sinister prospect for mankind:

> When this point is reached, domination in the guise of affluence and liberty extends to all spheres of private and public existence, integrates all authentic opposition, absorbs all alternatives.
> Technological rationality reveals its political character as it becomes the great vehicle for better domination, creating a truly totalitarian universe in which society and nature, mind and body are kept in a state of permanent mobilization for the defence of this universe. (Marcuse 1968, p. 31)

Convergence implies less diversity. Our current experience in the European Community is of more diversity, but the economic rationale behind the Community is improved efficiency which can only come if the number of manufacturers is reduced. For example, there is already over-production in cars as well as in agriculture.

Coping with the complexities of a world-wide business or a Europe-wide business raises questions about strategy and structure. There are many new relationships now within the European Community; this has encouraged mergers, takeovers, franchise operations, joint ventures, networking and more rationalization of divisional or regional structures. The future managers in Europe will need to understand the cultural and institutional differences in each country.

The need to manage people in different cultures brings more attention to expatriate policies. The structural forms of multinationals have important implications for the utilization of expatriates. In many developing countries it is now only possible to trade if a partnership is formed with the host country. Local subsidiaries may require assistance, but the relationships are different.

The need for sensitivity in moving in and out of different cultures is recognized by some of the older established multinationals, who try to prepare their managers for the new culture through techniques such as shadowing, 'looksees' (visits prior to appointment), briefings, formal courses and overlaps between the new appointee and the incumbent (Brewster 1988). The costs of expatriate failure are high, so it is surprising that all companies proposing to send someone overseas on a long assignment do not make extra efforts to reduce culture shock.

Language ability is itself a significant issue for companies with large overseas interests. British failure to educate their employees in this regard is often attributed to the assumption that others will speak English. The need for more than just language ability, but for an understanding of the culture, history and business environment of countries in Europe was only recognized by half *The Times* top 500 companies surveyed in 1989 (Tyson 1989).

The prospect of creating truly 'European' employees who can deal with customers and suppliers from all over Europe is now becoming a reality. The idea of the 'Euromanager' has emerged, that is, a manager whose career spans several EC countries. This implies harmonization in the conditions of service, qualifications and rewards, and above all new approaches to management development. Research has shown there are a number of contextual variables which influence the development of Euromanagers, the most salient being the company strategy in preparation for 1993 and beyond (Bournois 1990; Bournois and Chauchat 1990). The approach to management development was seen as dependent upon one of the following four main strategies.

1. **'Multinationals'**: to improve the companies current standing in their business sector (for example, Air France, Thomson, Midland Bank, Lufthansa).

2. **'Europe first'**: to develop a distinctive European strategy, in companies already of global standing (for example, Philips, Beecham Products, Rhône-Poulenc).

3. **Repositioning for Europe**: to focus on Europe for the first time as a single market area (for example, Henkel, Dumez, Casino BSN).

4. **Supranationals**: to excel in Europe whilst protecting their already strong home base (for example, Renault, Crédit Lyonnais).

These companies differed in their strategic objectives, saw different problems posed by 1992/3 and had different managerial populations with different training needs. The variation in strategy brings us back to our contingency approach. It is not possible to generalize about Euromanager policies which are different for each of the four groups. For example, the 'Europe first' group were developing virtually all their managers through European-wide processes, whereas those repositioning for Europe were currently only developing around 10 per cent along a European development track.

The convergence thesis is too broad to be accepted as explaining the organizational processes of industrialization. Variations in the business context, and culturally, cast doubt on the notion that all organizations will ultimately conform to one model. There is, nevertheless, a force leading to convergence, which comes from technological and market rationality. The process of change is so long-term, and we are all bound up in it to such a degree, it is almost impossible to see where this push towards convergence will lead.

Conclusions

This chapter has taken a broad sweep to see what significance international dimensions have for the study of organizational behaviour. There are four general conclusions to be drawn:

1. Culture has been shown to be all pervasive. However, national

cultures are mitigated by contingent factors at the organizational level of analysis.

2. Institutional and legal differences between societies are significant especially in creating particular organizational forms, and they influence the decision-making processes in organizations. There is difficulty in separating cultural from institutional influences, since these interact.

3. Technological and market conditions are most important, and transcend national cultures and institutions in their effects on organizational strategies. Corporate culture can, if it is powerful enough, overcome national cultural influences, although how permanent this supremacy is, and whether there is informal as well as formal acceptance of corporate cultures, is in doubt.

4. There are forces for convergence. This has implications for individual and societal values and for personal freedom. The technological and market forces which are pushing towards convergence are mediated by variations within organizations, and any degree of convergence in organization form seems to be a very long-term possibility.

Case study

International business: The case of Airbus Industrie

Background

Airbus Industrie was created as a consequence of the need to have in Europe a viable, efficient and profitable aircraft industry in order to compete with the giants of the United States: Boeing and McDonnel Douglas. Instead of fighting each other, European manufacturers, prompted by their governments, sought to pool resources in a collaborative venture in which the enormous research and development costs, typically of around $3–4 billion could be shared, along with the commercial risks. The costs of developing new airliners to compete with the United States had simply become too great for a single manufacturer to sustain.

Business structure

The consortium was established in December 1970 under French law in the form of a 'grouping of mutual economic interest' (Groupement d'Intérêt Economique – GIE). There are now four aerospace companies which make up the shareholders of Airbus Industrie: Aérospatiale, which has 37.9 per cent, Deutsche Airbus of Germany (37.9 per cent), British Aerospace (20 per cent), CASA (Spain) (4.2 percent) (see Figures 9.2 and 9.3).

These companies control the management of Airbus Industrie like a board of directors – covering its general policy and administrative and financial rules. They are also suppliers who deliver parts of aircraft to Airbus Industrie in accordance with sub-contracts. The value of the work they do is roughly equal to the constituent companies' shareholding. By 1990, Airbus had achieved profitability, with 600 aircraft in service with 68 operators, and firm sales of 1,650 aircraft.

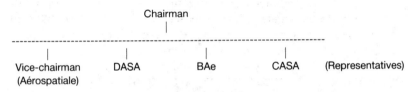

Figure 9.2 The organization

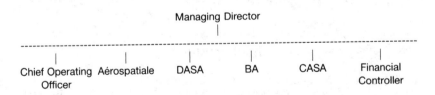

Figure 9.3 The executive board

The legal structure

As a 'GEI' Airbus Industrie exercises normal management control, but is not a limited liability company. However, it does have well-defined corporate objectives, and is able to interact with its customers as a single entity. The partners retain an independent capability to develop and sell other aerospace products, and these member companies can also sub-contract parts of their airbus work to other sub-contractors.

The organization

The assembly of the aircraft is at Toulouse in France, to which the complete constituent parts are delivered from the United Kingdom, Germany and Spain. As at 1990, the company employed 1,464 people of different nationalities. There are differences, therefore, in their management styles, their problem-solving approaches and their education and training.

People were not distributed to the different functions according to their nationality, but were appointed entirely according to their ability.

According to the managing director:

> Our strength lies in the fact that we have turned these differences to good account by allowing each to express his or her views before deciding on what action to take. The people involved in such a process must be flexible, willing to adapt, understanding and well prepared to be part of a team. . . . We did not deliberately set out to create an Airbus 'Esprit de corps'. It simply evolved from our day-to-day activities. (Taken from Jean Pierson, *European Success in Global Competition*, Henry Ford II Scholar Award Lecture. Cranfield 1991, p. 17)

As he sees it, the lessons to be learned for international collaboration are as follows:

1. Agreement on goals among the partners.

2. No conflicts of interest between the partners.

3. The principle of equity agreed between the partners.

4. Risks and costs shared according to contribution.

5. Encouragement of motivation and commitment by a multicultured dialogue, devised through the human resources policy.

References

Barsoux, J.L. and Lawrence, P. (1990), *Management in France* (London: Cassell).

Bournois, F. (1990), 'Européanisation des grandes entreprises et gestion des cadres', Doctoral Thesis, Université Jean Moulin, Lyons.

Bournois, F. and Chauchat, J.H. (1990), 'Managing managers in Europe', *European Management Journal*, March, vol. 8, no. 1, pp. 3–18.

Brewster, C. (1988), *The Management of Expatriates* (Cranfield: HRRC, Monograph No. 2).

Brewster, C. and Tyson, S. (1991), *International Comparisons in Human Resource Management* (London: Pitman).

Child, J. (1972), 'Organizational structure, environment and performance. The Role of Strategic Choice', *Sociology*, vol. 6, pp. 1–2.

Child, J. and Tayeb, M. (1983), 'Theoretical perspectives in non national organizational research', *International Studies of Management and Organization*, vol. 12, pp. 23–70.

Daniels, J.L. and Frost, C. (1991), *The Global Frontier* (New York: Harper and Row).

Deal, T.E. and Kennedy, A. (1982), *Corporate Cultures* (Reading, Mass.: Addison-Wesley).

De Bettingies, H.C. (1973), 'Japanese organisation behaviour: A Psychological Approach', in D. Graves (ed.), *Management Research: A cross cultural perspective* (Amsterdam: Elsevier Scientific Publishing).

Duncan, R. (1972), 'Characteristics of organisational environment and perceived uncertainty', *Administrative Science Quarterly*, vol. 17, pp. 313–27.

Evans-Pritchard, E.E. (1976), *Witchcraft Oracles and Magic Among the Azande*, (Oxford: Oxford University Press).

Heller, F., Drenth, P., Koopman, P., Rus, V. (1988), *Decisions in Organisations. A Three Country Comparative Study* (London: Sage).

Hofstede, G. (1984), *Culture's Consequences* (London: Sage).

IDE (1981a), *European Industrial Relations* (London: Oxford University Press).

IDE (1981b), *Industrial Democracy in Europe* (London: Oxford University Press).

Kerr, C., Dunlop, J.J., Harbison, F.H. and Myers, C.A. (1960), *Industrialism and Industrial Man* (London: Heinemann).

Lane, C. (1989), *Management and Labour in Europe* (Aldershot: Edward Elgar).

Lévi-Strauss, C. (1955), *Tristes tropiques* (London: Pan Books).

Lévi-Strauss, C. (1962), *La Pensée sauvage* (London: Weidenfeld and Nicolson).

Lévy-Bruhl, L. (1923), *Primitive Mentality* (London: Macmillan).

Loveridge, R. and Mok, A. (1979), *Theories of Labour Market Segmentation* (Leiden: Martinus Nijhoff).

Marcuse, H. (1968), *One Dimensional Man* (London: Sphere Books).

NEDO (1987), *The Making of Managers*, A Report on Management Education,

Training and Development in the USA, West Germany, France, Japan and the UK (London: HMSO).

Ouchi, W. (1981), *Theory Z. How Amercian Business Can Meet the Japanese Challenge* (Reading, Mass.: Addison-Wesley).

Pascale, R.T. (1978), 'Zen and the art of management', *Harvard Business Review*, pp. 153–62, J6.

Smith, P.B. (1984), 'The effectiveness of Japanese styles of management. A review and critique', *Journal of Occupational Psychology*, no. 57, pp. 121–36.

Tayeb, M. (1988), *Organizations and National Culture* (London: Sage).

Tyson, S. (1989), *1992: An investigation of strategies for management development* (Cranfield: HRRC).

Index

Index

socialization, 13, 17, 110, 114, 214
socio-technical system, 27, 142–3, 144, 149–51, 162
solidarity, 48, 90
specialization, 135
stability needs, 18
staffing levels, 36–7
static theories, 10–12, 14–15
steady state theory, 39–40
stereotypes, 37–9
strategic planning, 60
strategy, structure and, 153–6
stress, 30–1, 123–4
structure: of groups, 43; strategy and, 153–6
sub-systems, 140, 141
sub-units, 94, 134, 146, 166–7, 172
success criteria, 193–4
supervisory index, 160
supporting (leadership role), 77, 78
supranationals, 223
synchronization (life stage), 127–8
Synectics, 64
synergy, 49
systems theories, 140–3

T groups, 174, 175–80
task: dominated team roles, 66–8; grouping, 161–2; orientation, 66, 72–3,

77–8, 168; structure, 75–6; system, 142–3
tasks: core, 157; group, 57–9
Taylorism, 31–2, 137
team roles, 66–8, 80–3, 181
technical maps, 189
technical systems, 90, 142–3, 145
technocentric approach, 163
technology, 146, 148–9, 163–8, 210
Theory X / Theory Y, 139, 214, 216
Theory Z, 169, 218
time (group resource), 61–2
trade union power, 89–90
training, 105, 218; T groups, 174, 175–80
trait theories, 108–9, 110–12
transaction costs, 147–8
transition, 124–5, 128–9; cycles, 126–7; life stages, 105–8

uncertainty avoidance, 214, 215–16
unemployment, 27

valence concept 22
values, 45, 119–20, 178–9, 185, 188, 213, 218; conflict and, 50–4

Western Electric, 33, 48, 137
work groups, 90, 94, 142–3
work history, 130–2